G·L·E·A·N·I·N·G
R·U·T·H

A Biblical Heroine and Her Afterlives

Jennifer L. Koosed

The University of South Carolina Press

© 2011 University of South Carolina

Published by the University of South Carolina Press
Columbia, South Carolina 29208

www.sc.edu/uscpress

Manufactured in the United States of America

20 19 18 17 16 15 14 13 12 11   10 9 8 7 6 5 4 3 2 1

Library of Congress Cataloging-in-Publication Data

Koosed, Jennifer L.
    Gleaning Ruth : a biblical heroine and her afterlives / Jennifer L. Koosed.
      p. cm. — (Studies on personalities of the Old Testament)
    Includes bibliographical references and index.
    ISBN 978-1-57003-983-6 (cloth : alk. paper)
    1. Bible. O.T. Ruth—Criticism, interpretation, etc. I. Title.
    BS1315.52.K66 2011
    222'.3506—dc22
                                    2010051371

This book was printed on Glatfelter Natures, a recycled paper with 30 percent postconsumer
waste content.

• CONTENTS •

• SERIES EDITOR'S PREFACE •

Critical study of the Bible in its ancient Near Eastern setting has stimulated interest in the individuals who shaped the course of history and whom events singled
out as tragic or heroic figures. Rolf Rendtorff's *Men of the Old Testament* (1968)
focuses on the lives of important biblical figures as a means of illuminating history,
particularly the sacred dimension that permeates Israel's convictions about its God.
Fleming James's *Personalities of the Old Testament* (1939) addresses another issue,
that of individuals who function as inspiration for their religious successors in the
twentieth century. Studies restricting themselves to a single individual—for example, Moses, Abraham, Samson, Elijah, David, Saul, Ruth, Jonah, Job, Jeremiah—
enable scholars to deal with a host of questions: psychological, literary, theological,
sociological, and historical. Some, such as Gerhard von Rad's *Moses* (1960), introduce a specific approach to interpreting the Bible and hence provide valuable ped-
agogic tools.

As a rule these treatments of isolated figures have not reached the general pub-
lic. Some were written by outsiders who lacked a knowledge of biblical criticism
(Freud on Moses, Jung on Job) and whose conclusions, however provocative, re-
main problematic. Others were targeted for the guild of professional biblical critics
(David Gunn on David and Saul, Phyllis Trible on Ruth, Terence Fretheim and
Jonathan Magonet on Jonah). None has succeeded in capturing the imagination of
the reading public in the way such fictional works as Archibald MacLeish's *J. B.* and
Joseph Heller's *God Knows* have done.

It could be argued that the general public would derive little benefit from learning more about the personalities of the Bible. Their conduct, often less then exemplary, reveals a flawed character, and their everyday concerns have nothing to do
with our preoccupations from dawn to dusk. To be sure, some individuals tran-
scend their own age, entering the gallery of classical literary figures from time
immemorial. But only these rare achievers can justify specific treatments of them.
Then why publish additional studies on biblical personalities?

The answer cannot be that we read about biblical figures to learn ancient history,
even of the sacred kind, or to discover models for ethical action. But what remains?
Perhaps the primary significance of biblical personages is the light they throw on

the imaging of deity in biblical times. At the very least the Bible constitutes human perceptions of deity's relationship with the world and its creatures. Close readings of biblical personalities therefore clarify ancient understandings of God. That is the important datum that we seek—not because we endorse that specific view of deity, but because all such efforts to make sense of reality contribute something worthwhile to the endless quest for knowledge.

James L. Crenshaw
Duke Divinity School

· PREFACE ·

The book of Ruth is about relationship, and the four main chapters of this work explore Ruth's personality as she interacts with the other characters in the story. Not only is one's character both formed and expressed through relationships, but one's character is also embedded in social context and geographical location. Place is not incidental to personality. Therefore questions of society and land are also important, especially in Ruth, where the agricultural setting is key to the plot. In the three "Agricultural Interludes," I explore the world in which Ruth lives—the land she walks, the fields she works, the food she eats.

My readings of Ruth's character are indebted to feminist biblical scholarship and literary theory, and my understanding of Ruth's place has been influenced by feminism. Carol Meyers has been a pioneer in the research methods and theoretical models of archaeology and anthropology that are attuned to gender dynamics in the society of ancient Israel. Meyers begins her work by dismantling the assumptions of male domination, that the private and public spheres are distinct and separate, and that the private is dominated by women and hence devalued in the life of the community. Using cross-cultural anthropological analysis Meyers points out that the boundaries between the private and the public were not clearly demarcated in preindustrial societies, particularly ones based in subsistence agriculture and lacking complex social hierarchies. Activities that are centered in the home, then, may be informal but are not unimportant. It is our own more contemporary Western biases that understand informal, home-based activities and networks (which are centered on women) as less important and subservient to public activities and institutions (which are dominated by men). Gender asymmetries, which certainly do exist in every known culture, do not necessarily indicate male privilege. Feminist historical, archaeological, and sociological studies no longer assume that patriarchy means simply the suppression and devaluation of women. Rather, women always have power, however circumscribed their situations. And in subsistence economies, where social and political life is rooted in the extended family, women may have much more informal power than what has been traditionally presumed. Meyers writes: "The dynamics of life in the self-sufficient family household involved a wide variety of agrarian tasks necessary for survival. Except perhaps for metal tools and implements, individual households produced all the necessities of daily life—food, clothing, simple wooden tools and plain, utilitarian vessels. Providing these essentials involved a carefully orchestrated division of labor among all family members, male and female, young and old. Clearly, the survival of the household as a whole depended upon the contributions of all its members. . . . In such situations, households are typically characterized by internal gender balance rather than gender hierarchy."[1] In a book that foregrounds women's relationships and informal networks and focuses on the procuring of food, such archeological and anthropological analyses are essential to interpretation.

I begin laying the anthropological foundation of analysis by addressing the centrality of food in the story of Ruth. Food is more than the motivator of the plot. It is also intimately linked to gender, sexuality, reproduction, and ethnicity. Although underattended in biblical studies in general, and in the study of Ruth in particular, the examination of food and foodways has risen to prominence in anthropology. I draw on both anthropological and archaeological studies to examine agriculture and eating in Iron Age Judah.

Ruth is first introduced with Orpah, and Orpah functions as Ruth's counterpart. Consequently the reader's first understandings of Ruth's character are formed through contrast with Orpah. I employ postcolonial criticism and include a reading of H. Rider Haggard's best-selling novel *King Solomon's Mines* (1885). Ruth and Naomi's relationship is then examined. Dialogue dominates the narrative of Ruth, and Ruth and Naomi are the first to engage in conversation. The words that Ruth speaks to Naomi (1:16–17) are some of the most passionate in the Bible, and yet Naomi does not respond to them directly. The ambiguity of their interaction in Ruth 1 sets the stage for sexual and gender ambiguities throughout the biblical book. I focus on feminist and queer theory and examine Fannie Flagg's reading of Ruth and Naomi's relationship in her novel *Fried Green Tomatoes at the Whistle Stop Cafe* (1987).

I then return to food and foodways in order to argue that the problem the plot of Ruth moves to resolve is a crisis in bread production. The cereal grains, primarily in the form of bread, provided the foundation of the ancient diet. Alone, Ruth and Naomi did not have the means to produce their own bread so they had to find a way to integrate themselves into a bread production network. The final acceptance of Ruth into the Israelite community is predicated on Ruth's incorporation into Israelite foodways.

In the fields Ruth meets Boaz, and their relationship is my next subject. Is Ruth's marriage to Boaz a matter of expediency or a real romance? In either case Ruth and Boaz's interactions underscore Ruth's poverty and vulnerability. Yet her interactions with Boaz also are some of the most comic as he behaves in a kind but bombastic manner while she gently mocks his pomposity. Also examined is the question of the theology of this beloved biblical book. Again I use primarily feminist criticism and pair my biblical interpretation with a reading of a contemporary novel—in this case, Jane Hamilton's *The Book of Ruth* (1988).

Looking back to several key moments in the advancement of life on earth, I then examine the invention of agriculture through the domestication of cereal crops and the effects agriculture had on human culture and society. Even farther in the past is the evolution of photosynthesis, its crucial role in the production of all organic matter and therefore in the development of life itself. Ruth stands in the fields of grain, each leaf transforming the inorganic to the organic, each seed a nexus of sunlight, water, and soil. The influence of grain on the way Israel structured time, both secular and sacred, can be seen throughout the biblical text. The influence of grain on the way Israel structured society, in terms of both gender and class, can be seen in the book of Ruth.

Next I address the questions of kinship that arise because of the legal arrangements made at Bethlehem's gate. On the surface all's well that ends well—Boaz and Ruth marry and immediately conceive a son. The child is born and Naomi's own emptiness is finally filled. Yet curious displacements take place as Ruth and Boaz drop out of the narrative entirely and Naomi is proclaimed the boy's mother. In the context of queer criticism I examine nonconventional kinship patterns in Ruth against the backdrop of reproductive technologies and the remaking of kinship patterns in the contemporary United States. B. D. Wong's memoir *Following Foo: The Electronic Adventures of the Chestnut Man* (2003) provides insight into the changing meaning of family.

I conclude *Gleaning Ruth* by examining Ruth's liturgical afterlives in Judaism and Christianity. It may seem to contemporary English readers of Ruth that the genealogy (Ruth 4:18–22) functions as a neat ending, closing the narrative; however, in Hebrew narrative genealogies begin rather than end stories. The final genealogy is the book's way of resisting the "happily ever after" ending a reader might expect from this idyllic tale and beginning every one of Ruth's afterlives. The gleaner becomes the gleaned. As Ruth moves through different times and cultures, she opens herself up to theologians and rabbis, to writers and directors. All come to pick from her bounty, with each to create according to his or her need.

· ACKNOWLEDGMENTS ·

I would first like to thank James Crenshaw for suggesting to me that I write on a personality of the Old Testament. His support and encouragement, as well as his generous readings of my work, are more than a junior scholar could ever hope to expect from someone so admired. Editor Jim Denton approached his task with a patience that made me wonder if any author ever gets a manuscript in on time. Thanks are owed him and everyone at the University of South Carolina Press who helped this project progress smoothly from proposal to book.

Albright College has provided me the precious gift of time through a semester-long sabbatical (spring 2009) and a semester-long family leave (spring 2010). I hope that this book is ample demonstration that their family-friendly policies help to create and sustain a community of scholars. Happy people simply teach better and write more. My colleagues at Albright also deserve special thanks. I am grateful to the religious studies department for suffering my leaves without complaint, and especially to Bill King for taking on the duties of department chair one more time. The faculty bridge club provided a much-needed weekly respite—wine, cards, and conversation are a wonderful way to end the week. And thanks to those who attend the monthly Scholar Session and Poker Séance for scotch, cigars, and reading a draft of chapter 6.

As the book of Ruth links agricultural fertility with human fertility, *Gleaning Ruth* connects the creative processes of writing and procreation. During my sabbatical spring I wrote the first full draft of this manuscript and also conceived my son. He grew and developed within me as I continued to write and revise. The delivery of the manuscript was delayed by his birth when I realized that I simply could not make my original February 1 deadline when Simon was born January 21. A remarkable amount of this book was written and revised—including this passage—typing with one hand while the other hand held a baby on my lap or to my breast. Consequently it feels appropriate to dedicate this book to Simon Raphael Seesengood, as well as to his father, Robert Paul Seesengood, without whom Simon would not exist, and *Gleaning Ruth* would be poorer. He never wavered in his confidence that I would be up to the task of writing while undergoing the changes wrought by pregnancy and new motherhood. He was always ready to listen to a new idea, read another section, or ask the right question. In both critique and praise, he is my best and most beloved reader.

GLEANING

I have harvested more than I have gleaned. The season would begin with the distinctive crank of the rusty orange-red tractor, which would shutter and spark into life then slowly clunk out to the back acres where we had the vegetable gardens. I would perch on the wheel rim, riding with my father as he performed his one agricultural task—overturning the soil, plowing the fields. Afterward he would fade into the background, and my mother and my sister would emerge and we would plant, weed, tend, harvest—another two generations of women in the field.

The story of Ruth is beautifully crafted, an idyll in four elegant movements.[1] A family immigrates to a new country in search of food. While there the sons marry local women. Over the course of time both the father (Elimelech) and the sons (Mahlon and Chilion) die, leaving the three women alone. Bereft of husband and sons, Naomi decides to leave Moab and return to her home country of Judah. At first her daughters-in-law follow her, intending to remain by her side. Faced, however, with the discouragement of Naomi as well as her sage advice (there is nothing for you with me but hardship; stay with your own mother and find a new husband who can give you a family), one daughter-in-law, Orpah, returns to her own mother's house. Ruth, the other daughter-in-law, journeys on, refusing to leave Naomi's side. Chapter 1 ends with Ruth and Naomi arriving at Naomi's home village of Bethlehem.

Chapter 2 tells the tale of the two poor women. They arrive in Bethlehem with nothing and thus must rely on the ancient social welfare systems in order to eat. Ruth goes out into the fields, happening upon the barley harvest of a rich man who, unbeknownst to her, is a distant relative of her dead father-in-law. She begins to glean. Boaz, the rich relative, arrives, and she catches his eye. He speaks to her, grants her special favors and special protections, and so her gleaning is bounteous. When she returns to Naomi at the end of the day and recounts the story, she learns that Boaz is a relative. She continues to glean in his fields through both the barley and the wheat harvests.

Once the harvests are complete Naomi devises a plan. She instructs Ruth to sneak up to the threshing floor after the men have worked, eaten, drunk, and fallen asleep. Ruth is to approach Boaz, uncover his feet, and wait for his instruction. He awakes with a start and she reveals herself to him, asking for his protection as next of kin. Flattered, he vows to come to her aid—but then reveals to her that there is another man who is a closer relative than he. He asks her to stay the night with the promise that he will resolve the matter in the morning. At the end of chapter 3, as dawn breaks, he fills her apron with barley and sends her home to Naomi.

The focus of chapter 4 shifts from the world of women and the private setting to the public world of men. Boaz goes to the city gates where the men of the community sit and dispense judgment. When the other relative passes by, Boaz calls him over and explains the matter at hand—Naomi has land that needs to be redeemed by a kinsman, but she also has a daughter-in-law from Moab. At first interested in the land, the closer relative ultimately declines both the land and the woman. Boaz then declares himself the redeemer of the land and the taker of Ruth. The two marry, a son is born and named Obed, and the narrative ends with a genealogy connecting the story of Ruth to the family of David. Out of famine, bereavement, and poverty comes a future royal dynasty. A story that begins with the death of sons ends with the birth of sons.

The story of Ruth is beautifully crafted, but the narrative is not as simple as first appears. Tod Linafelt opens his commentary on Ruth with the observation: "The more time I have spent with the book the more convinced I have become that it is exceedingly complex and ambiguous."[2] As the book, so the woman: Ruth's character is unsettled and unsettling.[3] The questions about her character are not just the questions of readers millennia later, uncertain now of meaning. Rather, these questions are integral to her character. Both Boaz and Naomi ask Ruth, "Who are you?" at key points in the narrative (Ruth 3:9, 3:16), an inquiry not easily answered by simple proximity.[4]

Despite the common characterization of her narrative as an "idyll" and the familiar "fairytale" elements, the suggestion of Ruth's complexity should not be surprising. These four short chapters of scripture have continued to engage and interest readers for millennia, a feat that would be impossible were the title character flat and the story simple. In fact the illusion of simplicity may seduce the casual reader into deeper reflection; intriguing personalities do draw others into their world.

Linafelt continues: "The task of the commentator is to enable the reader to apprehend and negotiate the uncertainties of the text and, when possible, to demonstrate how these uncertainties are not pesky problems to be solved but rather are integral to the narrative art of the book."[5] Following Linafelt's lead, I explore rather than explain the many facets of the personality of Ruth.

Doppelgangers and Other Doublings

The writer of Ruth employs a doubling motif in various ways at various levels throughout the narrative. First, most of the characters are presented in pairs: Naomi and Elimelech, Mahlon and Chilion, Ruth and Orpah.[6] Boaz has his pair in the unnamed relative whose claim to Elimelech's property precedes Boaz's claim. Even Obed may have a double. Jack M. Sasson argues that the peculiarities at the end of the book can be explained by positing an original story in which Ruth gave birth to two children—Obed and an unnamed brother.[7] Important moments in the plot often turn on the doubles making diametrically opposed decisions: Orpah turns back to Moab while Ruth continues on to Judah (1:14); Boaz accepts what the other relative declines (4:6).

On a deeper level, several of the narrative motifs rely on binary oppositions that structure the plot of Ruth. Elimelech's family first leave Bethlehem because they are full of family but empty of food, and Naomi returns empty of family but, since the famine has subsided, she comes home to a full "House of Bread" (the literal meaning of *Bethlehem*). The interplay between fullness and emptiness continues throughout the narrative. Other binary oppositions—women/men, poor/rich, threshing floor / before the gate, private space / public space—are also integral to the plot.

The very way language works in the book of Ruth is through multiple levels of doubling. First there is a poetic substratum that underlies much of the spoken dialogue in Ruth, and many of the dialogues are structured in couplets.[8] For example, Ruth's first speech—her passionate plea to Naomi (1:16–17)—contains six poetic couplets. Second, the author of Ruth doubles meaning through wordplay, especially punning.[9] Third, a "striking characteristic of Ruth" is the number of key words that occur only twice.[10] Examples include *lads* (1:5, 4:16), *security* (1:9, 3:1), *lodge* (1:16, 3:13), *brought back / restorer* (1:21, 4:15), *empty* (1:21, 3:17), *covenant brother / circle* (2:1, 3:2), *substance/worthy* (2:1, 3:11), *wings* (2:12, 3:9).[11] As Edward Campbell argues in his commentary: "Double occurrences of the same word are not simply a matter of repetition; they constitute brackets, as plot problems are transferred from one set of circumstances to another, from difficulty to be overcome to resolution of that difficulty."[12]

In addition these doublings form inclusio, bracketing devices. Note that with each pair enumerated above, the first instance is toward the beginning of the book (either in chapter 1 or 2) and the second occurrence is toward the end (either in chapter 3 or 4). Campbell suggests that the entire narrative is structured through the use of smaller inclusio and chiasm in the construction of the larger ones that frame the entire narrative.[13] The smaller units are marked by the doubling and reversal of other word pairs—El Shaddai / Yahweh in 1:20–21a becomes Yahweh / El Shaddai in 1:21b, for example.

Finally, there are peculiarities in the Hebrew that involve doubles. In several instances when Ruth and Naomi are discussed together, instead of the expected feminine plural, a masculine plural is used (examples include "with you" in 1:8). Such instances may be the result of a possible dual feminine archaic form (which is what Campbell argues[14]). An equally unprecedented plural form of the word for *legs* or *feet* is used when there is discussion of Boaz's body in chapter 3 of the book of Ruth (3:7).

One way to read these multiple pairings and doublings is that they encode the centrality of relationship. Relationship has often been cited as one of the primary themes of Ruth based on the plot alone—two women from two religions, two cultures, two ethnicities join forces to cross over from one country to another and see what life brings. For example, Judith A. Kates and Gail Twersky Reimer introduce their edited volume of essays on Ruth by noting that Ruth's "central figures are women, its central story (or stories) is relationship."[15] In general, character is not formed in isolation and cannot be understood outside of interaction with others. In a book that foregrounds relationship in theme, plot, and structure, this is even more apparent. In order to explore the personality of Ruth, it is necessary to explore the personalities of Orpah, Naomi, Boaz, and Obed as they interact with and help to define Ruth's own character. The four primary chapters of my work are organized around these four central relationships.

I have entered into a new series of relationships too. When I elected to write this volume, my greatest fear was that it would be a dull read. What could I add to the study of Ruth; what could I say that has not already been said? I am deeply in debt to the previous scholarship on Ruth with which I have been in dialogue. It was only when I gave up the spring hope of planting to embrace the fall reality of gleaning from somebody else's bounty that this book began to come together.

Feminist interpreters have been particularly interested in the book of Ruth, and I have been particularly influenced by their approaches. Feminist interpretation of the book of Ruth formally begins with Elizabeth Cady Stanton's *The Woman's Bible,* published in 1898.[16] Stanton's reading falls far short of many of today's academic standards. She assumes the historical reliability of the story, even the historicity of Matthew's genealogy listing Rahab as Boaz's mother. She speculates freely about the daily lives of Ruth and Naomi in Bethlehem, including how they spent their evenings together (dining on "herb tea, bread and watercresses" and talking about practical matters[17]) and whether or not they kept pets (yes—they had "doves, kids and lambs"[18]). Finally she is guilty of certain anachronisms (picturing Obed's baptism[19]). Yet in terms of her focus on the women and the strength of their relationship, Stanton is decidedly feminist in her positive analysis of this biblical book.

As innovative as Stanton's work on the Bible was in the nineteenth century, and as prevalent as feminist biblical scholarship is today, there is no direct line from *The Woman's Bible* to, say, *The Women's Bible Commentary,* edited by feminist biblical critics Carol A. Newsom and Sharon H. Ringe and published in 1992. Stanton did not found a school of thought, nor were her biblical interpretations engaged by her successors in the women's movement. Women in the academy may have given some encouragement to the project, but they did not participate in the committee she formed to examine the biblical text, nor did they later build on her work.[20] Traditional historical-critical studies did not focus on gender in Ruth despite the prominence of the female characters and their relationship. Even Louise Pettibone Smith, one of the first female modern biblical scholars, wrote on Ruth but did not explore the gendered aspects of the text.[21] It was not until the revival of the women's movement in the 1960s (second-wave feminism) that feminist biblical scholarship emerged once more.

Since Stanton's early foray into feminist readings of Ruth, the book has been met with mixed reviews in feminist commentary, exemplified by two early treatments: articles by Phyllis Trible and Esther Fuchs.[22] Phyllis Trible's 1976 essay on Ruth, which she then expanded into a chapter in her 1978 *God and the Rhetoric of Sexuality,* is the first full feminist analysis that regards Ruth positively. Much like Stanton's interpretation but without the assumptions of historicity or the conservative and traditional language, Trible's essay portrays Ruth as a model of *hesed* and the bond between Ruth and Naomi to be primary.[23] The word *hesed* appears throughout the book of Ruth, applied to Ruth's actions primarily. It is, however, notoriously difficult to translate because there is no one English word that captures the full meaning of the Hebrew. The term encompasses actions and attitudes of love, kindness, mercy, care.[24] Ruth embodies all of these values in her interactions with the other characters in the book.

Esther Fuchs's work is an example of the negative evaluation some feminist interpreters have given Ruth. Fuchs makes the connection between Ruth's journey and Abraham's. Yet for Fuchs Ruth leaves her home and accepts Yahweh for the love of Naomi, not because of her own personal faith commitments. Other commentators (including the rabbinical ones) hold Ruth in higher regard because she abandons her home and accepts Yahweh without the kind of direct contact and assurance of reward that Abraham is given in Genesis 12. For example, Trible writes: "Not even Abraham's leap of faith surpasses this decision of Ruth's. . . . There is no more radical decision in all the memories of Israel."[25] In contrast, Fuchs regards her commitment as derivative: "Ruth, on the other hand, is a means in the process of restoring *man's* name to the world; that of Mahlon, her husband, and of Elimelech, her father-in-law. Her battle is not for monotheism [like Abraham's] but for the continuity of patriarchy."[26] All of Ruth's actions, including the subversive and unconventional ones, are in the service of bearing a male child to continue the line of the fathers. "Thus, Ruth is the paradigmatic upholder of patriarchal ideology."[27]

The last thirty-five years have seen more complex assessments of the characters in the book of Ruth from feminist perspectives, as the very term *feminist* also has become more complex. No longer are feminist studies preoccupied with the question "Is this text good or bad for women?" Rather, feminist studies examine the complex cultural constructions of femininity and masculinity, the representations of sexuality, and the diverse perspectives of the marginal.

In the final analysis the ultimate double may be Ruth herself. As a brief look at feminist interpretations alone demonstrates, readings of her are bifurcated. Is she passive or active; submissive or aggressive; obedient or disobedient; protofeminist or pawn of the patriarchy; heterosexual or lesbian; kind or predatory? Does Naomi use her or does she use Naomi and/or Boaz? She is subject to such divergent assessments because of her complexity and because, as in most Hebrew narrative, her inner voice is absent from the telling of her story. As a result readers can rely only on her spoken words and her actions in order to discern her personality. Yet her actions are exaggerated; her speech is misleading; there are gaps between what she says and what she does. Consequently she emerges Janus-faced, a trickster in the fields and on the threshing-room floor.

Gleaning as Metaphor and Method

To glean is to follow behind, picking up what others leave. Gleaning was, and is, a common agricultural activity but most of us no longer live in communities that are familiar with it. Contemporary gleaning in industrialized and urbanized cultures consists of a wide range of other practices. The context has changed, but the impulse to pick through, pick up, and assemble anew has hardly abated. Because Ruth has continued to live outside of her narrative, readings of her are well informed by her afterlives in literature, art, film, and liturgy. With her documentary *The Gleaners and I* (2001), Agnès Varda has been one of my primary reading companions. Her camera moves from large-scale industrialized farms to urban dumpster diving, from antique malls to her own mantelpiece exploring the world of modern-day gleaners in France.

Even though Varda does not mention Ruth in her documentary, the biblical heroine might easily be considered a shadow presence, following behind and beside the contemporary gleaners Varda documents. For me, Ruth's entry follows a chain of images and associations that begin with the painting that opens the film: Jean-François Millet's painting of women gleaning wheat entitled *The Gleaners*. The viewer just catches the black-and-white reproduction as Varda points her camera at a dictionary entry for *gleaning*. As the camera moves back another painting in black-and-white appears underneath the first painting—Jules Breton's *Woman Gleaning*. Varda notes that Millet's painting is used to illustrate all the dictionary entries she has found, so she follows the image to its original in Paris's Musée d'Orsay. Later in the documentary she pursues Breton's painting (also frequently found in dictionaries), traveling to a museum in Arras, France. Here she even poses like the woman in Breton's painting, sheaves of wheat balanced across her shoulders.

Breton's and Millet's images come together midway through the film when Varda stops to explore an antique mall/junk store. She finds the two paintings combined in the work of an anonymous amateur artist—Millet's group of stooping gleaners in one corner, Breton's upright single gleaner in the foreground. Clearly the dabbler had access to the same dictionary entries that Varda perused.

Millet (1814–1875) painted many rural scenes, particularly of peasants working in the fields. He drew primarily on the French agricultural worker. Breton (1827–1906), painting after Millet in a similar style and tradition, also made the French countryside with its workers central to his artistic endeavors. Millet's and Breton's works are not only used to illustrate multiple dictionary and encyclopedia entries on gleaning, but also occasionally to illustrate editions of the book of Ruth. Connections between the French paintings and Ruth are easily made in the minds of readers and illustrators. The paintings are two of the best known artistic depictions of gleaners, and Ruth may be the best-known gleaner in literature. Millet also painted pictures explicitly about Ruth—for example, his *Harvesters Resting (Ruth and Boaz)*—in which the nineteenth-century French field-worker becomes the model for workers in the Iron Age fields of Ruth's own gleaning.

There is even sometimes a confusion between the nineteenth-century French peasant and the biblical heroine and even between the works of Millet and Breton. Cynthia Ozick opens her essay simply titled "Ruth" by discussing the only two pictures that hung on the wall of her childhood home. One was a painting of her paternal grandfather. The other was a reproduction—perhaps cut from a magazine or a calendar—of *The Song of the Lark*. Ozick describes the painting:

> A barefoot young woman, her hair bound in a kerchief, grasping a sickle, stands alone and erect in a field. Behind her a red sun is half swallowed by the horizon. She wears a loose white peasant's blouse and a long dark skirt, deeply blue; her head and shoulders are isolated against a limitless sky. Her head is held poised: she gazes past my gaze into some infinity of loneliness stiller than the sky. . . . There was no lark. It did not come to me that the young woman, with her lifted face was straining after the note of a bird who might be in a place invisible to the painter. What I saw and heard was something else: a scene older than this French countryside, a woman lonelier even than the woman alone in the calendar meadow. It was, my mother said, Ruth: Ruth gleaning in the fields of Boaz.[28]

Not only does Ozick believe for years that the painting is of Ruth, but she also thinks that it is the work of Millet. Only much later does she discover that it is not by Millet at all—it is the work of Breton.[29]

From Breton and Millet to Ruth, by way of Ozick, the book of Ruth is my subtext when I watch Varda's *The Gleaners and I*. A film does not need explicit reference to a biblical figure to be read in conversation with the Bible. In *Screening Scripture* George Aichele and Richard Walsh bring contemporary movies into conversation with biblical texts in ways that illuminate both.[30] As Aichele and Walsh point out, there is "a third member of such conversations—namely the scholar making the comparison."[31] Despite the fact that many interpreters hide their role in the conversation between movie and text, "it is that often reticent, third member of the conversation who actually voices and indeed dominates the conversation."[32] Consequently "The 'real' (material) justification for any connection between scripture and film is the scholar whose specific experience and interpretative reading alone supplies the connection."[33] As is aptly demonstrated in several of the essays in *Screening Scripture* and then by Richard Walsh in his later book *Finding St. Paul in Film,* the interpreter is the nexus where the film is brought into dialogue with the Bible. Walsh writes: "The films discussed below, then, relate to Paul only as my interpretations of the films and of Paul render a Paul as the films' precursor."[34] To paraphrase Walsh in terms of my project, *The Gleaners and I* relates to my characterization of Ruth only because of my interpretations of both Ruth and the documentary. And rather than watching the film in order to see how it interprets the biblical text and thus uses the Bible to create and deepen its own meaning, here the interpretive dynamic is reversed. I watch Varda's documentary in order to see how it illuminates Ruth, creating and deepening meaning in the biblical text.

The Gleaners and I is not only a part of the content of my interpretation; it is also integral to the method of my reading. Therefore some background on Varda and her filmmaking techniques is essential to the present study. Varda began making films, feature-length and shorts, dramas and documentaries, in 1954. With her first film *La Pointe courte* (1954), she became the first woman in France to direct a full-length movie on her own. Sometimes referred to as the "grandmother of the French New Wave," Varda is known for her focus on women, the poor, traditional crafts, and the minutiae of everyday life.[35]

The French New Wave describes the period 1959–1965, but it is grounded in the earlier film theories and practices of Jacques Doniol-Valcroze, André Bazin, and Alexandre Astruc. Bazin in particular laid the theoretical foundation of the New Wave through his articulation of the *auteur* theory or "theory of the author." In an essay published in the early 1950s Bazin argued that the true author of a film is the director not the screenwriter or the textual writer. The director uses the camera, lighting, movement, and framing like a pen, and such components of a film convey meaning just as much, if not more so, than the spoken dialogue and plot. Although the official period of the French New Wave is over, its impact was profound, and there are still filmmakers who follow its traditions and act as *auteurs.* Varda was one of the earliest embracers of this aesthetic and she still makes film today based on its essential ideas.[36]

The two most prominent and distinctive features of works created as a result of the auteur theory are montage and the highlighting of the director's subjectivity. Film historian Rémi Fournier Lanzoni notes that

> the real innovation of the auteurs lay in their theory on montage (mainly a denunciation of temporal continuity), rather than a direct intervention of the director's intellect, which best illustrated its radical change for visual input (absence of the use of wipes or traditional filmic punctuation, juxtaposition of contradicting shots, and so forth). The revolutionary "editing" point of view broke new ground with its visual discontinuity, spatial-temporal ellipses, and the absence of logical connections, thus indirectly reminding the audience of the inevitability of an active spectatorship. For the promoters of authorism, the new concept of editing was to differentiate cinema from traditional filmed epics, and, in general, the conventional Hollywood linear narrative.[37]

Visually a movie that employs techniques of montage looks strikingly different from a more typical film, in which one scene flows into the next as the narrative arc rises and falls. Montage juxtaposes images in ways that are potentially jarring, even confusing, to the viewer, and this disruptive cinematic form mirrors the nonlinear narrative content of the story being told.

In tune with the theory of authorism's highlighting of the role of the director in the creation of meaning, New Wave directors drew attention to their role in ways that were at odds with the conventional invisibility of the filmmaking process. These directors narrated their stories "through personal themes and an ostentatious subjectivity."[38] In a sense every film they made was, at one level, a story about themselves.

Such innovations in approach created a dialogue between filmmaker and film viewer. Instead of the director hiding and presenting a seamless, straightforward narrative for the audience to consume passively, the *auteur* showed his or her hand and drew the viewer into the film as active participant. Instead of presenting a clear and conventional narrative sequence, the use of montage, disrupted chronology, and obvious editing also drew the viewer into the film as it engaged him or her intellectually, not just emotionally.

In emblematizing the French New Wave, Agnès Varda is eclectic, combining "any approach that suit[s] her needs: subjective point-of-view shots, a soundtrack that capture[s] secondary characters' conversations, an open ending with the denouement left unsettled, and an earnest desire to let the course of suggestion and ambiguity bec[o] me part of the viewing."[39] The subtle incorporation of her own subjectivity and her use of montage draws the reader into the narrative as a partner in the making of meaning. This describes her feature films, but even more pointedly describes her documentaries.

The original, French title of *The Gleaners and I* is *Les Glaneurs et La Glaneuse,* which means "The Gleaners and the Gleaner." Varda's use of "La Glaneuse," the feminine singular, embeds her own self into the title of her work, indicating to the viewer that she is just as much a subject of her film as she is its creator, just as much in front of the camera as behind it. Her use of a small hand-held camera throughout the filming allows her an extraordinary amount of freedom and flexibility. Not only does she document her own gleaning—Varda is particularly drawn to heart-shaped potatoes and a clock with missing hands—but she easily can and does turn the camera onto her own body as well, thus making its aging another motif of the film. Her voice—asking questions and making observations—is also a constant presence.

The images of her own body are interwoven with the more expected images of women in the fields, artists collecting discarded objects, and homeless people digging through the trash. Most striking, however, is the inclusion of images that have no direct relationship to either Varda's own self or the subject matter at hand. For example, as she tells the viewer, she accidentally leaves her camera on as she walks across a field. The resulting image of a lens cover twisting and dancing above the ground becomes a part of her film. In another brief scene a dog stands on the side of the road, bright red boxing glove tied inexplicably around its neck. Such images come and go without explanation. Her use of montage thus becomes a form of gleaning, gleaning images that bear no obvious relationship to each other or to the subject of the film. She makes the connection between what gleaners do and what she is doing with her camera explicit in an early scene in which she is seen posing like the figure in Breton's *Woman Gleaning,* next to the painting itself. She drops her bundle of wheat and picks up her hand-held camera—the traditional agricultural gleaner becomes the contemporary artistic gleaner. The only thing that ties all of the images together is Agnès Varda herself.

My task in this study is to take the source material—the Hebrew and Greek texts, the traditional commentaries, the modern monographs, the literary allusions, the peer-reviewed articles, the artistic representations, the liturgical practices—and arrange, edit, juxtapose. My method is eclectic as befits a gleaner, employing such criticisms as feminist, literary, postcolonial, and queer, and also availing myself of the full harvests of historical, archaeological, and sociological methods. An eclectic approach also befits a complex personality, as different questions reveal different aspects of character. My portrait of Ruth will not be bound by any one methodological approach; my portrait will be like any personality—multifaceted. As Ruth shadows Agnès Varda, as she makes cameo appearances in novels and other works of literature, as she haunts paintings, I follow behind, gleaning images and ideas to create my own portrait of Ruth.

Matters Historical and Literary

My understanding of Ruth is not bound to the historical context out of which Ruth emerged, because Ruth herself has continued to live and thrive outside of her original setting. Ruth's death is never recorded in the biblical scripture, and, as a literary figure, Athalya Brenner argues that she never dies: "many of us biblical women live on, an open-ended kind of existence not achieved by ordinary mortals . . . in and outside the biblical text that wasn't interested enough in us to record death and to bury. . . . As literary female figures we live everlastingly, eternally, perpetually, as long as the canonical text is still alive, occupying various niches and fulfilling varied roles in the individual and collective cultural memory of Western and, to a lesser extent, Eastern and especially Islamic cultures."[40]

In her book *I Am . . . Biblical Women Tell Their Own Stories,* Brenner takes advantage of the lack of a death narrative in order to assemble a variety of biblical women together in a type of academic conference. One by one each explores her own biblical persona and literary afterlife, telling, as the book's title indicates, her own story. Neither Ruth, Naomi, nor Orpah die in the biblical text; thus they are left to wander in and out of other narratives, pieces of art, film, and biblical commentary.

At the same time, it is not immaterial that I was conceived in Kent, Ohio, soon after the day that the National Guard opened fire on unarmed student protestors at Kent State University, killing four. It is not immaterial that we left the pink apartment building when I was two years old. My parents had bought my paternal grandparents' house in Granger Township, a rural community poised midway between Akron and Medina. How, exactly, these accidents of birth shape the document I sit here now in Reading, Pennsylvania, writing is an open question, better left to other interested parties (if there are any) to analyze. But affect my reading and my writing, they certainly do. Ruth herself is not a historical figure, but somebody created her, told her story, wrote it down. Whoever it was left traces of him or herself,[41] entangled in the letters on the page.

There are two dominant ways of understanding the context out of which Ruth emerged. The first is to see the book of Ruth as an answer to a question about David's ancestry. Kirsten Nielsen's commentary exemplifies this position. For her Ruth is clearly the product of a pro-David campaign, seeking to legitimate his Moabite origins, origins that were so well known that they could not be simply denied. The precise historical moment when such a defense would have been necessary is an open question for Nielsen. It could have been as early as David's, Solomon's, or Rehoboam's reign or as late as Hezekiah's or Josiah's. The author of the tale, however, was most certainly a member of the royal court between the tenth and the seventh centuries B.C.E. "The court provided not only the essential financial resources but also the environment that could produce an artist of the caliber of Ruth's author."[42]

Nielsen and others who hold this position on the provenance of the story of Ruth concede that the book of Ruth may be fictional but assert that it does preserve a historical datum in its ascription of a Moabite ancestor to David. In the words of William Rudolph, "It is out of the question that a tale would have invented a Moabite grandmother for the greatest and most celebrated king of Israel, prototype of the Messiah. Therefore this central narrative affirmation must be historical."[43] Such a position is maintained even though the books of Samuel call only David a son of Jesse and do not climb further back on the family tree. Addressing the absence of Ruth or any other Moabite ancestor in the biblical texts devoted to David's story, some commentators believe that they see further proof of David's Moabite ancestry in the story of his taking his parents into Moab for refuge (1 Sam. 22:3–4).[44]

There are, however, several problems with positing that David did indeed have a Moabite great-grandmother and then placing the book of Ruth in the context of court propaganda. First, the story in 1 Sam. 22 is not evidence of David's blood ties to Moab. From one perspective such a reading assumes the basic historical reliability of the stories in Samuel-Kings—if the narrative says that David took his parents to Moab then he took his parents to Moab. Yet in the current state of scholarship, such historical reliability can no longer be assumed.[45] From another perspective one does not need to argue that there is an actual historical memory here; rather one could argue that the presence of this story indicates that readers would have found it plausible for David's parents to seek refuge in Moab because of the well-known historicity of David's Moabite roots. Although this argument sidesteps the question of the historical reliability of Samuel-Kings, it still maintains the historical core of David as part Moabite, which raises other questions. If his Moabite roots were so well known, why did the author(s) of Samuel remain silent about them? In addition David himself seeks asylum in Philistia and even offers his military services to the enemy king (1 Sam. 27–28). Does this mean that he also has a Philistine ancestor? Of course not—such an argument is never made. David is portrayed in Samuel as an opportunist, alternatively forming alliances with foreign powers and then fighting these same foreign powers depending on what suits his needs. Whether at the level of history or story, David's parents' flight to Moab demonstrates nothing about the veracity of the genealogy at the end of Ruth.

Second, it is a fallacy to argue that no one would have made up a Moabite ancestress for David because such ancestry would have been too scandalous, so therefore it must be true. André LaCocque uses the example of Jesus' genealogy in the Gospel of Matthew to make his point against such arguments. In Matthew's genealogy of Jesus, Ruth, Tamar, Rahab, and "the wife of Uriah" are all listed as ancestors of Jesus. The genealogy highlights precisely the women who have questionable ethnic backgrounds and irregular sexual histories. LaCocque draws attention specifically to Rahab. In constructing a genealogy of Jesus that encompasses Abraham through David, the Jewish scriptures do include Ruth, Tamar, and Bathsheba. One could question the author of the Gospel's reasons for highlighting these women, but the presence of the women in the genealogy comes straight from Jewish scriptures. However, the addition of Rahab, based on no known tradition of her connection to this family line, is most probably an invention of the Gospel writer. Why would the Gospel writer make up a Canaanite prostitute ancestor for the messiah Jesus? There are numerous interpretations of this text but no one tries to argue that Rahab is a part of Jesus' genealogy because Rahab really is an ancestor of Jesus. If it is probable that someone invented a Canaanite prostitute's ties to the messiah Jesus, then it is just as probable (if not more so) that someone invented a Moabite great-grandmother for the king David.[46] LaCocque asserts that the genealogy at the end of Ruth is fictitious.[47]

The second way of understanding the context out of which Ruth emerged is to focus less on the issue of David's legitimacy despite his Moabite origins and more on the general issues surrounding intermarriage. LaCocque critiques the position that Ruth is court propaganda because he understands the book to be written in the postexilic period, not to justify David but to justify Moabites.[48] Tikva Frymer-Kensky also holds this position. She sees the book of Ruth answering several questions that would have arisen in the postexilic context of the Persian Period (533–333 B.C.E.). Those who were exiled and then returned would have seen themselves in Naomi's situation. The first question the book answers is the one about property—should those who return be able to recuperate their ancestral land? Second, many of the returnees would have had foreign peoples return with them—again, as Naomi came home with Ruth. What is the status of these people who come with the returning Judahites, possibly even married to them? And third, what should the relationship be between the returnees and those who stayed in the land? "The telling of the Ruth and Naomi story in the paradigmatic, even allegorical fashion of the book of Ruth should best be seen in the context of these issues."[49] The book of Ruth answers these questions in ways opposed to the answers provided in the books of Ezra and Nehemiah. In the book of Ruth those who return to Judah are entitled to recuperate their land. Foreign partners who accompany the returnees should be welcomed and incorporated into the community. The returnees, the "people of the land," and the foreigners who voluntarily join themselves to the people of Israel all work in concert to assure the prosperous future of Israel as a whole. "In this way, the ancestry story and the genealogy of the great king of Israel's past point the way toward the nation's glorious future."[50]

There are multiple interpretations and explanations of the genealogy that do not depend on its being a historical datum, thereby making the story of Ruth a part of David's political propaganda and situating it during the monarchical period.

Frymer-Kensky's understanding of the function of the genealogy resembles the function of the genealogies that open the first book of Chronicles. They are constructing a particular past not for the sake of conveying factual information but in order to produce a certain vision of the future postexilic community. In the case of Chronicles the vision is a utopian one.[51] There is an element of utopian fantasy in Ruth as well, as the Moabite widow proclaims her "till-death-do-us-part" loyalty to the Judahite god and the Judean people. Linafelt proposes another way in which the genealogy functions in terms of the story: "that the book of Ruth was written as and intended to be a connector between these two books [Judges and 1 Samuel]."[52] Genealogies in Hebrew narrative open a story, not conclude one, in every case except for the book of Ruth. For Linafelt the genealogy does open a new story—the story of David's rise to power and succession to the throne of Israel.[53]

Other aspects of Ruth's genre also point to the Persian Period. Short stories, especially short stories with women as their central heroes, proliferated in the Persian through Hellenistic periods. Examples include Esther, Judith, and Susanna. LaCocque's work *The Feminine Unconventional* groups Susanna, Esther, Judith, and Ruth together based on similar literary characteristics and themes.[54]

Ruth is a short story, but the genre can be defined even further. In discussing her own attitude toward the book of Ruth, Vanessa L. Ochs proclaims: "It's so implausible. In the abstract, of course, I can easily imagine a drama of devotion between human beings who share suffering, or devotion between two women who are bound to each other by circumstances. But the specific scenario makes me raise my eyebrows."[55] Ochs goes on to speculate that perhaps the improbability is what is intended by the author. By making the story so improbable, the love Ruth demonstrates is brought into even sharper relief. Ruth, perhaps, is the embodiment of "irrational, undemanded love."[56] The excessive responses not only of Ruth but also of Boaz are key to Campbell's interpretation as well. For Campbell and others who see a deep theological core to this book, humans model God in how they treat each other and Ruth and Boaz respond with more than what is strictly required by law or custom.[57]

A rarely explored aspect of the story begins with Ochs's raised eyebrows but does not end by domesticating the oddness and excessiveness of the situation by meditating on the great unconditional love of God. The book of Ruth *is* strange. How many young widows devote themselves so passionately to their mothers-in-law? How many people throw themselves face down in the dirt as a gesture of gratitude? How many marriages are contracted in secret, in the middle of the night, after a drunken revelry? Well, the general scenario here is probably more common than many would admit. The point still obtains: after reading Ruth for nearly twenty-five hundred years the inconsistencies, incongruities, and peculiarities of the book pass largely unnoticed. Highlighting instead of downplaying the oddities of the story brings a comedic element to light.

Although Ruth is not generally associated with comedy, the book has appeared in a few recent comic writings. Fannie Flagg's *Fried Green Tomatoes at the Whistle Stop Cafe* is engagingly written and the comedy is even more evident in the movie version, *Fried Green Tomatoes*. Woody Allen also employs Ruth in a parody of his own. In his short story "Hassidic Tales, with a Guide to Their Interpretation," Allen writes six vignettes about rabbis and their questioners, following each vignette with a commentary. In the first tale a man goes to Rabbi Ben Kaddish in order to ask where he can find peace. In response Rabbi Kaddish yells, "Quick, look behind you!" and then, when the man turns, takes a candlestick and hits him in the back of the head.[58] Allen's commentary on the tale provides an alternative version of the story. Instead of hitting the questioner with a candlestick, in the second version "the Rabbi leaps on top of the man in a frenzy and carves the story of Ruth on his nose with a stylus."[59] Many Jewish professionals seem to be invested with a talent for writing miniscule Hebrew letters, as mezuzot, teffilin, and this story attests.

Without reference to Ruth's cameos in contemporary comic fiction, Nehama Aschkenasy argues that Ruth should be read as a dramatic comedy.[60] To support her thesis she draws on the literary theory of Aristotle, Northrop Frye, Henri Bergson, and Dorothea Krook, as well as the on plays of Shakespeare and Molière. Comedic plots begin in crisis and move to a happy ending, are tightly constructed, and entail unexpected reversals of fortune. Comedic dialogue is humorous, full of verbal play (puns, similes, hyperboles), and quick and clever repartee. The setting of comedy is frequently the spring, and the characters move back and forth between private and public domains.[61] The ways in which the book of Ruth corresponds to these basic elements is clear. Ruth's plot moves from the tragic deaths of Elimelech and his sons to a wedding and the birth of a son.[62] Its plot is singular, lacking subplots and thus complying with Aristotle's criterion of unity of action.[63] Ruth's story is told primarily through witty dialogue, is set in the spring, and deals with issues of fertility.[64]

Aschkenasy draws particular attention to the reversals of fortune and the overturning of societal expectations in the book of Ruth. In particular Ruth and Naomi conspire to deceive the patriarch Boaz, employing the standard comic troupe of the "bed trick," and then Ruth proposes marriage to the man herself.[65] The crucial moment in many comedies is "the moment of chaos that is characterized by the breaking of all boundaries, by making merry, and by eating and drinking excessively."[66] The climax of the story of Ruth is the threshing room scene. Boaz, the community pillar, participates in this spring harvest ritual by drinking so much that he cannot make it home at night but must sleep on the floor of the threshing room with the other laborers. The celebration already entails ritual of reversals of decorum and inversions of normal behavior. It is easy for Ruth to take advantage of the already topsy-turvy situation to secure her future.

Aschkenasy draws the reader's attention to other comic moments in the text: Naomi's exaggerated and even bawdy speech about her getting pregnant and Ruth and Orpah waiting for her sons; Ruth and Boaz's first scene together where she gently mocks him; Ruth's continued gentle mockery in the threshing-room scene; Boaz filling her apron with a ridiculously large amount of grain and sending her home with her belly bulging. There are many comic elements in the closing scenes of Ruth as well: Boaz baiting the alternative redeemer who then frantically backtracks to get out of the situation; the singsong phrase the text uses to refer to him rather than by a proper name (*peloni 'almoni*); removing his shoe to seal the legal arrangement. Aschkenasy suggests that this unnamed relative fulfills the comic role of communal scapegoat as defined by Frye. The expulsion of the scapegoat is the way in which "society purges itself of the spirit of chaos that has temporarily seized it."[67] In this case the unnamed relative expels himself by refusing Ruth and removing his shoe. His "expulsion" allows the plot to resolve with the proper wedding, after the improper bedding, of Ruth and Boaz. Order is restored. Too often it is assumed that a book of sacred scripture must be solemn and pious, that comedy is antithetical to any holy purpose. But biblical books were not written as sacred scripture—canonization followed the writing, reading, and circulating of the story for perhaps hundreds of years. And laughter is not automatically profane. If one shifts one's expectations the book of Ruth abounds in humorous, even absurd situations; if one shifts one's expectations the character of Ruth looks out from between the pages, wryly grins and winks at the reader.

· 2 ·

AGRICULTURAL
INTERLUDE NO. I

There are no famines in northeastern Ohio; want comes from other circumstances, not climate or soil. The plum trees came down first, infected by black knot. Then the pear trees had to go too. We abandoned the apples and the cherries to the worms. I spent most summer afternoons in the branches of the cherry tree behind the great evergreen, at the edge of the apple orchard. I hid books up in its branches. I would eat, slowly opening up the cherry first to look for bugs, carefully examining the sweet flesh before putting it in my mouth. No one ate the apples. Only one of the peach trees would produce—one perfect peach, every other year. The grapes grew with wild abandon, never pruned, seemingly impervious to blight and pest. The blueberries were subject only to the birds in the morning. The vegetable gardens had many enemies—deer, groundhog, rabbit. And yet there are no famines in northeastern Ohio; the land always produces.

The plot of Ruth is motivated by the absence of food and ends with its abundance. But the agricultural setting is not just a backdrop, and food is more than what is eaten by hungry Moabites and Israelites. Food sustains the body, and it is linked intimately with such aspects of the body as sexuality and reproduction. The interplay between emptiness and fullness in Ruth is the interplay between empty and full bellies with empty and full wombs. The plot plays with the interconnections of food, sex, and reproduction throughout. Food also defines ethnicity, and the family's movements from famine to fullness are also movements that cross national borders and ethnic identities. Although the biblical story focuses on Ruth, both Ruth and Naomi are border crossers. Whereas most readers focus on Ruth's crossing (sometimes called conversion) in terms of her vow to Naomi or her marriage to Boaz, underlying the story is a more elemental crossing, the transfer of systems of food, a journey into different foodways.

I

In the opening words of L. P. Hartley's novel *The Go-Between*, "The past is a foreign country: they do things differently there."[1] The journey begins for Ruth's readers by traveling back into the past, to a time without presidents or prime ministers, to a past even before there were kings. The story of Ruth is set in the period of the judges, when the people of Israel were a loosely configured confederacy of tribes, probably even less organized than the biblical books of Joshua and Judges suggest. The opening words of Ruth take the reader back to this time, but the syntax of the opening phrase is unusual.[2] It reads woodenly but literally: "And it was [*vayhi*] in the days of the judging of the judges, and there was [*vayhi*] a famine in the land . . . " (Ruth 1:1ab). Many biblical books begin with the word *vayhi* ("and it / there was"), sometimes as a reference to time and sometimes as a reference to an event,[3] but only Ruth opens with its repetition. The next phrase, "the judging of the judges," also is unusual. It contains, as Jack M. Sasson points out, "a noun in masculine plural 'constructed' to an infinitive that, itself, is dependent on the word following."[4] If the explanation of the grammatical construct sounds confusing, it is. Common Hebrew redundancies often sound strange in English and are routinely altered in translation.[5] But these two repetitions (the double "and it was" and the "judging of the judges") even sound strange in Hebrew. The writer encodes the doubling motif, twice, in the first five words of the story. The text takes us to a time of even greater specificity, not just a time of judges but also a time of famine. The second "and it / there was" [*vayhi*] introduces the famine that will plague the people of Bethlehem and compel the family of Elimelech to leave their home and sojourn in the land of Moab. The irony of the situation is lost in English but painfully evident in Hebrew—there is a famine in Bethlehem, a famine in the "House of Bread." The doubling motif continues at the level of binary opposition and what Linafelt calls "the dialectic between emptiness and fullness."[6]

II

The contemporary food writer M. F. K. Fisher remarks, "It seems to me that our three basic needs, for food and security and love, are so mixed and mingled and entwined that we cannot straightly think of one without the others."[7] The book of Ruth exemplifies Fisher's observation for the author tangles all three needs up together. The underlying plot motivation, from beginning to end, is the search for security in the form of food and love (or at least marriage). Agricultural fertility is linked chiasmicly with human reproductive fertility, and agricultural work is likened to sexual congress. Naomi has two sons in the land of famine; in the land of bounty her daughters-in-law do not reproduce. Naomi's family is intact in the land of famine; in the land of bounty her husband and sons die (1:3–5). When she begins her journey back to Bethlehem Naomi makes specific reference to the emptiness of her womb (1:12–13); when she enters the town she tells the women that she left full (presumably of biological fruit) and returns empty (without sons or the potential of having sons) (1:21). The story reaches resolution only when the fertility of the land comes together with human fertility. The journey back to Beth-lehem occurs because the famine has ended, but the story ends only when Boaz fills first Ruth's apron with grain (3:15) and then her womb with seed (4:13).

Travel to the past entails the exploration of different ways of knowing. The link between human fertility and the earth's fertility in Ruth is more than just a pretty metaphor, a neat literary device to structure the plot. As with all cultures that developed before the advent of scientific epistemologies, the mechanisms of reproduction were not fully known in the ancient Near East. Lacking knowledge of the ovum, it would seem as if a man "plants" his "seed" in the "ground" of the woman's womb. Food, the product of the earth's fertility, and pregnancy are further linked because a full womb mimics a full belly—large and protruding. Regardless of time or place pregnancy also changes a woman's relationship to food. It brings sharp food cravings and pronounced food aversions. A favorite food may now induce nausea and vomiting. Even the most committed vegetarian may crave red meat; even the most dedicated carnivore may blanch at the sight or smell of steak.

A story that relies on the play between fertility and infertility invites the question, What associations with and experiences of fertility did the author assume in his or her readers? The contemporary platitude "she's eating for two" is not entirely accurate, but it is correct to say that a pregnant woman's body has embarked on a construction project of staggering proportions—the construction of another human body from scratch. The sperm and the ovum have united to provide the blueprint, but now every single cell must be built up from the elements and assembled into systems so complex that modern biology and medicine still cannot fully explain them. The raw elements of the project are oxygen, water, and the minerals, vitamins, and other substances provided by food. A pregnant woman must consume enough calories to fuel and nourish her body and to power the creation of another body—about three hundred extra calories a day. A pregnant woman must consume enough substances to be digested and reassembled into that other body; specifically she has a meteoritic increase in her iron, folic acid, calcium, and protein needs. The particularities of the nutritional data would have been unknown, but the experience of pregnancy would have provided a different kind of data set, and food is a constant preoccupation of the pregnant.

To take just one example of nutritional needs, iron deficiency is a common problem today among pregnant and nonpregnant women alike, among women in industrialized and nonindustrialized countries.[8] Like other contemporary women with health insurance and therefore access to the best prenatal care the United States has to offer, I took prescription prenatal vitamins for a year before I conceived and during the forty-one weeks of my pregnancy and will continue to take them through my months of breast feeding. Even so I developed anemia by my twenty-eighth week of pregnancy and had to supplement the prenatal vitamin and my healthy, balanced, twenty-first-century American diet with additional iron pills. Iron deficiencies must have been even higher in ancient Israel, among agriculturalists and pastoralists alike. The high cereal and low meat consumption of the agriculturalist can lead to anemia, as can the low fruit and high dairy intake of the pastoralist since vitamin C aids and calcium impedes iron absorption into the blood. Whereas anemia alone will not lead to death, "iron deficiency affects brain function and the immune system, and can reduce working capacity."[9] Anemia becomes particularly dangerous during labor and delivery since some bleeding always occurs and substantial bleeding sometimes does. A woman who is already anemic is at a higher risk for death in childbirth because she is less able to recover from this bleeding. Infant and maternal mortality rates in times of famine must have been particularly high. The irony of Ruth's opening scene deepens—it is precisely in the land of bounty (Moab) where infertility reigns and death overtakes grown sons.

III

Information about human fertility would have been based in the experiences of pregnant women and the observations of the women and men who watched over them. Information about the earth's fertility would have been more widely experienced since both women and men, the young and the old participated in farming. In their study of life in ancient Israel Philip J. King and Lawrence E. Steger observe: "The gap between us and ancient peoples continues to widen as we become further removed from our agrarian roots. Today less than two percent of the population in the United States are farmers. In ancient Israel, it was just the opposite."[10] The biblical story is told within a particular context, and the author (like any author, then or now, there or here) assumes that the reader shares a certain cultural knowledge. The story of Ruth is set in the early Iron Age or Iron Age I (1200–1000 B.C.E.), although it was most probably written in the postexilic or Persian Period (538–333 B.C.E.). The centuries between these eras wrought many changes in the political, social, and religious life of the people of Israel. These centuries did not, however, alter the basic agricultural orientation of society, nor did the methods of food production change significantly. Diet also remained largely the same.[11] Recently, through the archaeological turn to everyday life and material culture, scholars have been able to recover some of what the biblical authors assumed about how people lived and how they filled their time, time which was largely spent producing, preparing, and consuming food.

The environment of the ancient Israelites both shaped and was shaped by their activities as farmers: "The environment is not merely a passive and static stage on which cultural evolution takes place, but, indeed, a set of dynamic processes inducing that evolution. At the outset, the environment conditions the material life of a society. Reciprocally a society's responses to the opportunities, challenges, constraints, and hazards presented by the environment tend to modify the environ-ment. Thus a society's interaction with the environment inevitably affects its values and attitudes—indeed, its entire worldview."[12] Agricultural metaphors abound in the Bible (especially metaphors derived from viticulture); both creation myths are preoccupied with water and God is frequently portrayed as the giver and with-holder of rain; food-production systems shape the Israelite cult through animal and grain sacrifice; the uncultivated desert acts as a liminal space where human and divine can meet. On every page of Hebrew scripture the agricultural experiences of the Israelites infuse the biblical worldview.

Even the Israelite calendar was at base an agricultural calendar and the Israelite holidays were essentially harvest festivals. The celebrated salvific events (Exodus, Wilderness Wanderings, Sinai) were attached to the celebrations only later. The Gezer Calendar, which dates to the end of the tenth century B.C.E., is a twelve-month calendar further divided into eight agricultural seasons, beginning with the fall harvests: "His two months are (olive) harvest, His two months are planting (grain), His two months are late planting; His month is hoeing up of flax, His month is harvest of barley, His month is harvest and feasting; His two months are vine-tending, His month is summer fruit."[13] Time was marked by the rhythms of planting, tending, harvest.

The book of Ruth stands out in the biblical corpus in part because of its agricul-tural setting. The Bible as a whole reflects the agrarian society that produced it, but no other biblical book foregrounds actual agricultural practices, embedding both characterization and plot into them. Ruth's narrative chronology is marked by famine and its end, by the seasons of barley and wheat harvesting. The characters move in and out of the fields, on and off the threshing room floors. As if to empha-size further the agricultural significance of Ruth, the word *field* (*sadeh*) is used repeatedly, including in some unusual ways. For example, the phrase *fields of Moab* or *field of Moab* is used seven times in the book of Ruth (1:1, 2, 6 [twice], 22; 2:6; 4:3). The word *field* can refer to land or territory, but such is not the typical Hebrew way of referring to other countries.[14] The word *field* is also used nine other times with reference to land in Judah (2:2, 3 [twice], 8, 9, 17, 22; 4:3, 5). Oddities and repetitions are not accidental. They continually reinforce the agricultural setting as the characters in the book move from field to field. Readers of Ruth travel back in time, to a moment during the era of the judges when famine swept the land to find themselves standing in the fields of food production.

IV

First, survey the field. The basic geography of the book of Ruth can still be discerned in the geography of Israel and Jordan today. Bethlehem is located five miles south of Jerusalem, 2,350 feet above sea level on well-watered, fertile, and productive soil.[15] Moab is the land east of the Dead Sea, bordering on Israel. In antiquity the population of Moab was concentrated on a plateau 3,000 feet above sea level between the Dead Sea and the Arabian desert. The soil was thin then, as it is now, but the winter rains were plentiful and cereal crops could be cultivated.[16] The farming method was dry farming—meaning that agricultural productivity relied on the water from annual rainfalls captured in porous soil.[17] Neither the Israelites nor the Moabites could rely on periodic rains or on irrigation. The winter rains, which began in the fall and lasted until spring, were everything. In the northern area of the hill countries of Israel, average rain fall could be as high as forty inches, whereas in the southern area, average rainfall is about sixteen inches;[18] twelve inches are necessary for a productive growing season.[19] The amount of precipitation was the key factor in determining crop success or failure, but the distribution and timing of that rain also played a role. Rains that came too soon or too late, rains that were too light or too heavy, could devastate a particular crop just as easily as no rain at all.[20] Even though the village was in a productive area, located in the southern regions of the hill country, Bethlehem had a margin for error that was extremely narrow.

The land the Israelites had settled by the time of the Iron Age was not a land that gave up its fruits readily. The ancient Near East (today's Middle East) is an intermediate region that lies between the continents of Asia and Africa and includes parts of these continents. It inhabits an intermediate climate zone, "between the humid or subhumid environments of southeastern Europe and the hyperarid environments of the great desert belt."[21] Poised unstably betwixt and between, the Israelites struggled to eke out an existence: "They had to cope with the adversity of the rugged hills and erodible soils of Canaan, the barrenness of the deserts of the Negev and Judea, the prolonged droughts alternating with capricious flash floods that occasionally inundated the valleys and lowlands, the violent westerly rainstorms that lashed the land in winter and the searing easterly winds that desiccated the land in summer, the occasional earthquakes that emanated from the numerous geological faults, and the proximity of the storm-prone Mediterranean Sea."[22] Their geography left them vulnerable to both environmental crises and political upheavals. Famine was always a concern.

This is the land that Naomi and her family farmed. When famine threatened their very lives, they walked out of Judah and into Moab. When death finally found the men, Naomi and Ruth walked back to Naomi's homeland. The Dead Sea lies between the two lands at 1,329 feet below sea level, the lowest point on earth. Ruth and Naomi had to descend 4,329 feet to cross the Dead Sea and then ascend 3,679 feet into the Judean hill country. The text records no conversation between the two widows as they made this difficult journey, the terrain perhaps reflective of their mood, the landscape a metaphor for their state of mind.

V

Now, inventory the fruits of the field: land used to pastor flocks, land used to grow grain, land for vegetables and fruits. Beyond the generalizations (grains, legumes, fruits, vegetables), reconstructing the Israelite diet, especially in the Iron Age, is challenging. What is eaten cannot be excavated; what is decomposed can not be found. And early archaeologists were unconcerned with the texture of daily life—any plant remains that managed to survive the millennia were disregarded. Only recently have archaeologists begun to seek out such remains and to recover and record them.[23]

Anthropological research has not been much better. Since W. Robertson Smith anthropological studies on the food of the Bible have been preoccupied with the legislation around the consumption of meat.[24] Following Smith's lead contemporary cultural anthropologists such as Mary Douglas[25] and Marvin Harris[26] have sought to understand the Levitical food regulations, which delineate the animals permissible for consumption along with methods of slaughter and preparation.[27] As anthropologist Sidney W. Mintz notes, this bias for the unusual—"food prohibitions and taboos, cannibalism, the consumption of unfamiliar and distasteful items—rather than [the] everyday [foods that are] essential features of the life of all humankind"[28]—is a failing throughout the history of anthropological research. Fruits, vegetables, grains, and dairy products were permissible among the ancient Israelites and therefore have merited little attention from researchers interested in food. Yet customs and rules shape all food consumption. Simply because all is permitted does not mean that all is partaken. Any individual eats a very limited diet in comparison with the range of plant and animal matter that could be consumed, limits imposed not just by personal taste but also, and even more forcibly, by cultural context. And food choice is only the beginning of the story. As Roland Barthes asks, "For what is food? It is not only a collection of products that can be used for statistical or nutritional studies. It is also, and at the same time, a system of communication, a body of images, a protocol of usages, situations, and behavior."[29] Such meanings are not just attached to meat eating; even grains, fruits, and vegetables are a "rich symbolic alphabet" in the language of culture.[30]

Even though, as Nathan MacDonald notes, "There is scarcely a page in the Old Testament where food is not mentioned,"[31] there have been only a few forays into more comprehensive approaches—archaeological, anthropological, or even literary—to the food in the Hebrew Bible.[32] Researchers who do speak to the subject integrate the little archaeological remains we have, cross-cultural comparisons, literary references in both the Bible and the occasional inscription, and knowledge about what the Levant produces today. If the readers of Ruth were to look up from the fields of barley and wheat that are so integral to the story, they would see vineyards, olive-tree orchards, fig, date, and pomegranate trees, lentils, chickpeas, broad beans, and various nut trees. They might even have seen the occasional vegetable garden growing onion, leek, melon, cucumber.[33]

VI

When Elizabeth Cady Stanton wrote her entry on the book of Ruth in her *Woman's Bible,* she pictured Ruth and Naomi sitting down together every night to talk about the day's adventures, sipping herbal teas and eating watercress sandwiches. The picture is quite genteel, and clearly influenced by Stanton's own culinary practices. When examining the question of any society's food practices, it is never enough to describe climate and soil and to list the types of food available. Ruth may have walked past fields of lentils, orchards of almonds, plots of melon on her way to the barley fields. These foods were grown, but such information is not sufficient for an accurate representation of what constituted the typical Israelite diet. There would have been a wide variety of practices depending on what foods were available any given year in any given locale due to political, social, and environmental vagaries; and, more germane to Ruth, what foods were available to particular people based on their gender and class status.[34] To take just one example, archaeological investigation may indicate that a certain village raised enough livestock to supply everyone with a portion of meat daily, but this does not mean that animal protein was evenly distributed throughout the community. More nuanced analyses are required to portray accurately the diet of the average Israelite. Two poor widows forced to glean the fields of rich neighbors did not sit down to the refined repasts that Stanton imagined, nor did they dine on the full bounty that the fields of Bethlehem had to offer.

Ruth's culinary narrative is a story of gender, class, and ethnicity. Her status as a poor widow is marked by her need to glean. The ways in which food marks her ethnicity are harder to discern from the narrative itself. What follows is, admittedly, speculative, but is based on the general principle that "the role of food in generating and sustaining national identities is well documented in literature on food and foodways."[35] Different food practices maintain cultural boundaries, and the Israelite food practices certainly set them apart from their neighbors.

Cultural meanings perforce encode food choice because of a fact of human biology: humans are omnivores. Our physical needs cannot be met by a diet limited to a few particular plants or animals, and our bodies are capable of extracting the necessary nutrients from a wide variety of sources. Omnivory on such a vast scale is unusual in the animal world and may be, in part, the reason for the evolutionary development of our intelligence. Without an innate preference for a limited diet (as koalas have for eucalyptus, for example), we had to develop the capacity to discern what was safe to eat from the poisonous (the chanterelles from the death caps), acquire the tools and technologies to transform raw inedibles to substances we could digest (grain in its raw form is nearly worthless to us, whereas processed it becomes "the staff of life"), and remember it all so that diet did not need to be reinvented in every generation.[36] The French sociologist Claude Fischler describes the "omnivore's paradox" thus: "On the one hand, needing variety, the omnivore is inclined toward diversification, innovation, exploration and change, which can be vital to its survival; but, on the other hand, it has to be careful, mistrustful, 'conservative,' in its eating: any new, unknown food is a potential danger."[37] Cultural traditions, rules, and practices help negotiate the paradox of omnivory.

All peoples have dietary restrictions and both official and unofficial regulations about what can and cannot be eaten. What constitutes "food" in general North American culture? We have certain categories of animals that cannot be eaten as food despite the fact that they are equally good protein sources as the animals permitted for consumption. We do not eat animals that have been classified as pets: dogs and cats especially. Not only are there strong social bans against using pets as food; there are also laws that prohibit treating dogs and cats like livestock. If one treated a dog as chickens are routinely treated, one would be arrested for cruelty to animals.[38] We do not eat most animals that are classified as rodents: rats, mice. We do not eat insects or spiders or worms. To even think about consuming such creatures evokes a negative visceral reaction. Ask North Americans about eating fried ants and chances are that they will experience a tightening of the abdominal muscles, they will screw up their faces, wrinkle their noses, and say some variation of "eew." The cultural proscriptions have been deeply inscribed into the body. How much more so if the dietary restrictions also had the force of divine mandate behind them? Beyond hygienic or environmental or economic reasons for certain meat prohibitions in Israel, especially the one that forbade the consumption of pig, kosher legislation erected cultural boundaries that would have been difficult to traverse.

As Ruth and Naomi walk back and forth across national borders, what native foodways do they cling to and which ones do they abandon? Food regulations maintain the boundaries between different peoples, but so do preferences of preparation. People in Central and South America roll meat, cheese, and vegetables into a tortilla; people in North America put the same between two slices of bread. What difference set Moabite apart from Israelite? Since meat eating was not a common practice among all Israelites and Moabites, were cultural distinctions less pronounced among the poor? All of the evidence indicates that Moabite ate differently from Israelite; none of the evidence can show precisely how.

VII

We draw our sustenance from the earth beneath our feet. The ways in which distinctive foodways define ethnicity or nationality go even deeper than what foods are eaten and how they are prepared. The fields are the very ground of our being. The

interconnections between soil and body are less pronounced in modern industrialized societies like our own. Especially in twenty-first century America most of the
food we eat has been grown elsewhere, transported over hundreds, sometimes
thousands, of miles. We eat out of season—fruits and vegetables are grown either
in warmer climes or in greenhouses heated with fossil fuels. We eat out of place—
most of our produce, meats, dairy, grains are transported from elsewhere by trucks
or trains or planes. We participate in a world cuisine: people on every continent
now drink tea and coffee. The flour for the bread I ate today was grown in the central plains, the orange in Florida; the cheese was made in Vermont.

Preindustrial agrarian communities also bought and traded foods. In Israel fish
came from the Galilee, from the Mediterranean, even from the Nile.[39] Communities
raised sheep and goats and sold their surpluses to neighboring villages. Pastoral
groups traded milk for grain. Even so, the bulk of the food consumed was produced
by the land the people lived on. The sun, water, soil, air of one place was trans-
muted into grain, figs, carrots, lentils. Such foodstuffs would then be consumed and
transformed into skin, heart, eye, hair. The links between a particular place and a
particular body would be intimate; each person would be laced into his or her environment and then linked to every other person in that place. All beings, in fact,
animate and inanimate, would be made out of the exact same elements, only configured and reconfigured in different bodies, in different ways, at different times.
When Ruth and Naomi crossed over each other's borders, their bodies began to
transform as they ate each other's food.

In her work *Borderlands / La Frontera: The New Mestiza,* Gloria Anzaldúa explores the lands along the borders of two countries and the mixed identities that
emerge among those who live along such lines. Specifically she addresses life along
the United States–Mexican border. Even though her experience grounds her in this
particular place, the idea of the borderland transcends: "The psychological borderlands, the sexual borderlands and the spiritual borderlands are not particular to the
Southwest. In fact the Borderlands are physically present wherever two or more cultures edge each other, where people of different races occupy the same territory,
where under, lower, middle and upper classes touch, where the space between two
individuals shrinks with intimacy."[40] Both Ruth and Naomi are border crossers.
Naomi sojourns in Moab for at least ten years; Ruth sojourns in Israel. It is this
more than anything that binds the women together. They have both experienced
the psychological borderlands of ethnic and cultural mixing; in fact they have both
eaten the foods of the other: "To live in the Borderlands means to put *chile* in the
borscht, / eat whole wheat *tortillas.*"[41]

When Naomi leaves Bethlehem in search of sustenance, she settles in Moab and
her body becomes one built by Moabite soil and water. She is integrated into the
community in part because she is eating its food and thus physically and literally

integrating her body into the land and people. When Ruth leaves Moab she does the same. As time goes on more and more of her cells are built with the soil, air, water, and sun of Bethlehem. Each new Bethlehemite cell replaces a Moabite cell. She is transforming—still Moabite but also other than Moabite, Judahite too, but not completely. Ruth's relationship to food tells her story of crossing over. Ruth is pushed to the margins by hunger, inhabits the margins through gleaning, moves across the border by adopting Israelite foodways and eating from the bounty of Bethlehemite soil, and hence is incorporated into the community as demonstrated but not affected by her marriage to Boaz.

· 3 ·

RUTH AND ORPAH

Naomi and her family cross the border into Moab looking for food.[1] While there her two sons find Moabite women to marry. Ruth and Orpah are introduced together and remain undifferentiated through the deaths of their husbands and the beginning of their journey with Naomi back to Judah. The pair divide only in their different responses to Naomi's advice to return to their own mothers. In an otherwise dialogue-laden text Orpah simply weeps and turns toward home. Because of her lack of articulate voice commentators have used her as a cipher for all sorts of concerns. In many traditional interpretations she serves as the negative foil for Ruth's faithfulness. Many contemporary commentators "mimic the biblical text by leaving her to return home unattended, both literally and critically."[2] Feminist interpreters seem divided between regarding Orpah's decision as "sound" or "dangerous."[3] Postcolonial readings regard her as a symbol of resistance against imperialism.[4] In tune with the book of Ruth's employ of various doubling motifs, Orpah functions as Ruth's doppelganger, her counterpart. But how exactly we are supposed to read the doubling is an open question—if Orpah's decision is "sound," is Ruth's "dangerous," or vice versa? If Ruth demonstrates *hesed* and loyalty, is Orpah selfish and cowardly? If Orpah is a symbol of resistance, is Ruth the betrayer of her people?

While probing Orpah's character and her relationship with and to Ruth, I became increasingly weary of one common understanding of Ruth's purpose and meaning—that the book provides a testimony in Israel against societal antipathy toward Moabites. I became not only weary but troubled by certain postcolonial readings that assumed the Israelite *oppression* of Moabites and then drew analogies between Israelites and white European colonial powers. In these readings Moabites are Botswanian, Maori, Asian immigrants to America, foreign guest workers in Israel, Native Americans . . . there is hardly a group whose suffering has not been equated to the supposed suffering of the Moabites at the hands of the Israelites. I read Ruth, carefully watching the dynamic between Israelite and Moabite, looking for the shock, horror, disgust expressed whenever Israelite encountered Moabite, the prejudice that commentators assured me was there. I did not, however, find it. Instead I found that the literary presentation of Moabites in the scripture is complex, ambivalent, sometimes unequivocally negative but just as often open to interpretation; and certain types of postcolonial engagements with Ruth are dependent on an equation between modern European colonization of Africa, Asia, Australia, and the Americas with ancient Israelite contact with Moab. An imperialism based on *racial* hierarchy is read back into Ruth, a time and place where, historically, neither exist.

Moabites

The book of Ruth opens with a situation that is common in biblical narrative as well as in human history—a privation that compels migration. In the face of famine Elimelech and his family travel to Moab in search of food.[5] In sparse biblical narrative details are not incidental and repetitions are never gratuitous. The fact that the family sojourns in Moab, along with the repetition of Ruth and Orpah's ethnic identity throughout the narrative, invites reflection and interpretation.

Since the narrative of Ruth fails to explain the significance of Moab, biblical scholars have turned to other scriptural texts to illuminate Israel's attitudes toward its neighbor. Genesis 19 is the first text ushered in to explain Ruth and Orpah's status. Fleeing a burning Sodom, Abraham's nephew Lot and his two daughters seek shelter in a cave. Believing themselves to be the only people left on earth, Lot's unnamed daughters take on the responsibility of reproduction. They get Lot drunk and, on successive nights, rape him. One daughter gives birth to Ben-Ami and the other to Moab, the eponymous ancestors of the Ammonites and Moabites, respectively (Gen. 19:30–38).

The pericope can be read in several different ways. On the one hand Lot's daughters were almost subjected to gang rape at their own father's urging (Gen. 19:7–8), thus their rape of him can be read as either a result of trauma or as poetic justice, in either case, justified. On the other hand their progeny are the product of deceptive, drunken incest. Incest insults are common throughout the world (even in our own society), and many argue that this story establishes the basic orientation of the Israelites to the Moabites—they are related to us, but something about them just isn't right. For example, Randall C. Bailey looks at the polemical use of sexuality, particularly in the way it brands the foreigner as morally degenerate.[6] He sees the incest insult in Genesis 19 as obvious and evident.

The tension that results from close relation but troubled relationship marks many of the interactions between peoples in biblical texts (other examples include Israelites and Edomites mirrored in the relationship between the twin brothers Jacob and Esau; Israelites and Ishmaelites whose eponymous ancestors are the half-brothers Isaac and Ishmael). The stories of the individual ancestors reflect the tensions and the ambiguities experienced in later times between the peoples. Reading the story of Lot and his daughters as a kind of ethnic slur is standard in biblical scholarship, but other scholars like Tikva Frymer-Kensky caution against assuming a negative interpretation of the story.[7] After all, the story itself does not condemn the actions of the daughters, and, generally speaking, the continuance of a male line, even if it is accomplished by unorthodox measures, is always rewarded.[8] Examples in Genesis especially abound and include the story of Rebecca counseling Jacob to deceive both Esau and Isaac in a way that fulfills God's plan for Jacob to inherit the blessing (Gen. 25:23; Gen. 27:5–28, 40), and Tamar dressing as a prostitute to deceive Judah, conceiving Perez and Zerah and thus continuing the line of promise (Genesis 38). Tamar is even proclaimed "righteous" for her act. Lot's daughters may be understood in terms of Rebecca and Tamar, their sons just as free of moral taint.

The ambivalence surrounding Moab continues throughout the Torah. In the book of Numbers the wandering Hebrews pass by and through territories under Moabite control.[9] Several stories illustrate conflict between the two peoples. In Num. 22:3–4 the Moabites fear that the Israelite hordes will devour them "as an ox licks up the grass of the field" (Num. 22:4b). King Balak sends Balaam on an ill-fated journey to curse the Israelites (Numbers 22). Immediately after Balaam's curses turn to blessings, Moabite women lead Israelite men astray either through licentious sex or improper worship or both (Num. 25:1–5). Yet in Deuteronomy's retelling of the journey from Egypt to Canaan a more cordial relationship between the two peoples emerges. In Deut. 2:8–9 Moses is commanded by God to leave the Moabites alone because, as descendents of Lot, they are under special protection and the land that they inhabit is theirs, given by God's own hand. Deut. 2:28–29 implies that the Moabites did provide food and drink to the migrating Hebrews.

The laws toward the end of Deuteronomy turn again to a negative assessment of their character and their consequent place in the community: "no Ammonite or Moabite shall enter into the assembly of the Lord. Even to the tenth generation none of their descendants shall enter into the assembly of the Lord, because they did not meet you with bread and water on your way out of Egypt, and because they hired against you Balaam son of Beor, from Pethor of Mesopotamia, to curse you. . . . You shall never seek their peace or their welfare all of your days, forever" (Deut. 23:3–4, 6 [Heb.: 4–5, 7]). These verses are clear condemnations of the people of Moab.

Outside of the Torah there are several references to Moab which again point to a cordial relationship between the peoples. David takes his parents there for refuge (1 Sam. 22:3–4). In Isaiah a long oracle indicates that Moab will be destroyed by the Assyrians, but the words of Isaiah are sympathetic not condemnatory. The people of Judah are urged to offer sanctuary to the fleeing Moabites: "Like fluttering birds, expelled from the nest, so are the daughters of Moab at the fords of the Arnon. 'Give counsel, make justice; set like night your shade at the height of noon; hide the outcasts, do not betray the fugitive; let the outcasts of Moab abide with you; be a hiding place to them from the destroyer'" (Isa. 16:2–4a).

Against this backdrop the attitudes of the author and audience of Ruth seem less than clear. What kind of Moabites are Ruth and Orpah? The kind who would screw their own father or the kind who would give sanctuary to the aging parents of a man on the run? The kind who are categorically excluded from the Israelite community or the kind who are given refuge in time of need? With few exceptions commentators cite the story of Lot and his daughters, negatively assessed, along with Deuteronomy's law against Moabite intermarriage to construct the attitudes of Ruth's original audience toward Moabites. Thus Mahlon and Chilion's marriages to Moabites are determined to be illicit, and a range of interpretative possibilities follow— from understanding the deaths of the men as punishment for their transgression of intermarriage to reading the whole book as a polemic against the prevailing prejudices against Moabites and their inclusion in the Israelite community.

Understanding the marriages of Ruth and Orpah to Israelite men as a violation of biblical proscription can be seen as far back as the Targum of Ruth.[10] A Targum is an Aramaic paraphrase of the biblical text, the paraphrase offering a space for interpretive comment. The opening verses of the book of Ruth as translated in the Targum read thus: "*They transgressed against the decree of the Memra of the Lord and they took for themselves foreign* wives *from the daughters of Moab.* The name of one was Orpah and the name of the second was Ruth, *the daughter of Eglon, king of Moab,* and they dwelt there for about ten years. *And because they transgressed against the decree of the Memra of the Lord and intermarried with foreign peoples, their days were cut short* and both Mahlon and Chilion also died *in the unclean land,* and the woman was left *bereaved* of her two sons and *widowed* of her husband."[11]

At every juncture the Targumist inserts a negative assessment of Moab and Moabites, clearly influenced by both the Deuteronomic laws and its theodicy—the sons violated the law and they are promptly (well, after ten years) punished through death, and possibly earlier through the barrenness of their wives. These same judgments are present in Ruth Rabbah, later rabbinic interpretations (midrash) of the book of Ruth. Ruth is ultimately accepted into the community only because there is an emphasis on her anachronistic status as a proselyte, despite the fact that biblical law does not make an exception for converts. The idea of conversion was probably quite foreign to the biblical writers, not because the biblical writers did not recognize the fact that non-Israelites could believe in Yahweh and join the community but because the concept of "conversion" relies on a more modern notion of "religion."

Many contemporary readings of Ruth, both Christian and Jewish, pick up on the assumed opprobrium. Ellen F. Davis notes at the beginning of her commentary: "The first sentence [of the book of Ruth] hints at a small drama. . . . Against this background, we can see that our story begins with a scandal, a public scandal of major proportions."[12] Davis continues in this vein and cites Jacob Neusner to support her position. Neusner, commenting on David's having a Moabite great-grandmother, "suggests that it would be analogous to a grandchild of Hitler running for prime minister of the state of Israel."[13] Other biblical commentators are more restrained. For example, Nielsen writes: "The text itself contains no evaluation of the sons' marriage; it simply states it as a fact, leaving the reader to consider whether the following events are a consequence of their marrying foreigners."[14] Yet she still understands the Moabite ancestry of David to be an embarrassing historical fact that must be addressed and justified.

The text of Ruth itself does not condemn the marriages between Ruth and Orpah with Naomi's sons or Ruth's second marriage to Boaz. If there are negative attitudes assumed about these marriages they are not made explicit in the text. The verses simply state "And they [Mahlon and Chilion] married Moabite women; the name of one was Orpah and the name of the second was Ruth, and they lived there about ten years. And then the two, Mahlon and Chilion, also died, and the woman [Naomi] was left without her two boys and without her husband" (1:4–5). As readers we can see the Israelite men's marriage to Moabite women as unremarkable as the text seems to or we can read the straightforward recounting of events as, to quote Erich Auerbach, "fraught with background." While the reader's decision to see more behind the text may be justified by Hebrew narrative's general reticence, the way a reader understands this background relies on decisions about what other biblical narratives and interpretive traditions to read in conjunction with the book of Ruth.

If we did not read Ruth with select portions of Genesis, Numbers, and Deuteronomy in our back pocket, would we condemn Orpah for returning to her mother? Would we see the people of Bethlehem recoil when Ruth enters the town? Would we see the other redeemer make a hasty retreat from his pledge to buy Naomi's land once Ruth's name is brought into the negotiation? Ruth and Orpah are certainly marked as foreigners in the story—the fact that Ruth is a Moabite is mentioned multiple times, gratuitously (1:22; 2:2, 6, 21; 4:5, 10). Their status as foreigners is certainly important for the story because it is repeated so frequently, but there are other, more positive, ways in which such marking can be read.

Ruth's status as foreigner may heighten the reversals of fortune with which the text as a whole plays, without necessarily portraying her foreignness as negative— she is a poor widow and, if that is not bad enough, she is a recent immigrant. No matter the specific situation, being in a place away from home, speaking a language that is not one's native tongue, negotiating new societal systems and cultural codes, places one at a disadvantage. In such a case the reader is supposed to feel even more sympathetic to her situation not regard her with more suspicion or prejudice. Most

of the characters who surround Ruth do not seem to regard her foreignness negatively. There are some actions that are open to interpretation—Naomi's silence after
Ruth's vow (1:18); the overseer's response to Boaz's initial query (2:6–7); the other
kinsman-redeemer's refusal to marry Ruth (if this is indeed what he is refusing,
4:6). Otherwise, Boaz speaks kindly to her and has clearly been hearing the gossip
of the town about her—gossip which is positive from the beginning. Boaz tells
Ruth: "I have been told all that you have done for your mother-in-law after the
death of your husband, and how you left your father and your mother and the land
of your birth and came to a people whom you did not formerly know. May the Lord
reward your deeds and may your reward be full from the Lord the God of Israel
under whose wings you have sought refuge" (2:11–12). When Ruth marries Boaz
she is blessed by the community (4:11–12), and in the end the women of
Bethlehem declare her better than seven sons to Naomi (4:15). The town is certainly a-buzz when Ruth accompanies Naomi home, but the people do not appear
to be scandalized when the Israelite woman returns with a Moabite daughter-in-law
in tow.

We can not draw clear and certain connections between a negatively interpreted
Genesis 19, the laws of Deuteronomy, and the characters in the book of Ruth. Not
only are there the issues outlined above, but there are also questions of the dating
of the texts, how accurately the texts represent social attitudes, and whether or not
the laws are proscriptive or descriptive, ideal or real. Take the case of Deuteronomy,
in which the law against admitting a Moabite into the community appears.
Historical-critical scholarship positions the writing of Deuteronomy toward the end
of the seventh century B.C.E. as part of Josiah's reforms. It cannot be assumed that
any given precept in Deuteronomy would have been known, let alone followed,
before this time. In fact it is clear that certain laws were not followed—in particular, Deuteronomy enjoins a centralization of worship that does not appear to be a
part of Israelite religion before Josiah's time (as both textual and archaeological evidence attests). Therefore in arguments that position Ruth as a book from the
monarchical period, Deuteronomy cannot be used to illustrate Israelite attitudes
toward and laws against Moabites.

At the beginning of the postexilic era Ezra and Nehemiah return to Israel to find
multiple marriages between Israelites and Moabites. Ezra and Nehemiah have to
argue vehemently against such marriages, a situation that would have been impossible if the laws of Deuteronomy were widely known and widely adhered to. The
books of Ezra and Nehemiah do not reflect widespread antipathy toward Moabites
but precisely the opposite. Only if one regards Ruth as a late postexilic document,
after Deuteronomy had been widely disseminated and its status approaching canonical, can its pronouncements against Moabites play a role in the writing of Ruth.
Mahlon's, Chilion's, and Boaz's marriages to Moabites bothered interpreters who

certainly accept Deuteronomy as authoritative (the writers of the Targum, Midrash, Talmud, and early Christian interpreters), but how far back Deuteronomy's influence goes is impossible to determine.

The Hebrew Bible has a mixed record in its assessment of intermarriage, not just with Moabites but with the many non-Israelites that come into contact with this group of people. Egypt is the state that enslaved the Hebrews—certainly a worse history of oppression than the Moabites refusal of hospitality. Yet Joseph marries an Egyptian woman, without comment by the text (Gen. 46:20); Solomon marries an Egyptian woman with ambivalent results (1 Kings 3:1)—it is a testimony to his power but also contributes to the split of his kingdom according to the Deuteronomist historian. Moses marries a Midianite and perhaps even a Cushite (Exod. 2:21 and Numbers 12). Those who question his marriage are punished (Numbers 12). Judah is married to a Canaanite (Gen. 38:2). Solomon's mother Bathsheba may be a Hittite—at the very least she is first married to one, and he serves faithfully in David's army (2 Samuel 11). In many of these cases such marriages are unremarkable, perhaps even implying that they were, if not common, also not rare. It is also possible that, far from being a mark against one's lineage, foreign women in one's ancestry were considered a mark of distinction.

It is common in mythology and legend to ascribe unusual or miraculous conception stories to heroes, kings, and deities. Sometimes these stories also transgress the normal ethics, laws, and customs of the people who tell the story. Heroes, kings, and deities are not bound to regular human mores. "Ancestors, gods, and gods-on-earth are special beings, marked in their specialness by their breaking of the taboos, including the one against incest, that restrain ordinary people. Breaking the taboos doesn't shame them; it heightens their sacredness."[15] Perhaps contemporary readers have it all wrong. The very aspects of the story that we regard as shameful—Lot's daughters conceiving children with him, for example—are the very ones the original audiences would have regarded as sacred. David would not have had to be defended against the charge of having a Moabite ancestress—it was this ancestry that helped strengthen his royal claims—and the story of Ruth could have been constructed to make such a point. There is no unequivocal evidence to regard the story of Ruth as one that assumes its audience's antipathy toward Moabite women. They may be indifferent to such marriages; in certain circumstances they may even be inclined toward them.

Orpah

Ultimately Ruth must be separated from Orpah because they do part and walk into very different futures, very different afterlives. Orpah is a minor figure in the book of Ruth. She is introduced in the same verse as Ruth herself as one of the Moabite wives of one of Elimelech and Naomi's sons (Ruth 1:4). It is not clear until the end of the story that Orpah was married to Chilion (in Ruth 4:10 Ruth is identified as the wife of Mahlon). Once the sons die Ruth and Orpah are referred to as Naomi's daughters-in-law, or literally, Naomi's "brides." The one Hebrew word (*kalah*) has both meanings, and the particular sense of the word is derived from context. The English expression *daughter-in-law* and the word *bride* have such different connotations that English readers may miss an important component of Naomi's (or the text's) attitude toward these two women. The former establishes a legal relationship and sounds more official than familial, but the latter conjures up images of love, affection, joy, and hope. Consequently Ellen F. Davis chooses to translate the Hebrew word as "bride-daughters" in order to retain the connotations of *bride,* a suggestion I follow below in some of my own translations.[16] The repeated use of this word in the opening chapter is also an aspect of the irony so deftly employed by the author of the tale. The two "brides" have just become widows.[17]

Orpah, like Ruth, begins the journey back to Bethlehem with Naomi: "And she arose with her bride-daughters. . . . And she went out from the place where she had been living with her two bride-daughters, and they walked along the road to return to the land of Judah" (1:6a, 1:7). At some unspecified point in their travels Naomi stops to tell both Ruth and Orpah to turn back, giving them both God's blessing. Both respond in the same manner, and they are undifferentiated in the narrative. They both are kissed by Naomi, and they both weep (1:9), saying to her "With you, we will return to your people" (1:10). The Hebrew sentence begins with the phrase "with you," thus emphasizing it and perhaps indicating the reason the bride-daughters embark on the journey to Judah: they want to stay with Naomi no matter where she goes. Naomi, however, continues to entreat them to return to their own mother's houses, affectionately calling them, "my daughters" three times in her speech to them (1:11–13). They continue to weep (1:14).

As Linafelt notes, "both rabbinic and modern interpreters have taken a negative view of Orpah's decision to return to Moab rather than continuing on to Judah with Naomi," but "the narrator does not offer any clue that we are to condemn her for the decision."[18] Both Ruth and Orpah decided to leave Moab and accompany Naomi to Bethlehem; both Ruth and Orpah resist Naomi's urging to return to their own mother's houses; both Ruth and Orpah weep. Any negative assessment of Orpah is as unwarranted, at this point, as any negative assessment of Ruth would be. It is not until the middle of verse 14 that Ruth and Orpah separate and differentiate. Together they both continue to weep: "And they lifted up their voice and they continued weeping." Then Orpah finally acquiesces and kisses Naomi goodbye. The Hebrew itself is poignantly succinct: "Orpah kissed her mother-in-law and Ruth clung to her" (1:14b). Both Orpah's and Ruth's responses, though different, are intimate gestures in biblical texts.[19] The Masoretic text leaves Orpah at the kiss and does not specify that she returns home, although her return is reflected in Naomi's next words to Ruth: "'Behold, your sister-in-law has returned to her people and to her god [gods];[20] return after your sister-in-law" (1:15).[21] The story ceases to follow Orpah at this point, not even recording her departure. Perhaps it was not Orpah who turned and left. Perhaps she stood in tears watching the other two continue on in their journey to Bethlehem. Perhaps she is still there in the middle of the road, looking west across the plain.

Commensurate with Ruth's folktale quality the names used in the story all seem to indicate character. Elimelech means "My God is king," Naomi means "pleasantness," and their two sons are named "Sickness" (Mahlon) and "The End" (Chilion).[22] The etymologies for Orpah and Ruth's names are a bit more obscure. Ruth may be a name derived from the word for *friend* or may be associated with water. Orpah may be derived from the word for *nape* meaning nape of neck. The idea expressed by this name is that Orpah's character is embodied in her turning away from Naomi and Ruth. All that was seen was the nape of her neck as she returned to her mother's home. Others see the connection to *nape* as indicating thick, luxurious hair. There may also be a connection to the Arabic for *scent, perfume, aroma* or another word that means "a handful of water."[23]

Although none of these meanings is definitive, traditional Jewish and Christian exegesis has focused on the nape of the neck, emphasizing Orpah's turning away from Naomi. She is condemned for this decision in ways that are not subtle. For example, in the midrash Ruth Rabbah, Orpah is punished on her way home by being gang raped by one hundred men and, as if that were not enough, a dog.[24] Other Jewish legends understand her to be the ancestor of Goliath—the sons of Ruth and Orpah, then, face each other as mortal enemies and Ruth's son triumphs. In these readings Orpah becomes the cipher for all negative assessments of Moabites, assessments that must be deflected from Ruth in order to adhere to the text's positive evaluation of her character and her connection to David. For both Jews and Christians Ruth is, after all, in the family tree of the messiah. Furthermore, since Moabites no longer exist in the real world of traditional Jewish and Christian commentators, all their anxieties about women who are ethnically and religiously other (Orpah returns to both her people and her gods) and all their anxieties about intermarriage with such women are focused in the commentators' fantasies about Orpah's fate. Orpah is the one subjected to unthinkable violence and even dehumanized through her rape by a dog. Such interpretations are excessive and unprovoked by the text itself.

Some recent feminist interpreters have sought to redeem Orpah. Athalya Brenner's interpretation of Orpah in her book *I Am . . . Biblical Women Tell Their Own Stories* draws on the midrashic method and is just as imaginative as midrash can be, yet it ultimately offers a much fairer interpretation of Orpah's character, grounded more in the neutral presentation of the biblical text. Since Brenner is telling a story and writes in the first person as if the narrator were the biblical woman herself, there are elements of Brenner's reading that have no grounding in the book of Ruth. For example, Ruth and Orpah are sisters-in-law but also blood sisters—same father, different mothers.[25] When all of the men were still alive, their household was harmonious and happy. The men died because of a mysterious virus and the women had to burn all of their property—houses and harvests—because of the community's fear of contagion. Naomi was ultimately forced out.[26]

But in her reading of Orpah's departure Brenner maintains the biblical text's neutrality and even continues to position Ruth and Orpah as doubles, two sides of the same coin. Orpah reflects on that moment at the crossroads: "Never mind the fact that, by turning away and returning to my home, I complied with Naomi's wish as explicitly expressed. Never mind the fact that Naomi never ever had anything against me, that I never had anything against her. Never mind that I did love her and Ruth with all my heart. . . . Ruth was too scared to go back and thought that casting her lot with the unknown (read: Bethlehem) would be better; whereas I was too scared to go forward in the direction of that same unknown."[27] In their division Ruth is the disobedient one whereas Orpah obeys Naomi's wishes; both make their decisions out of fear of the unknown; both cling to the familiar, although both define what is most familiar in different ways.

Postcolonial readers, especially those who combine feminist with postcolonial perspectives, have been particularly drawn to Orpah. Postcolonial readings have done much to bring Orpah out of the shadows and to reevaluate her character. Musa W. Dube, while not explicitly drawing on the creative reading method of midrash, uses her imagination to fill out Orpah's story and her character. Like Brenner, she gives her interpretation a narrative frame. "The Unpublished Letters of Orpah to Ruth" opens with members of a family sitting outside around a fire talking of the world.[28] One woman, Lesedi, who had been pursuing a degree in anthropology, had just returned home: "I kissed my professor goodbye and returned to my homeland, for I found the humanity of African people portrayed in less than human terms. In anthropological books African people, and other non-Western or non-Christian people, were described as savage, childish, lazy and sexually immoral. I just could not read anymore without insulting myself and all my people. That is why I quit my degree and returned to my mother's house in Botswana, to my Gods."[29] The allusion to the book of Ruth is clear as Lesedi adopts the subject position of Orpah—the one who returned to her mother's house and to her gods. Together Lesedi and Orpah will give voice to the postcolonial critique.

Next Dube turns to a collection of papers she found among Lesedi's—papers that purport to be the unpublished letters of Orpah to Ruth. The first letter begins with the story of the Moabites' origins. All of the elements from the story in Genesis 19 are present in Dube's retelling. There is, however, nothing morally suspect about either the inhabitants of Sodom and Gomorrah or the actions of Lot and his daughters, and Dube deletes the supernatural elements of the biblical account. The towns were built in a region of volcanic activity, and they were destroyed in a volcanic eruption. Lot and his son, his daughter-in-law, and his daughter had been, by chance, out of town when the natural disaster struck. When he realized what was happening Lot ran into town fearing for the safety of his wife. He was engulfed in ashes and turned into a pillar of salt. The Moabites are the descendents of Lot's surviving children.[30]

The second letter retells the story of Elimelech, Naomi, and their two sons. The family flees a famine in Judah for prosperity in Moab during the rule of King Eglon. Eglon himself provides them with hospitality, even adopting them into his own royal household. Orpah and Ruth are the two daughters of Eglon and Balak his only son. The five children grow up together in the court and the two girls marry Chilion and Mahlon when they all come of age. The third letter tells of the disaster—how Elimelech died and how Chilion and Mahlon tried unsuccessfully to usurp the throne from Balak. They killed Balak but were then killed by Balak's guards. Ruth and Orpah both chose the right path. It was right for one of them to accompany their mother-in-law, who was practically a mother to them both, home. It was right for one of the royal daughters to remain at home with her own mother. Ruth left and Orpah stayed. In the final letter Orpah entreats Ruth, "And when you have borne children, you should tell them these stories of the Moabites: of their origins, of their kindness, of their hospitality and of their struggles for survival."[31]

Dube understands the biblical account of Moabite origins and national character akin to the Western construction of Africans, particularly in the ascription of sexual immorality and in the understanding of God's punishing hand behind any tragedy. She then turns such constructions inside out to underscore the prejudices behind them. Like Brenner, she closely links Ruth and Orpah, first by understanding them as sisters and second by giving them identical motives for their opposite reactions to Naomi's words. The sisters divide and part in order to comfort and cling to their mothers. Contrary to hundreds of years of traditional interpretation and scholarship, Orpah is as good, loyal, and loving as Ruth.

Postcolonial Inventions and Interventions

Postcolonial studies "emerged as a way of engaging with the textual, historical, and cultural articulations of societies disturbed and transformed by the historical reality of colonial presence."[32] As a method of reading, postcolonial interpretation first analyzes "the diverse strategies by which the colonizers constructed images of the colonized" and second studies "how the colonized themselves made use of and went beyond many of those strategies in order to articulate their identity, self-worth, and empowerment."[33] Fernando F. Segovia famously delineates three postcolonial optics that are employed when reading biblical texts. The first optic analyzes the imperial context out of which the Bible emerged, from the Assyrian to the Roman Empire. The second optic examines how the biblical text was read and used to support the colonial contexts of the last five hundred years. The final and third optic looks at how the Bible has been redeployed as an act of resistance to colonization.[34]

Postcolonial and other "voices from the margins"[35] are drawn to the book of Ruth because the heroine is a poor, foreign widow (multiply marginalized) who emerges triumphant, and the minor character Orpah resists assimilation by returning home and retaining her own ethnic and religious identity. Within the context of the recently named minority criticism, Gale A. Yee identifies the attraction to the book of Ruth because it "conjoins issues of gender, sexuality, race/ethnicity, immigration, nationality, assimilation, and class in tantalizing ways that allow different folk to read their own stories into the multivalent narrative of Ruth and Naomi."[36] She then lists more than two dozen engagements with the book of Ruth written by scholars foregrounding their distinctive ethnic/racial, national, and gender identities.[37]

Musa Dube has turned to the book of Ruth several times. Her article "Divining Ruth for International Relations" focuses on the relationship between Ruth and Naomi as representative of the relationship between Moab and Judah.[38] As in many postcolonial readings, the standard Western exegetical methods are eschewed in Dube's work. In this article Dube's hermeneutical lens is a southern African divination method employed for healing. When ailing people go to traditional healers of southern Africa, these healers consult various kinds of divining sets in order to diagnose the issues causing the illness. Divining sets are the objects used to help the healer in his or her diagnosis, and Christian healers regularly include the Bible among the objects they use in divination. Dube reads Ruth to divine the relationship between Moab and Judah, to determine whether or not it is healthy, and then to see if it provides insight into ethical international relations today, especially relations that involve Africa in general and Botswana (Dube's country of origin) in particular.

The first international movement in the story is Judah into Moab as Elimelech's family sojourn to Moab in search of food. From a healer-divination perspective the relationship between Judah and Moab is unhealthy because when Judah enters Moab death and infertility result. Dube infers a famine in Moab that kills the Israelite men and eventually causes Naomi to flee back to Bethlehem. Ruth accompanies her for the same reason Naomi accompanied Elimelech—not out of love or loyalty or commitment but because they are family and she has no choice.[39] Moab is forced into Judah.

Ruth's experience in Judah is diametrically opposed to Naomi's experience in Moab. Whereas Naomi encountered death in Moab, Ruth encounters life in Judah.

Moab was bitter for Naomi, but Judah is pleasant for Ruth. Behind the issues of fertility, both human and agricultural, is divine blessing and protection—it was absent in Moab but present in Judah.[40] For Dube the story characterizes Moab as a "god-forsaken land whose resources (Ruth) can be tapped for the well-being of Judah."[41] The story then is a story of colonization and domination, in which one country exploits the resources of another. Ruth (Moab) is compelled to serve Naomi and Boaz (Judah) as a slave is compelled to serve her master.[42] Dube then likens such exploitation to Europe's relationship to Africa.[43]

Equating Judah with colonizing oppression and Moab with the colonized oppressed is not unique to Dube. It is common in postcolonial readings of Ruth. Judith E. McKinlay reads the white New Zealand colonizers as the Israelites and the native Maori people as the Moabites, equating the story with the racial politics of Aotearoa New Zealand. The way she blends all these different times and subject positions is exemplified in the following statement: "While I cannot read as an ethnic Moabite, although colonizers have a long history of presuming to be surrogate indigenous readers, women of both races are, at least to some degree, Moabites."[44] Brenner reads Ruth against the background of foreign workers in the modern state of Israel, workers who primarily come from eastern Europe and the Far East. Like Dube, Brenner also denies Ruth's choice in her following of Naomi. As a foreign worker she is forced into service; she is invisible, works a menial job, and tries to use hard work to come to the attention of the dominant culture. A similar blending and blurring of then and now, there and here, occurs in Brenner: "a female foreigner can perhaps be integrated into Judahite, or Israelite, or Israeli society through marriage—if and when the additional issue of class does not occur."[45]

Essays such as Dube's, McKinlay's, and Brenner's offer important critiques of situations of exploitation that have taken place in the recent past and still take place today. However, the equation of Iron Age or even Persian-period Israel with the colonizing powers of Europe in Africa, New Zealand, and the Middle East is to attribute power to Israel that it simply did not have. Israelites are not European colonizers; Israelites are not even Israelis. Equating Israel with white colonial powers and Moab with dark colonized peoples is to imply a past racial hierarchy that also simply did not exist. Moabites and Israelites are of the same race, and as Semitic peoples who live next to each other in an area smaller than New Jersey they looked identical to one other and shared a largely identical material culture.[46]

Historical anachronism, reflecting on how the book of Ruth interacts with one's own social location or autobiography, and using one's imagination to interpret the biblical book do not necessarily result in "invalid" readings. I am not leveling a charge of eisegesis; rather my critique is grounded in ethics, the ethics postcolonial readings themselves demand. Historical anachronism can sometimes lead to undeserved, and therefore unethical, indictments. And even though the people of Iron

Age or Persian-period Judah are long dead, it is unjust to malign their character without sufficient evidence. Allow me to reiterate: postcolonial interpreters are drawing attention to situations of oppression in our own historical moment that do need to be addressed and redressed. However, using unjust invectives against others does not affect justice for one's own community. In addition some postcolonial biblical interpreters fail to attend to the unique contexts of the literature they are reading and instead go for an easy identification that attenuates historical specificity. Quite frankly such readings are not only lazy, but they also turn postcolonial criticism into a type of structuralism—collapsing all empires, all ethnic difference, all cultural contact into a universal rubric of oppressor-oppressed based on modernist ideologies.

The narrative context of the book of Ruth is the early Iron Age when both Israelites and Moabites lived in loose confederacies of tribes and no imperial power held sway. There was not even a monarchy to establish national boundaries and identities on either side. The author's context is most likely the Persian period, when both the Israelites and the Moabites were equally subject to the same empire—the Persian Empire. Even if we were to understand the dynamic between Moabite and Israelite in the book of Ruth as a dynamic influenced by their status as colonized subjects in Persia, we would need to be cautious about importing into the biblical world our understandings of colonialism derived from the modern practices, strategies, and intrusions of Europe into the Americas, Asia, Australia, and Africa. Especially since the Persian Empire is not explicitly present in the text of Ruth—Persians are not constructing their colonized "other" nor is the subaltern writing back in the book, the oppressed is not challenging the oppressor. Anxieties about intermarriage may be an aspect of the text and may be present because of the pressures of colonization, but the argument must be carefully made, not assumed, in order to read Ruth in postcolonial perspective.

In the case of the book of Ruth Segovia's second optic can be the most illuminating. Rather than reading the history of Israelites and Moabites and identifying Israelites as the colonial oppressors of Moabites, the second optic reads the history of *interpretation* in order to analyze how the story was employed in the modern context to further the aims of colonization. Ruth did not live in a postcolonial context of oppression, fighting against Israelite prejudice and subjugation; however, the *book* of Ruth has lived in a postcolonial context of oppression, interpreted by white Europeans and Americans to justify the exploitation of others. Ruth enters into colonial discourse in a variety of ways. Two different deployments of the book of Ruth exemplify this process: H. Rider Haggard's wildly popular novel *King Solomon's Mines* (1885) and the political use of Ruth in colonial America. [47]

H. Rider Haggard engages the book of Ruth in his story of colonized Africa. In many ways the story is the polar opposite of the book of Ruth. Instead of being a book that revolves around relationships between women, Haggard's novel is a book by a man, about men, for men. It is even dedicated "to all the big and little boys who read it," effectively excluding women readers from the first cracking open of the cover. Mothers are particularly absent. The main character—Allan Quatermain—has a son whom he frequently mentions; however, he refers to the boy's mother only once and that is in a disparaging way, indicating that all women are ingrates. The book commences with Sir Henry Curtis's search for his brother, with whom he quarreled and parted after the death of their father—again, no mention of their mother.[48] The only character who has a mother is Umbopa, the African man who begins the story as one of Quatermain's servants. Umbopa's mother had died long before the novel begins, but her sacrifices for and protection of her son are lovingly remembered. After the coup that kills his royal father she escapes their village with him when he was just a young boy. She gets him to a safe place, raises him until he is old enough to hear and understand their story, and then dies.[49] She is positively portrayed but absent nevertheless.

There are two female characters that inhabit the novel, and they are binary opposites. They are both African women of Umbopa's people. Foulata is young, beautiful, and good. She falls in love with Captain John Good, Quatermain and Curtis's other compatriot in their African adventure. Gagool is ancient, shrunken, and evil. She is witch who controls King Twala, the one who usurped Umbopa's throne. She is responsible for countless murders and other evil deeds in the story. Despite the fact that both of these characters are women, both are removed from this category by the narrator. Not only is Gagool removed from the category of woman, she is even removed from the category of the human from her first introduction. She is, perhaps, more than three hundred years old, shriveled, shrunken, and almost animal-like in movement and appearance. Quatermain calls Gagool more of a fiend than a female.[50] He then continues even to exclude Foulata from the category "woman" (through he hesitates for a moment over her) because she is African and not a viable love interest for any white man.[51] Regardless of who wrote the book of Ruth (a man or a woman), regardless of the feminist assessment of Ruth's character (positive or negative), it cannot be denied that the book is woman-centered, its main characters are women, and its plot highlights women's relationships and informal social networks. In its hypermasculinity *King Solomon's Mines* is the antithesis of Ruth; yet in other ways the novel engages one of the text's primary themes: love and marriage across difference.

The entire novel owes its plot to a biblical tale, one about the great-great-great-grandson of Ruth—Solomon. According to 1 Kings 9:28 and 1 Chron. 29:4, Solomon had mines in Ophir. Ophir has never been positively identified. The novel's premise is that the biblical Ophir is in southern Africa. The three main characters set out in search of Sir Henry's brother, who set off himself several years earlier in search of Solomon's mines. In addition to the biblically inspired plot there are frequent biblical allusions throughout the story. Despite its reliance on the Bible the narrative's attitude toward the Bible is less than reverent. The first mention of the Bible is at the beginning of the tale: "I am not a literary man, though very devoted to the Old Testament and also to the 'Ingoldsby Legends.'"[52] The latter is the work of the English satirist and humorist Thomas Ingoldsby (whose real name is Richard Harris Barham [1788–1845]). It is "a collection of clever and absurd prose stories and poems, most of which were based on medieval fables and legends."[53] Thus the Old Testament is subtly equated with such satirized legends. Throughout, the biblical allusion is mixed with allusions to other histories (particularly Roman) and stories (particularly Shakespeare). The Bible exists on a level equal to these popular and fictitious tales.

Among the many references, allusions, and even citations of biblical text, there are two allusions to the book of Ruth and one to Moab. Both of the allusions to Ruth are spoken by Foulata. Foulata is the most graceful and beautiful young woman of the people Kukuana. She had been chosen to be sacrificed to the gods but is saved by the three white men who had traveled into the land of the Kukuana looking for Solomon's mines.[54] Good plays a particularly prominent role in her rescue and she becomes quite attached to him. Later, after a great battle between the usurper Twala and the rightful king Umbopa, Good falls sick with internal injuries and an infection. She nurses him back to health, never leaving his side. When he is well again and informed of her heroic devotion, he goes to thank her. She responds, blushing: "'Nay, my lord; my lord forgets! Did he not save *my* life, and am I not my lord's handmaiden?'"[55] Her words to Good, in particular her self-designation as his handmaiden echo Ruth's words to Boaz (in the King James translation) when they first meet in the barley fields (Ruth 2:13), and when she confronts him on the threshing-room floor (Ruth 3:9).

The second reference is again spoken by Foulata to Good. Toward the end of the novel, when all of the issues in the village have been resolved and Umbopa restored to his throne, she decides to accompany the three white men farther in their search for Curtis's brother and Solomon's mines. When they are on the threshold of the caves known as the Place of Death, Good asks her if she is going to continue with them. She is afraid and hesitates, but then says: "'Nay, my lord, whither thou goest, there will I go also,'"[56] thus quoting Ruth's well-known speech of undying devotion. Her devotion may have been undying, but Foulata herself dies soon after pledging these words. In a chamber in the Place of Death Gagool moves a stone over the entrance, thus trapping Foulata and the men inside. Foulata attempts to stop Gagool but is stabbed by her instead. As she is dying she confesses her love to Good, who holds and kisses her. She reflects that it is better that she die since black and white cannot marry: "'Say to my lord, Bougwan, that—I love him, and that I am glad to die because I know that he cannot cumber his life with such as I am, for the sun may not mate with the darkness, nor the white with the black.'"[57] She continues, even more poignantly: "Even now, though I cannot lift my hand, and my brain grows cold, I do not feel as though my heart were dying; it is so full of love that could live a thousand years, and yet be young. Say that if I live again, mayhap I shall see him in the Stars, and that—I will search them all, though perchance there I should still be black and he would—still be white."[58]

The reference to Moab comes in between the two allusions to the book of Ruth. When the three men approach the mountains of the Place of Death, where the mines and the treasure rooms are, they find three great stone statues. These are the Silent Ones worshipped by the Kukuana people. While Quatermain is standing there wondering whose hands carved them and for what purposes, he remembers: "Whilst I was gazing and wondering, suddenly it occurred to me—being familiar with the Old Testament—that Solomon went astray after strange gods, the names of three of whom I remembered—'Astoreth the goddess of the Zidonians, Chemosh the god of the Moabites, and Milcom the god of the children of Ammon'—and I suggested to my companions that the three figures before us might represent these false and exploded divinities."[59] Hence the identification between Ruth and Foulata is further strengthened. Now Foulata too worships the god of the Moabites.

Haggard thus takes two verses from Ruth—one spoken to Boaz, the other to Naomi—and puts them in the mouth of Foulata, spoken to Good, the man she loves. In this fictional context both lines express romantic love and devotion. The primary point of the biblical story as it is commonly read—faithfulness, love, and marriage that crosses ethnic and religious difference—is referenced through Foulata's love of Good. Haggard's tale, however, ultimately denies the lesson of the biblical story. In his world the *hesed* of an African woman is not enough to recommend her for marriage to a European man. No matter her personal merit, the racial divide is simply too great to cross.

King Solomon's Mines is written in the colonial context of nineteenth-century England by an author fully immersed in the prejudices of his day. It is a colonial novel in which the white Europeans enter Africa to exploit the land and the people for both adventure and wealth. There are noble Africans, but they are generally the exceptions that prove the rule of African inferiority and depravity. The white men even bring salvation to the Kukuana people by helping them defeat the evil usurper and put the rightful king back on the throne. As for Foulata, in every way she is a fine woman—not only in appearance but in intelligence and demeanor as well. The narrator has to keep conceding this point even as he expresses his basic prejudice. However, it would be a mistake to conflate Allan Quatermain's attitudes and opinions with those of H. Rider Haggard. In many ways the narrator is the most bigoted character in the book, and there are times when he even appears ridiculous in his

European arrogance. For example, the way in which Foulata's death is recorded is clearly meant to evoke the reader's sympathy. She dies at the service of European greed (she would have never been in that chamber had not the three white men insisted on finding the wealth of Solomon's mines), and she sacrifices herself in an attempt to save them. Even Good never recovers from the death of this beautiful woman. But Quatermain expresses a glib relief, calling her murder "a fortune occurrence" that will prevent "complications."[60] Quatermain's voice is not identical to Haggard's.[61] By using the lines from Ruth, is Haggard suggesting that his society is not following biblical principles in its racism? Is Haggard introducing ideas more subversive than his plot would suggest or his narrator admit? The Bible in colonial contexts is complex, even when employed by the colonizer.

Laura Donaldson explores this complexity in another context—the colonial United States.[62] Her reading of Ruth focuses on the ways in which the Bible was used to justify the West's imperial policies and further subjugate colonized peoples. Donaldson does not invent imperial oppressions that did not exist in the biblical world; rather she looks at how colonizers constructed colonial identities through their own use of biblical texts. Donaldson acknowledges that the translation of the Bible into native languages and the adaptation of Christianity has been part of the history of victimization and culturecide. At the same time, however, native peoples have also read the Bible for themselves in ways that can "exceed the bounds of imperial exegesis."[63] Donaldson calls her interpretive space the "contact zone," a space that resembles Gloria Anzaldúa's borderlands, and is defined by Mary Louise Pratt as "the space of colonial encounters where people who are divided both geographically and historically come into contact with each other and establish ongoing relations, usually involving conditions of severe inequality and intractable conflict."[64] Donaldson reads Ruth in this contact zone with an eye to understanding how the Bible and its interpretations have affected native peoples and seeking to have more native interpretations heard.

She starts with the Moabites and their origins: "The belief in Moabite women as a hypersexualized threat to Israelite men prophetically augurs the Christian attitude toward the indigenous women of the Americas."[65] Thomas Jefferson wrote *Notes on the State of Virginia* in 1787 and gave it to Charles Thomson, who was then secretary of Congress. Thomson remarked on the work, and Jefferson included his remarks in the published version. In a section about the forwardness of Indian women Thomson wrote: "Instances similar to that of Ruth and Boaz are not uncommon among them. For though the women are modest and diffident, and so bashful that they seldom lift up their eyes, and scarce ever look a man full in the face, yet being brought up on great subjection, custom and manners reconcile them to modes of acting, which, judged of by Europeans, would be deemed inconsistent with the rules of female decorum and propriety."[66] Jefferson follows Thomson's comment by including a citation from Ruth 3:7—the scene in which Ruth uncovers the "feet" of a drunken and passed-out Boaz. Donaldson is not arguing that the text itself presents the foreigner Ruth as hypersexualized but that she was read that way in colonial interpretation. The determination to read native women as hypersexualized, despite the description of them as modest, diffident, and bashful, demonstrates the way in which the prejudice dictates the interpretation of the data—whether the data of experience or the data of a text.

For Donaldson, Ruth is a paradigm of the assimilationist strategy proposed by many European Americans as the "solution" to the Indian problem—convert them to Christianity and consume them through marriage to European Americans.[67] Since Ruth and Orpah are often read as opposites, Ruth's assimilation is countered by Orpah's resistance to it. "Is there no hope in the book of Ruth? Is it nothing but a tale of conversion/assimilation and the inevitable vanishing of the indigene in the literary and social text? In fact there does exist a counter-narrative—a kind of anti-Pocahontas—whose presence offers some small hope to the Native reader: the sign of Orpah, sister-in-law of Ruth and the woman who returned to her mother's house."[68] In fact Donaldson argues that Orpah is the book of Ruth's central character. Orpah is a hero in this reading, choosing her own religion, culture, and people in the face of a power that seeks to eliminate them.

Donaldson's postcolonial interpretation succeeds where others fail precisely because she does not ascribe the power dynamic between colonizer and colonized to the text itself, to Israelites and Moabites in the Iron Age (or in the Persian period). Rather she stays focused in the history of interpretation and its consequences. She then redeploys the text by holding up Orpah as the hero of the story.

In the history of colonial interpretation of biblical narrative, the oppressors equated certain biblical peoples and characters with the indigenous peoples they were in the process of colonizing in order to justify and even sanctify their actions. It is a powerful move, then, for the colonized to emerge out of the situation by turning the very texts around and back onto the colonizers. If Ruth and Orpah were used to perpetuate sexual stereotypes of Native American women, then Ruth and Orpah can be reconstituted in "a more inclusive, amenable and attractive text."[69] As such even Dube's article "Divining Ruth for International Relations" can be appreciated as an act of resistance. Audre Lord famously cautioned, however, about using the master's tools to dismantle the master's house.[70] Whereas poststructuralist theories of power and ideology may counter that there is nowhere to stand completely outside of the master's house, no tool that is not implicated in the master's history, her caution still bears weight. Postcolonial interpreters can read from their social location, entering into the story of Ruth in a variety of ways in order to invert and subvert the oppressive structures to which they have been subjected. However, all readers need to be wary that in the use of the master's tools they do not inadvertently build an addition onto the master's house, inadvertently perpetuate oppressive structures and attitudes, even if these are shifted onto someone else.

McKinlay says that Ruth is "not a good story for Moabites,"[71] but this is an assumption that reads *conflict* every time the text speaks of *difference*. Whereas the Moabite identity of the two women is frequently remarked on, it is not once disparaged. We are blinded by our bias for the melting pot, where race, skin color, ethnic background, custom, religion—in other words *difference*—are not remarked on in polite society. Certainly Ruth and Orpah's Moabite status marks them as different in this story, but we should not automatically read this difference as prejudice or inferiority. Difference may be positively construed especially if it is difference acknowledged and accepted without being erased.

Many postcolonial readings of Ruth fall subject to what Trinh T. Minh-ha identifies as an equation between difference and conflict. Minh-ha works to break down the binary oppositions between difference and sameness, oppositions that are dependent on the positing of essences, by arguing that the difference of which she speaks "is not opposed to sameness, nor synonymous with separateness. . . . There are differences as well as similarities within the concept of difference."[72] This complex interrelationship between difference and sameness serves to foster creativity for Minh-ha, not conflict.[73] Readers of Ruth who see a deep hatred of and conflict between Israelites and Moabites in the story assume the conflict in the reiteration of difference. Ruth is perhaps more productively read not as a story of conflict but as a meditation on life in the borderlands between difference and sameness, the creative space that opens up when two countries, cultures, ethnicities, religions, people touch.

Living in the Borderlands

The analogy between Gloria Anzaldúa's Borderlands and the borderlands between Moab and Israel, between Orpah, Ruth, and Naomi is not exact. Anzaldúa's Borderlands are places of conflict where the United States has exerted its hegemonic power over Mexico, where white skin is privileged over dark, where "pure" ethnic backgrounds are valued over "mixed" heritages, heterosexuality and traditional masculinity and femininity over anything queer. Yet, the concept of the Borderlands is not bound to the physical border culture in which Anzaldúa grew up. And conflict does not define even her conflict-ridden space. It is also a space of creativity: "Living in a state of psychic unrest, in a Borderland, is what makes poets write and artists create."[74]

Out of the creative space of the Borderlands, the new *mestiza* consciousness emerges. Anzaldúa writes in a way that embodies it by blending English and Spanish, poetry and prose, autobiographical narrative and theory: "From this racial, ideological cultural and biological cross-pollinization, an 'alien' consciousness is presently in the making—a new *mestiza* consciousness, *una conciencia de mujer.* It is a consciousness of the Borderlands."[75] She then shifts into poetry. In the poem "Una lucha de fronteras / A Struggle of Borders" Anzaldúa walks in and out of different cultures, even inhabiting all cultures simultaneously: "*alma entre dos mundos, tres, cuatro, / me zumba la cabeza con lo contradictorio.*"[76] The strength of the *mestiza* is in her plurality. As someone who contains difference within her sameness, she cultivates "a tolerance for contradictions, a tolerance for ambiguity. . . . She has a plural personality, she operates in a pluralistic mode—nothing is thrust out, the good the bad and the ugly, nothing rejected, nothing abandoned. Not only does she sustain contradictions, she turns the ambivalence into something else."[77] As with Minh-ha, difference becomes the site of a profound creativity.

Ruth and Orpah are both *mestizas,* continually walking out of one culture and into another. Robert Maldonado reads Ruth with Anzaldúa's work *Borderlands,* using Anzaldúa to explore the image of La Malinche.[78] La Malinche was an Aztec woman who, as a child, was sold into slavery to the Mayans by her mother. When Cortés arrived in Mexico he acquired her and gave her to one of his men, and when he defeats the Aztecs, married her to another of his soldiers. She is identified with the conqueror and his conquest of Mexico to such a degree that her name is a byword for betrayal.[79] Ruth is La Malinche, the one who crosses borders and mixes with the ethnic other. Yet Maldonado resists a singular reading of Ruth as betrayer of her people. By identifying Ruth with La Malinche Maldonado probes and even deepens the ambiguities in the book of Ruth.[80]

Ruth is *mestizaje.* She can be identified with Malinche, but she is not simply a traitor to her people like La Malinche. She had agency. "A *malinchista mestizaje* biblical hermeneutics, then, is a multi-level reading of betrayal. . . . To jettison the tradition involves loss even as does embracing it."[81] Some postcolonial critics understand Ruth's crossing as a betrayal of her people—she is absorbed into the oppressor's culture. Some postcolonial critics understand Orpah's refusal to cross as a defense of indigenous cultures against Western hegemony. Yet border crossing is ambiguous; it involves gains and losses, betrayals and loyalties. Ruth may have forsaken her people to cling to Naomi, but one cannot simply write her off as a traitor. Turning back would have been a loss too. Orpah may be the hero of the story for indigenous women, but she weeps when she turns away from Naomi to return home. Is there any way to love across borders that does not involve a betrayal, whether or not one stays or goes?

Although both the text and the reader tend to focus on Ruth's immigrant status, Naomi is also a border crosser—Naomi is also *mestiza.* In fact Naomi blazes the trail for living in the borderlands. Perhaps this, more than anything, binds the women together. Orpah stays but is still a border crosser too, one who crosses in terms of marriage, family, culture, not physically. She encounters difference and incorporates it into her life without leaving the place she calls home. She then weeps, kisses, and embraces those who continue to travel and traverse the borderlands.

Who Gleans in Your Fields?

In Varda's documentary *The Gleaners and I* many of the gleaners are immigrants to France from Africa and Asia. Some are people born in France but who are considered ethnically "other." (Varda spends some time in a gypsy encampment, for example.) Most of her gleaners are women; all of her gleaners are poor. To glean one must traverse a border, step over a property line, enter into a field that is not one's own. Gleaners, almost by definition, are people who inhabit margins; they are also people who cross borders and live in Borderlands. More than racial or ethnic identity, more than nation of origin, the Borderlands in the book of Ruth are those of class difference.

According to Chris Weedon, feminist postcolonial critics serve as essential interrogators of the postcolonial project. Feminist postcolonial studies draw attention to the importance of difference, to the complexity of theoretical concepts, literary texts, and lived experience. Terms such as *hybridity, the postcolonial condition, the postcolonial subject* or *woman"* are not universal, transhistorical concepts. Each has a historical specificity that is sometimes lost.[82] The biblical stories cannot be churned through the interpretive method of postcolonialism in a way that flattens the differences between now and then, between different times of colonization and different types of imperialism. The biblical stories cannot be read in ways that flatten the differences within the Bible itself. "All postcolonial feminist critics, wherever they are located, can contribute to making the existing social relations that produce hierarchical difference visible. This work is a fundamental prerequisite for social change and requires the *positive recognition of difference* in the struggle to redefine its meaning and reshape its material effects."[83] Postcolonial theory can illuminate the book of Ruth and postcolonial interpretation can open up new vistas of meaning—as long as Ruth, Orpah, and Naomi are allowed to speak with their own voices and not become just puppets mouthing contemporary woes.

· 4 ·

RUTH AND NAOMI

O rpah turns and goes back to her own family, leaving Ruth and Naomi together on the road. It is their relationship that will now shape the narrative. Naomi is the first to speak in the biblical book, to both Ruth and Orpah, but Ruth is the first to respond with words of her own. Robert Alter argues that the first statement of dialogue is key to the character of the speaker.[1] The biblical preference for direct rather than indirect speech is particularly pronounced in the book of Ruth; dialogue dominates the narrative. Of the book's eighty-five verses, fifty-nine contain spoken speech—sixty-nine percent of the story is told through dialogue.[2] Ruth and Naomi's first dialogue has been evaluated in a variety of ways, each reading examining what the two women do and say to determine how they feel toward one another.

Once Naomi persuades Orpah to leave her Ruth continues to cling (Ruth 1:14). The word for *cling* (*dabaq*) is not a common word in biblical texts. Its earliest appearance is in Gen. 2:24, after the speech the first man makes to the woman made from his rib: "Therefore, a man forsakes his father and his mother and clings (*dabaq*) to his woman and they become as one flesh." This intimate ideal, which may even suggest the closeness of sexual intercourse, is woven into marriage ceremonies and is the foundational text on which many theologies of marriage are based. When read with Genesis Ruth's clinging to Naomi is understood in terms of a husband's clinging to his wife. As he leaves mother and father Ruth is also leaving her home and her biological family. However, not every instance of *cling* is in reference to married partners. In Proverbs the word is applied to friendships closer than the relationship between brothers (18:24). In Psalm 119 the speaker clings to God's decrees (v. 31). Even in the book of Ruth itself the author uses the word throughout the narrative as a kind of leitmotif. In addition to its use to describe Ruth's hold on Naomi, it is used three times in chapter 2 when Boaz urges Ruth "to cling" to his female workers while in the field, and when Ruth and Naomi later talk about his instruction (2:8, 21, 23).

While Ruth hangs on her and Orpah turns away, Naomi again speaks. Naomi's second speech is directed to Ruth alone, urging her to follow her sister-in-law who has returned "to her people and to her god [gods]." Ruth now utters her best-known words: "Do not entreat me to forsake you, to turn from you; for wherever you go, I will go; and wherever you lodge, I will lodge; your people, my people; and your God, my God; where you die, I will die and there I will be buried. Thus may Yahweh do to me and more if even death intervenes between you and me" (1:16–17). Ruth uses the personal name of the Israelite god only here, swearing by Naomi's god's name and thereby emphasizing her commitment to Naomi. Naomi says nothing in response.

Many commentators—I among them—have asserted that the book of Ruth is about relationship; yet *relationship* is simply an association or connection. An association between two people can be fraught with all kinds of emotions; it can be reciprocal or one-sided; a burden or a joy; dangerous, loving, or indifferent. That the book of Ruth is about relationship seems almost self-evident—but *relationship* is an empty form, open to be filled by the reader's own imaginings. How one reads the bond between Ruth and Naomi is determined more by what the reader considers plausible than by what is explicit in the text. And how their relationship is read influences every other aspect of the book—how the character of each is understood, how the other relationships in the book are interpreted (particularly Ruth and Boaz's), and how their actions are assessed. What is the relationship between Ruth and Naomi? Is it one of two women coming together in a man's world in order to survive and model *hesed* (Phyllis Trible) or is the relationship one-sided, Ruth's devotion met by Naomi's coldness (Danna Nolan Fewell and David Miller Gunn) or are the two women in love with each other (Rebecca Alpert, Mona West)? To these possibilities I would like to add one more: Ruth and Naomi are engaged in a verbal sparring in their first exchange, one that employs hyperbolic speech. Ruth's first words do not necessarily reveal either love or loyalty to either Naomi or the Israelite god; rather Ruth's first words announce her as a verbally adroit trickster, as a jester of words.

Two Women Against the World

The first feminist interpreters of the book of Ruth had a positive assessment of Ruth and Naomi's relationship.[3] Elizabeth Cady Stanton's reading, while overly sentimental and even pious, does see their bond as one of mutual love and support. Phyllis Trible, the first modern feminist interpreter to address the story, also highlights the bonds of sisterhood that unite the women. Her approach to both feminism and the biblical text is more sophisticated than Stanton's, however, which leads her to address the ways in which the women manipulate the male-dominated legal system in order to guarantee their survival and to remain together.

Trible calls the story of Ruth "a human comedy."[4] The centrality of the women and their bond is signaled for Trible by the fact that "precisely at the point where third-person narration yields to dialogue, where introduction leads to action, women take over the story."[5] Naomi cares deeply about the well-being of her daughters-in-law, and she is realistic about the patriarchal world in which they live. Both would have more prosperous futures if they remarried and their chances of such a course of action are better among their own people. Orpah yields to Naomi's sound advice, but Ruth chooses Naomi. Here Trible assumes that Naomi is much older than Ruth and the difference in age is another aspect of the radicality of the commitment: "A young woman has committed herself to the life of an old woman rather than to the search for a husband, and she has made this commitment not 'until death us do part' but beyond death. One female has chosen another female in a world where life depends upon men."[6]

Even though Boaz's wealth and social standing make him a paragon of patriarchal power in the Bethlehem community, even though Ruth will later take Naomi's advice and pursue a marriage to Boaz, Boaz is not in charge and marriage is not the goal. Rather the plot moves only at the initiative of the women: Naomi's motivation is Ruth's survival and Ruth's motivation is loyalty to Naomi.[7] For Trible the story of Ruth is one of two women who "make their own decisions [and] work out their own destinies."[8] Even when Boaz enters into the narrative, he reacts only to the women's plans and proposals. The power in the story is not transferred to him until the end when he goes alone to the city gates to work out legally and publicly what Ruth had proposed privately on the threshing-room floor. And even here the transfer of power is not complete because the narrative returns to the women's world of childbirth, nursing, and baby naming as the women of Bethlehem rejoice with Naomi and conclude the story.

Ruth and Naomi model feminist relationality because they move across the borders that male-dominated society has constructed to disrupt sisterhood—their relationship crosses ethnic, religious, and generational differences. Ruth in particular is a model for feminists because her primary bond is with another woman, and her loyalty to Naomi replaces the conventionality of the marital bond. Even as she pursues marriage to Boaz, she remains first and foremost committed to Naomi. They are two women who carve out a life together outside the parameters of patriarchy. Trible's interpretation is also deeply theological. In fact Trible proposes that the book "suggests a theological interpretation of feminism: women working out their own salvation with fear and trembling, for it is God who works in them."[9] Trible understands the chance happenings in the book to be a code for God's activity. Thus since Ruth and Naomi are encouraged and validated by God, God is also an encourager and validator of feminism.

Traditional Jewish and Christian interpretations also infuse the book of Ruth with theological import but read Ruth's commitment to Naomi as a vow to the Israelite god, not one to Naomi per se. In the Targum Ruth is the model proselyte to Judaism and love of the Israelite god is her motivation for following her mother-in-law into Bethlehem. The paraphrase amplifies the dialogue between Ruth and

Naomi by inserting statements about Jewish law, each of Ruth's phrases turned into answers to particular legal questions Naomi poses. For example, Ruth states "Where you go, I will go" in response to Naomi's statement of Sabbath law: "We are commanded to keep Sabbaths and holy days so as not to walk beyond two thousand cubits." Ironically the next legal requirement that Naomi presents is "We are commanded not to lodge together with gentiles" to which Ruth responds "Wherever you lodge, I will lodge." Naomi continues, speaking of the 613 commandments, the forsaking of idolatry, the crimes to which the death penalty applies, and the separate cemeteries for Jews.[10] For the Targumist Ruth's commitment to Naomi is really a commitment to the Jewish people and Jewish law as defined by the rabbis. Ruth then becomes the paradigm for the one who converts to Judaism. This tradition is an important aspect of the book of Ruth even today. Jewish conversion ceremonies are often linked to the reading of Ruth during the holiday of Shavuot (the Festival of Weeks), and female converts frequently take Ruth as their Hebrew name.

Two Women in Love

Ruth's speech to Naomi (1:16) is one of the most passionate in the Bible. It is frequently used in marriage ceremonies, and her language harkens back to the first statement of marriage in Genesis (2:24). The lesbian facet of Ruth's speech has been noted at least as early as Jeannette H. Foster's groundbreaking study *Sex Variant Women in Literature* (1956).[11] Foster in fact gives the book of Ruth pride of place: It is the first extant written work to feature a lesbian bond, even if the portrayal is "delicate" and the authors of the work unaware of the "full significance, of an attachment which, however innocent, is nevertheless still basically variant."[12] This aspect of the speech has been recently picked up by queer biblical commentators who see the words as an indication that Ruth and Naomi are romantically, even sexually, involved with each other.

Rebecca Alpert begins her lesbian midrash on the book of Ruth by enumerating the ways in which lesbians have already appropriated Ruth and Naomi's relationship for both conversion and commitment ceremonies. As Jewish lesbians have sought greater integration into the wider Jewish community, many have sought role models in the past. Such a search is necessarily hampered by the fact that for millennia "lesbian love has not been spoken of in public."[13] Lesbian historiographers therefore have learned to read "between the lines through imaginative reconstruction."[14] For readers attuned to the reality of lesbian love, passion, and commitment, the words that Ruth speaks to Naomi are resonant with their experience. After all, as Alpert points out, if the words were spoken between a man and woman, the romantic and sexual bond between the two would be assumed.[15]

Other issues in the story resonate with lesbian readers, in particular the way in which Ruth and Naomi's relationship crosses boundaries of age, race, nationality, and religion."[16] Alpert notes that lesbian relationships do this in greater percentage than heterosexual relationships. Together they raise a child. Together their bond is not just romantic but also one of deep, abiding friendship. What remains central for Alpert, though, is the sexual bond. "A Jewish lesbian midrash on Ruth requires that we read between the lines of the text and imagine Ruth and Naomi to be lovers. To lesbians, this is not implausible."[17] Ruth's obvious sexual relationship with Boaz does not vitiate a lesbian interpretation of her relationship with Naomi because in a heterosexist, patriarchical society heterosexual marriage would have protected and provided for the two women.

Alpert situates her reading within the Jewish tradition of midrash. She acknowledges that hers is an imaginative reconstruction, grounded in her personal experience, but avers that such a reading is rooted in traditional Jewish reading practices. The purpose of midrash is not to uncover the history behind the text or what really happened. The purpose of midrash is to open up possibilities within the tradition. Certainly the writer/translator of the Targum cited above is no less imaginative than Alpert, reflecting his or her own concerns with intermarriage and his or her own understanding of Jewish law. "Making room for lesbian interpretations of the Book of Ruth is a way of welcoming lesbians into the contemporary Jewish community."[18] In every generation the concerns of the Jewish community are expressed through its midrash.

Alpert's reading of Ruth and Naomi is also an example of queer biblical interpretation. Queer biblical interpretation is an outgrowth of feminist and gender studies. It focuses on issues of sex and sexuality in the biblical text, and it is unabashedly committed to the social and legal equality of gay, lesbian, bisexual, transsexual, transgender, and intersex peoples. Queer biblical interpretation also plays with the various meanings of *queer* in its approaches and strategies, disrupting a myriad of conventional readings and methods.[19] The relationships between David and Jonathan and Ruth and Naomi were the first to be critically examined through the hermeneutical lens of queer theory, and understanding Ruth and Naomi's relationship as a romantic one is now commonplace. For example, in the entry on Ruth in *The Queer Bible Commentary* Mona West states that the book "is unique in the canon of Hebrew scriptures and Israelite patriarchal society because it celebrates one woman's love for and devotion to another."[20] West agrees with Alpert that the book presents a model of relationship that crosses boundaries of age, religion, ethnicity, and nationality and hence resonates with lesbian experience. For West, "Ruth is our Queer ancestress."[21] Her relationship with Boaz is a strategy for survival; her marriage provides protection for her relationship with Naomi, protection from both violence and poverty.

Both heterosexual and lesbian readings of Ruth privilege one of Ruth's relationships over the other—Boaz and Ruth's relationship in one, Naomi and Ruth's relationship in the other. A rarely explored possibility is the one of bisexuality. Resisting the erasure that comes from both straight and gay communities, Celena M. Duncan speaks from her own experience and reads the book of Ruth as a "bisexual midrash."[22] She too claims the traditional Jewish interpretive strategy of midrash in order to give license to her imagination. In her reading Duncan explores her own two major relationships—one with a woman and one with a man. Her own journey of self-discovery is matched with the journeys of Ruth, Naomi, and Boaz.

Duncan retells the story of Ruth using the form of narrative rather than a more scholarly genre. First she imagines that Naomi's sons chose Moabite women against the wishes of their mother. Naomi had to work to get over her ethnic prejudice. When the men all die and Naomi decides to return to Judah, Ruth acts on her developing bond with Naomi in a way that strengthens and deepens that bond. Naomi is silent, but it is the silence of acceptance: "Even so, in her silence, Naomi accepted what the younger woman offered, a bond of support, companionship, assistance, loyalty, and love. Are these not the elements of a marriage? It was a bond unbreakable by death because the God of Naomi forged it; they were both being drawn forward by God, who was weaving a grand tapestry that would forever include the names of these two humble women. God broke the boundaries that had separated the two, and who would break apart or deny what God has wrought?"[23] As is evident, Duncan's reading is informed by and informs a particular theological orientation. The god of Israel, the god of the world, has created sexual diversity as part of the rich tapestry of diverse life. Similar to the way Trible's god affirms the feminist bonds of sisterhood, Duncan's god affirms sexual diversity as a fundamental, divinely mandated good.

For Duncan God's guidance also graces Ruth and Boaz's interactions. "Whether it was done consciously or not, Boaz, Ruth, and Naomi worked together to bring down the false and negative boundaries thrown up in the name of ethnicity, age, race, religion, and gender boundaries that separate and divide. At the same time that those boundaries were coming down, the three, as God's agents, were erecting true boundaries—ethical and moral boundaries—that must exist if the reign of God is ever to be fully realized in the world. To the modern observer, they created a bisexual family."[24]

The strength of Duncan's reading is that it does not privilege one relationship over the other, especially since there is nothing in the text itself to justify such privileging. Since the book of Ruth does not reveal Ruth's feelings toward either Naomi or Boaz, what is obvious to one reader is not to another. In fact Ruth's only words of undying devotion are to Naomi (1:16–17), and the only person she is said to love is Naomi (4:15). In some ways a romance between Ruth and Boaz is less supported in the text itself, more dependent on the imagination of the reader, than a romance between Ruth and Naomi. Those trained to be sensitive to love between women (whether or not the interpreter is personally same-sex oriented), see love between Ruth and Naomi just as clearly as readers who seek heterosexual romance are sure of Ruth's love for Boaz. Duncan sees both.

The 1987 novel *Fried Green Tomatoes at the Whistle Stop Cafe* by Fannie Flagg features a relationship between two women named Ruth and Idgie in which the biblical Ruth's passionate speech to Naomi figures prominently.[25] The book is composed of two interwoven narratives, one set in Alabama from the 1920s to the 1960s, the other set in the Alabama of the 1980s. Despite the disjunctions of time and place, the novel shares many themes with the biblical book of Ruth. First the novel is about relationship, friendships which cross the boundaries of race (especially prominent in the story set in the early part of the twentieth century) and generation (seen most clearly in the more contemporary setting). Second the novel is not limited in its definition of *family* to the biological bonds of a nuclear family. The central family is the one that Ruth and Idgie form together. Indeed most of the families in the novel are not traditional. Idgie Threadgoode herself comes from a family that stretches the biological definition of the word. The Threadgoode family consists of a married couple, their nine children, and a girl named Ninny. The novel never explains where Ninny came from or who she was before she entered the family—she is simply taken in and raised like one of their own. Sipsey, the African American woman who works for the Threadgoodes, also has indeterminate roots. She came to the household when she was ten or eleven, said that she was looking for a job, and never left.[26] Sipsey did not give birth to any children, but one day a woman was giving away a child at the railroad stop. She said that her husband had been in prison for three years and she could not go back home with a baby. When Sipsey heard she ran out of the house to the railway station, and got that baby.[27] He was her son and grew up in the Threadgoode house too. Families are created through love and commitment, not necessarily marriage and birth.

The novel's Ruth shares much with the biblical Ruth as the biblical Ruth is generally understood. She is sweet and kind and good. "She had light auburn hair and brown eyes with long eye lashes, and was so sweet and soft-spoken that people just fell in love with her on first sight. You just couldn't help yourself, she was just one of those sweet-to-the-bone girls, and the more you knew her, the prettier she got."[28] Together Ruth and Idgie open a restaurant that becomes the heart of the town. Much of their story is set during the Great Depression, and Ruth and Idgie give everything they can to people in need. The two women feed the hungry in their community, they take in any man who is tramping, they serve African Americans despite being threatened by the KKK. In short they treat all people, especially those on the margins of society, with human dignity. Together they embody *hesed*.

The central relationship is between Ruth and Idgie. They meet when Ruth boards at the Threadgoode's house one summer. She is from Georgia but she is working at the church in Whistlestop. Idgie is still a teenager—wild, already refusing to wear dresses and eat at the dinner table. Ruth is in her early twenties, older and more mature than the young Idgie. Idgie immediately develops a crush on the visitor, a crush that is acknowledged by the entire family. In fact Mr. and Mrs. Threadgoode react as if there were nothing strange or threatening about their teenage daughter's crush on another woman.[29] Ruth soon realizes that she loves Idgie too, but she is the only one in the novel who seems to appreciate the full implications of their love for one another: she decides to leave to marry a man in Georgia. The only doubt or hesitation about the relationship is expressed by Ruth herself: "It was because she loved her so much that she had to leave. Idgie was a sixteen-year-old kid with a crush and couldn't possibly understand what she was saying. She had no idea when she was begging Ruth to stay and live with them what she was asking; but Ruth knew, and she realized she had to leave."[30]

Ruth marries Frank Bennett in Valdosta, Georgia. Her husband repeatedly beats and rapes her. When Ruth's mother dies, she finally decides to escape his tyranny. She tears a page out of her Bible, puts it in an envelope, mails it to Idgie, and waits for her to come. The page is from the book of Ruth: "And Ruth said, 'Intreat me not to leave thee, *or* to return from following after thee: for whither thou goest, I will go; and where thou lodgest, I will lodge: thy people *shall be* my people, and thy God my God.'"[31] Ruth uses her namesake's vow to another woman to express her own love and commitment to a woman. Idgie and her family drive to Georgia the next day to bring Ruth home.

When Ruth arrives back at the Threadgoode house, Idgie's parents want her to remain with Idgie forever. Ruth speaks to Idgie's parents alone, and pledges herself to Idgie, much to their happiness and relief.[32] When Ruth gives birth to Frank Bennett's baby, he is named after Idgie's favorite brother who was tragically killed—Buddy—and he takes Idgie's last name. He is referred to by everyone in the town as Idgie and Ruth's boy. Like her namesake, Flagg's Ruth also leaves her home, travels across borders to be with a woman, lodges with her, is embraced by her community, and finally bears her a son—a boy who everyone acknowledges belongs to the two women.

Although the characters in the novel treat Idgie and Ruth's relationship as natural and normal, the novel never uses the word *lesbian* or *lovers* or describes the bond between the two women. The subtlety results in an ambiguity. For some readers (and viewers of the movie) Ruth and Idgie are clearly in a same-sex relationship; for others the conclusion is not so clear.[33]

Sexual and Gender Ambiguity

The text is ambiguous about Ruth and Naomi's relationship, which allows the actualization of all three readings (heterosexual, lesbian, bisexual) depending on the perspective of the interpreter. It is this ambiguity that is highlighted by J. Cheryl Exum. Exum begins her article on the book of Ruth with a painting by Philip Hermogenes Calderon entitled *Ruth and Naomi*. What is so intriguing about the painting is that despite the title, which would seem to imply the presence of only two figures, there are three—two of whom are embracing while the third looks on. Consequently there is no clear correspondence between the signifiers (the names in the title) and the signified (the figures in the painting). Adding to the ambiguity is the fact that the gender of one of the figures in the embrace is difficult to determine. The ambiguous one is taller than the other with darker clothes; the face is in profile and partially shaded. The woman embracing this figure has her head thrown back, and the ambiguous one's arms encircle the woman, bringing her in tight against the body. The poise looks passionate, romantic, erotic.

The possibilities of identification are as follows: the two figures embracing are Ruth and Naomi, the scene is illustrating Ruth's "clinging" and her vow to Naomi, and the figure who stands to the side is Orpah. The other possible identification is that the two figures embracing are Boaz and Ruth, the scene is illustrating their union at the end of the biblical book, and it is Naomi who stands to the side, look-ing on approvingly. Exum conducted an informal poll and found that the people who were shown the picture had strong preferences for one or the other interpreta-tion and often thought their own understanding of the painting to be obvious.[34] In particular those who interpreted the embracing figures as Ruth and Boaz pointed to the sexual charge in the positioning of the two bodies, and the fact that the one fig-ure is much taller than the other. Such details could indicate only a heterosexual couple. Those who interpreted the embracing figures as Ruth and Naomi could point to other clues in the painting. First there is no scene in the Bible showing Boaz and Ruth embracing with Naomi looking on—in the biblical story Ruth and Boaz's embrace comes under the cover of night and Naomi and Boaz never appear in the same scene together. The fact that the solitary figure is carrying some kind of bundle is also understood as evidence that the embracing figures are Ruth and Naomi. The bundle indicates travel and suggests that the third figure is Orpah, who began the journey to Bethlehem with the other two women.

Rather than taking a position herself on the identity of the three figures, Exum uses the painting as her starting point for an exploration of the sexual and gender ambiguity in the book of Ruth. Readers could not have such opposing views of this painting, Exum argues, if the book itself were not already ambiguous in terms of the gender roles and relationships between the three protagonists. Exum writes: "There is a striking blurring of gender roles, indeed of sexually determined roles—husband, wife, mother, father—in this tale, with Naomi symbolically holding all four of these roles."[35] When Naomi places Obed on her breast and the women of Bethlehem proclaim the boy to be her son, she functions as both husband to Ruth and wife to Boaz, father to Obed and mother to Obed. When she calls Ruth "my daughter" she places herself in the position of Ruth's mother. When she instructs Ruth to go down to the threshing floor, because of an oddity in the Hebrew she also becomes the seducer of Boaz.

This last point of Exum's requires further explanation. The oldest complete Hebrew text of the Bible is the product of a group of Jewish rabbis called the Masoretes. They were not only preservers and copiers of older Hebrew manuscripts; they were also responsible for adding the vocalization (the vowel sounds) to the consonantal text. They were also scholars who made notes in the margins, catalogued vocabulary and grammatical features, and made decisions about inconsistencies. The text they produced—the Masoretic Text (MT)—is the Tanak used in Jewish liturgy and the Hebrew Bible used in academic investigation. It is also the basis of most English translations. In the MT Naomi tells Ruth: "And wash and anoint yourself and put on your mantle, *and I will go down* to the threshing floor. Do not make yourself known to the man until he has finished eating and drinking. When he lies down, mark the place where he lies down, and go and uncover his feet, *and I will lie down,* and he will tell you what to do" (3:3–4; emphasis added). Because of the obvious incoherence of these instructions, the Masoretes altered the two places where Naomi seems to be inserting herself into the seduction scene so that all of the commands are directed to Ruth. Even though the Hebrew is written with Naomi going down and lying down, it is to be read with Ruth performing all of the actions leading up to her waking of Boaz.[36]

The multiple subject positions inhabited by Ruth and Naomi and the gender ambiguity that results from their shifting positions are mirrored in another grammatical glitch in the Hebrew: there are seven times when a masculine ending appears at the end of a word whose referent is feminine, all but one of which occurs in the opening passage of the book of Ruth (1:7 twice; 1:9; 1:11; 1:13; 1:19b; 4:11). In every instance the referent is two women—either Ruth and Orpah, Ruth and Naomi, or Rachel and Leah. Two other irregularities also point to ambiguous gender roles in the book of Ruth: in Ruth 1:22 a masculine pronoun is used to refer to Ruth and Naomi, two women; and in Ruth 3:15 there is confusion in the ancient manuscripts about the gender of the person who left the threshing room and went to the city. The MT reads "and he went;" but multiple other manuscripts, including the Syriac and the Vulgate (the Latin translation), read "and she went." The context of the verse does not make the gender clear—both Ruth and Boaz leave as dawn breaks.

Commentators have a variety of explanations for these problems in the Hebrew grammar and the textual witness. For example, Campbell has proposed that what appears to be a masculine ending in the seven instances listed above is actually an archaic dual feminine form.[37] However, no historical-grammatical explanation can be conclusively demonstrated. Campbell's argument becomes quite circular. He states: "Since the Ruth text as we have it is quite scrupulous in its correct use of gender, these relics must be regarded as a distinct mark of archaic composition or at least of composition in a dialect retaining an otherwise lost grammatical feature."[38] Campbell can assert only that Ruth's grammar of gender is precise *if* the archaic dual feminine form actually exists and is present in the text, but here he uses the assertion as proof of his thesis. Even if Campbell is correct—that the book of Ruth is written during the monarchy and that early Hebrew had a dual feminine form that is identical to the masculine plural—the form is a peculiarity in the text that alters reading. As the narrative plays with masculine and feminine roles, the letters on the page play with the same binary oppositions. Identities and relationships can be read in multiple ways.

Who loves whom? Who marries whom? Who acts as mother to whom; who acts as father? Naomi, Boaz, and Ruth circle around each other, changing positions, interchanging identities, destabilizing binaries, and challenging our expectations as readers.

Trouble in Paradise

As divergent as these feminist, queer, and rabbinic readings are, they do share a common orientation toward the relationship between the two women: it is understood to be reciprocal. Ruth and Naomi care for one another and are motivated by similar impulses. There are, however, gaps in the text that, if exploited, call such mutuality into question.

Danna Nolan Fewell and David Gunn enter the story through Naomi's silent response to Ruth's vow. After Ruth's speech in 1:16–17 Naomi sees that the young woman is determined to accompany her to Bethlehem and "she ceased speaking to her" (1:18b). It is this silence that raises suspicions for them. Ruth may be committed to Naomi, but Naomi seems to be unmoved. "In our reading, Naomi's silence at Ruth's unshakable commitment to accompany her is not unexpected. Naomi is attempting to shake free of Moab and the calamity she associates with that place and its people. Resentment, irritation, frustration, unease may well lie behind her silence. Ruth the Moabite may even menace her future."[39] The entire journey seems to happen in this silence and when Naomi enters Bethlehem she is clearly still upset: "And she said to them, 'Do not call me Naomi; call me Mara, for Shaddai has made me very bitter. I went away full, and empty the Lord has brought me back'" (1:20–21). For Fewell and Gunn Naomi repudiates Ruth's love in her speech to the people of Bethlehem.[40] The relationship between the two is more antagonistic than earlier idealizations of either platonic or romantic love suggest.

Brenner also proposes a one-sided love affair, but in her assessment Naomi's feelings for Ruth are unreciprocated. Naomi is too depressed after the deaths of her husband and sons to pay much attention to her daughter-in-law. Ruth follows her home and takes care of their material needs, more out of necessity than love or loyalty.[41] When Ruth tells her about her first day of gleaning in Boaz's field, she is so happy that she jumps out of bed, hugs, and kisses her. "And then it happened. All of a sudden, as I was touching Ruth, a wave of . . . what? came over me. I couldn't understand what was happening. It was an electric shock, you'd say today."[42] Naomi has continued to burn with desire and even imagines that she and Ruth could set up a household together. But she never mentions her feelings to Ruth, and, after a few weeks, her reason and logic rein in her passions. Naomi pressures Ruth into seducing Boaz.[43]

Relationships are complex, motives are mixed, feelings are mercurial. It is common to read Naomi's urgent words to her bride-daughters as evidence of her care for them; it is common to read Ruth's vow as a declaration of her love and loyalty. But Fewell and Gunn and Brenner point out gaps in the narrative which may indicate tensions and complexities in their relationship. These tensions and complexities are present from the first words spoken in the story. As Alter notes: "In any given narrative event, and especially, at the beginning of any new story, the point at which dialogue first emerges will be worthy of special attention, and in most instances, the initial words spoken by a personage will be revelatory, perhaps more in manner than in matter constituting an important moment in the exposition of character."[44] Ruth's and Naomi's words reveal much about the character of each in manner and in matter.

There is a strong contrast between Naomi's speeches and Ruth's speech in terms of style. The three speeches Naomi employs in her attempt to dissuade her daughters-in-law from following her into Judah are long, repetitive, logical, formal, and characterized by "archaic syntactical constructions."[45] The second speech is particularly long, with arresting images: "And Naomi said, 'Turn back, my daughters, why do you go with me? Do I still have sons in my womb who could be your husbands? Turn back, my daughters, go your way for I am too old to have a man. Even if I had hope and tonight had a man and also gave birth to sons, would you continue to wait until they were grown? Would you shut yourselves off without husbands? No, my daughters, for my portion is more bitter than yours because the hand of Yahweh has struck me'" (1:11–13). Ruth's speech, in contrast, is "stripped down, staccato-like."[46] Each phrase is succinct, beginning with a verb in the second person and followed by a verb in the first person. Ruth's style is difficult to capture in English because certain phrases consist of only one or two words in Hebrew. For example, "your people will be my people" is six words in English but only two words in Hebrew. Naomi's long and logical speech reveals a carefully considered position. Ruth's short and emotional speech perhaps reveals a more impetuous character. Naomi realizes the consequences of Ruth's desire to follow her; Ruth simply wants what she wants.

Despite the other divergences in style both Ruth and Naomi use hyperbole and exaggeration in their attempts to persuade. Naomi's suggestion that she get a man that very night and conceive sons (presumably twins) and that the young widows wait some twenty years to marry the boys succeeds precisely because the idea is ridiculous. Will the women help to diaper their future husbands? Will the old widows shuffle down the aisle (or the ancient Israelite equivalent) with their young, strapping grooms? And even though readers tend to romanticize Ruth's speech and take it at face value, it is also extreme, over-the-top, overstated. No one would expect to hear such a vow from the wife of one's son. As we have seen, these words seem more appropriate spoken between lovers, but even in an amorous situation the vow is the hyperbolic sentiment of romance. Few lovers follow through on such commitment. Even couples with long, happy marriages stop at "till death do us part" and do not further commit to defying the separation of the grave.

This is not to say that the two women do not feel genuine affection for one another. As they stand on the road between Moab and Judah, Naomi seems genuinely concerned with Ruth's future well-being, and Ruth weeps and clings. But this affection, maybe even love, is complicated. Ruth and Naomi's relationship is marked by other moments of silence, disconnect, and intentional miscommunication. The cumulative weight of these moments suggests that the two women are wrestling with one another more often than they are living in harmony.

After Ruth's speech Naomi remains silent and the two women proceed to Bethlehem, presumably without saying another word. Once they reach the village Naomi speaks to the women who greet her. She changes her name to Mara ("Bitter"), and proclaims herself empty, seemingly ignoring Ruth (1:20–21). At the beginning of the second chapter the narrator reveals that Naomi has a rich kinsman (2:1). Yet Naomi does not give this information to her daughter-in-law. It is Ruth's idea to go and glean, and chance brings her to the fields of this very same rich kinsman (2:2–3). When she returns home to Naomi and tells her of her day, Naomi finally reveals that Boaz is Elimelech's relative. Ruth then proceeds to startle Naomi, perhaps to get back at her for concealing the existence of Boaz, perhaps to goad her into expressing some kind of concern. Boaz had urged Ruth to stick close to his female servants in order to avoid sexual harassment in the fields (2:8); yet Ruth tells Naomi that he instructed her to remain close to his male servants—a deliberate misstatement. Next Naomi devises a plan that involves Ruth sneaking into a barn full of drunken men, undressing Boaz, and waiting for him to tell her what to do. The plan may be placing Ruth in a dangerous situation; it is certainly placing her in an awkward one. Ruth does not protest but responds to Naomi's instructions: "All that you tell me, I will do" (3:5). For once, Ruth appears to be obedient to Naomi. But Ruth listens to Naomi's advice only to a point. Ruth does not uncover Boaz's feet and wait for him to tell her what to do; rather she uncovers his feet, waits for him to wake up, and then tells him what to do (3:9). When she returns to Naomi, again there is a gap between what happened between Boaz and Ruth as related by the narrator and what Ruth relates to Naomi. Boaz fills Ruth's apron with grain and sends her home. Ruth tells Naomi that he gave her the grain and said, "Do not return empty to your mother-in-law" (3:17). In the end Ruth disappears and Naomi takes the child born to her and Boaz. When the women of Bethlehem praise Ruth Naomi again remains silent (4:15).

Ruth's relationship with Naomi is marked by ambiguity, tension, and play. Commentators who attempt to define narrowly their feelings for one another foreclose on too many other possibilities that are present in the text. Is it love, friendship, romance, resentment, frustration, loyalty, longing, necessity? Yes. Such uncertainty does not obscure the meaning; such uncertainty is the meaning. The uncertainties and ambiguities build the portrait of Ruth as jester and trickster, a border crosser who embodies plurality. From the first, Ruth and Naomi engage in a verbal sparring match, each employing hyperbole and overblown rhetoric in order to persuade the other. Ruth's speech to her mother-in-law wins—she outmaneuvers the older woman whose silence is her concession. Ruth outmaneuvers Naomi, and she will best Boaz. She is lissome and lithe, loving deeply but strangely.

· 5 ·

AGRICULTURAL
INTERLUDE NO. 2

The root cellar held bushels of potatoes; the basement shelves with peeling paint held row upon row of tomatoes canned; applesauce, grape juice, strawberry jam, each in its mason jar; the freezer full of corn, beans, peas, blueberries; the honeycombs boxed and stacked.[1] My sister and I did not help much with the canning process—it was too hot, too precise. We would sit at the kitchen table and watch through the steam as my mother turned the summer into winter food. We shared the pink foam skimmed off the top of strawberries turned to jam.

When I follow Ruth and Naomi into Bethlehem, I have to bring my travel guide along. Journeys into other countries are also journeys into other cuisines. According to my guide (in this case biblical and other textual material, archaeological investigation, and cross-cultural comparison), the primary foods of the Israelites were the "Mediterranean triad"—bread, wine, and olive oil.[2] In addition to this three-legged foundation the people of the ancient Near East ate legumes, fruits, and vegetables. Some fish and dairy products also supplemented the Israelite diet. Meat, however, was eaten only on special occasions, more frequently by the wealthy than by the poor.[3] In other words Ruth and her companions lived low on the food chain, on local, sustainable foods. Grains were particularly important, forming the core of the diet. Cereal products were eaten at every meal in a variety of ways—parched or raw, as bread or porridge (like cream of wheat or oatmeal).[4] It is estimated that bread alone made up at least 50 percent of daily caloric intake.[5] Bethlehem means not only the "house of bread" but also the "house of food." The conflation of the two meanings for *bread* appears in languages across the ancient Near East. The dual meaning of *lehem* underlines the centrality of bread in the ancient diet—food is bread and bread is life. This is not a metaphor. Bread filled the stomach and fueled the body. The production of bread connected the self with the world and the self with others in ways both intimate and essential. One's relationship to and role in bread making defined gender and economic status in the family and the community. The back-story of Ruth is famine, but the crisis of food that compels the plot is a crisis of bread production. Alone, Ruth and Naomi could not produce their own bread.

I

I live in the easy cornucopia of a twenty-first-century American city. I buy my food in grocery stores and restaurants. I find neither in Iron Age Bethlehem. When I grow herbs or a tomato plant in containers on my back porch, I am a dilettante who plays with an agrarian past. Again I peruse my travel guide to follow Ruth and Naomi into the Iron Age. In some ways my diet is not much different. I, too, eat bread, use olive oil, drink wine. As a vegetarian my diet, too, consists primarily of cereal products, legumes, fruits, vegetables, dairy. But the similarities end when we leave generalizations behind and look at the specific food products, how they are produced and obtained, how they are incorporated into daily life.

Every week I bake a loaf of bread. In this practice I am unusual. Most people living in the United States buy mass-produced bread from grocery stores. Industrial breads are produced in large factories, quickly made with electric mixers and chemical leavening agents, shot through with preservatives and wrapped in plastic to sit on shelves for weeks at a time. Presliced and packaged, these breads bear little resemblance to the foodstuff upon which our ancestors built their diet. A few still do get their bread fresh baked from local bakeries, especially in some European countries where artisan breads are a long and cherished tradition. Slowly risen by yeast and touched by hands, these breads are more akin to the bread that sustained the human community for millennia. But even these breads, even my own loaves, do not require the kind of time and effort needed to make even the simplest flat bread in ancient Israel.

Bread is so simple and plentiful now that we barely think twice about it. Yet each one of basic ingredients of bread—flour, yeast, salt—represents a revolution in human understanding and manipulation of nature: "Bread is the most everyday and familiar of foods, the sturdy staff of life on which hundreds of generations have leaned for sustenance. It also represents a truly remarkable discovery, a lively pole on which the young human imagination may well have vaulted forward in insight and inspiration. For our prehistoric ancestors it would have been a startling sign of the natural world's hidden potential for being transformed, and their own ability to shape natural materials to human desires."[6] How did anyone discover that the seeds of certain wild grasses could be harvested, ground, combined with water and other ingredients, then baked or fried? The transformation of grain to bread must have seemed like a minor miracle to the earliest people.

II

Ruth and Naomi need to bake bread every day. The simplest bread is a flat bread that is made of only flour, water, and sometimes salt. Add yeast for the simplest of leavened breads. I bake my own bread, but I buy commercially produced flour, yeast, salt, sugar, oil—my ingredients take me no more time to assemble than does a quick trip to the grocery store. Ruth and Naomi's process is not so easy. I bake my own bread, but I do not participate in the growing and harvesting of the grain. I do not grind grain into flour. Ruth and Naomi must grow and harvest and grind; otherwise they do not eat.

Again, readers of Ruth find themselves standing in the fields of food production. Bread begins in these fields. The obtaining of grain is a complicated process that requires the coordination and cooperation of a whole society. Both societal structures and agricultural technologies must reach a critical level of sophistication in order for bread to be widely available. Because bread production takes a village, one's status in society dictates one's role in bread production. In other words tell me what you do in the process of bread making, and I will tell you who you are.[7] Ruth and Naomi's status in their society is most evident in what they have to do to obtain their daily bread.

In traditional bread-making practices men and women need each other.[8] The grain must be grown, the stalks harvested by cutting them down with flint sickles,[9] the sheaves stacked then carried to the threshing floor. The labor of farming may have been male dominated, but it was not male exclusive. The evidence from Ruth alone suggests that men may have been in charge of fields—Boaz owns the land where Ruth gleans, and a male servant oversees it—but both men and women contributed their labor to working these fields.[10] Ruth gleans behind both male and female servants, hired by Boaz to reap his harvest. Harvest time especially was a period when all available hands were necessary to secure the crops.

Once the cereal crop is harvested, the small edible seed must be separated from the inedible stem, leaf, hull, and chaff in processes of threshing, winnowing, and cleaning: "The threshing of the cereal took place on open, level surfaces, often elevated to catch the breeze needed for winnowing. . . . Threshing sledges fitted with flint studes or basalt embedded in wooden boards and drawn by oxen or donkeys were used to thresh the grain from the stalks (Deut. 25:4). The straw and chaff were separated from the grain by winnowing, that is, tossing the threshed grain into the air so the wind would carry away the chaff."[11] After winnowing, the grain was further cleansed, first by throwing it again into the wind with a wooden shovel and piling it into heaps, and second by shifting the grain through sieves.[12] Once it was ready to be made into food, grain was then stored in granaries and silos, either above or below ground, either public or private.[13]

The difficult work of threshing and winnowing was primarily a male activity, but women dominated the rest of the production chain. Since grain is not digestible in raw form, bread production continued through grinding, cracking, parching, soaking, boiling, roasting, leavening (a lot can be done with a handful of grain).[14] Just as the fields were spaces of communal activity, so were the "kitchens." To make the flour for bread, grain was coarsely ground between two basalt stones. The woman grinding the grain would kneel before the lower stone and move the upper stone back and forth. The grain was then transferred to a mortar to be ground more finely with a pestle. Archaeological evidence suggests that women worked in groups to grind the grain into the flour necessary for the family's daily bread intake.[15] For a basic bread, grinding the flour may have taken up to three hours a day.[16] It was also common for ovens to be positioned between domestic spaces suggesting that at least the implements for, if not the work of, baking was also shared.[17] The bread could be shaped and baked in a variety of ways—either flat and thrown on the heated interior walls of the *tabun* or *tannūr* (a beehive-shaped oven in the exterior courtyard) or on a griddle over the fire or rolled into balls and fried in oil.[18]

If the woman desired to make any kind of risen bread, the leavening came from yesterday's batch of bread dough.[19] Yeast is naturally present in the air, and a mixture of flour and water left to sit will eventually begin to bubble as the yeast settles on the mixture and begins to consume it. This dough then becomes the starter dough, a piece of which will leaven the next batch, which in turn will leaven the next, a process that can continue for decades, maybe even longer.[20] Today we know that yeast is a microorganism that eats the sugars in the grain. As it metabolizes those sugars it excretes carbon dioxide as a waste byproduct. Meanwhile the water mixes with the flour and the flour's gluten proteins form chains that knit together. The carbon dioxide from the yeast gets trapped in the spaces between the proteins, which causes the dough to expand. The bread rises. How mysterious this process must have seemed to those who first stumbled on it.

Salt is not just for flavoring—in a yeasted bread, especially, it is a necessary component.[21] "At 1.5–2% of the flour weight, salt tightens the gluten network and improves the volume of the finished loaf."[22] Salt also retards yeast reproduction and thus slows the rate of the rise. The slower rate is easier to regulate, allows the bread gluten more time to develop into stronger structures, and therefore produces a bread lighter with a firmer texture, a richer taste, and a longer shelf life. In the ancient Near East salt could be obtained through the evaporation of sea water from the Mediterranean or the Dead Sea. For me bread making is a simple affair, a leisurely afternoon in the kitchen; for Ruth and Naomi the process was long, arduous, and a matter of life and death.

Meat eating may be more interesting to most biblical scholars and cultural anthropologists, but it was bread making that structured time and relationship. In ancient Israel life revolved around the family and food production,[23] and the primary food was bread. The biblical text takes us into a world where time was divided by plantings and harvestings, where the weather was watched with careful intensity. Even where people in the United States still farm (somebody still grows the wheat, grinds it, and makes it into bread), farming is powered by fossil fuel and corn not sun and grass; it is undertaken by individuals and corporations not families and villages. In biblical times it was bread production above all else that knit the family and the community together in particular ways of interdependence.

Ruth and Naomi arrive in Bethlehem outside of these bread-making networks. Grains are planted in the fall, but the two widows enter Bethlehem during the first of the spring harvests (1:22). It is too late to grow their own. They have no material resources so they cannot buy or barter for grain either. At the end of the narrative it is revealed that Naomi does have a piece of land, and some commentators wonder why the two women did not use this land for food production. Land is, however, not worth anything if one does not have the resources to work it. One needs capital to acquire the seed and to hire the workers, especially for a labor-intensive crop like grain. The soil needs to be prepared, the crops sowed in the proper season, tended, harvested, threshed, winnowed, cleansed. Owning a piece of land simply is not enough to provide Ruth and Naomi with the bread they need. When they cross the border into Judah and then enter into Bethlehem, they are two poor women who arrive out of time.

III

The journey of Ruth and Naomi has taken them back to Naomi's home at a time when famine has ceased. There is bounty in the land, but the two widows have no immediate access to it. In order to provide for their basic needs law and custom allow them to glean in the fields of the wealthy, in fields controlled by men. Gleaning is a public announcement of their poverty, as standing in a soup-kitchen line or paying for groceries with food stamps is today. Ruth's gleaning marks her as a poor woman in Israelite society.

Not only does the circumstance of Ruth's gleaning indicate her economic and gender status, but the type of grain Ruth gleans also speaks the language of poverty. Ruth begins her gleaning during the barley harvest, which further underscores her dependence and destitution. "Barley (*Hordeum vulgare*), coarser than wheat and inferior, was considered the bread of the poor; it was also fed to animals."[24] Barley is a little easier to grow—it is more salt-resistant and requires less water than wheat. Fewer resources, then, are necessary for its production. Barley bread is also inferior to wheat bread because barley has a lower protein content. It does not produce the strong networks of gluten that provide the structure that allows a good wheat bread to rise. Consequently it was the grain of the poor, not just in Israel but also across the Near East.[25]

In addition to providing Ruth the grain she needs to make bread, the act of gleaning begins to incorporate her into the community of women and the networks of bread production. "Women's networks in small agricultural communities function in several important economic and social ways."[26] In her search to define *gleaning* at the beginning of *The Gleaners and I,* Varda interviews an older woman as she stands on the edge of a field in the French countryside. The woman reminisces about her youth, how her mother always told her to glean, not to waste anything in the fields. All the local women would go to the fields to glean wheat and sometimes rice. She pauses in her memories to demonstrate: she stoops down, picks up some fallen sheaves, puts them in her apron. She continues: it was hot work, gnats and mosquitoes were constant nuisances, and the women would return home exhausted. They were tired but they were also happy—they would laugh together, drinking coffee at the end of the day. The work was hard but the bonds formed between the women sustained them, and an apron full of grain meant a belly full of bread.

We label Ruth an idyll; the pastoral setting appears quaint, simple, innocent, charming. In reality the agricultural context of Ruth is fraught with danger and anxiety; the circumstance of farming is one of back-breaking labor. Ruth's skin has been darkened and weathered by the sun and wind, her hands are calloused, her arms muscled. Like everyone living in a subsistence society she lives on the edge of disaster, a couple of bad harvests away from starvation. Food is meaningful in every society at all times; food is invested with even more particular and poignant meanings when it is grown and produced in perilous circumstances, when a bad crop or two threatens death not just higher prices in the grocery store. It is invested with even more meaning when one spends most of one's time growing and preparing it, and when this must be done in relationship with others.[27]

IV

Carole Counihan and Penny van Esterik introduce their reader about food and culture by explaining how "food touches everything. Food is the foundation of every economy. It is a central pawn in political strategies of states and households. Food marks social differences, boundaries, bonds, and contradictions. Eating is an endlessly evolving enactment of gender, family, and community relationships . . . ; we see how food-sharing creates solidarity, and how food scarcity damages the human community and the human spirit. We see how men and women define themselves differently through their foodways, and how women across cultures so often speak through food and appetite. . . . Food is life, and life can be studied and understood through food."[28]

Everyone must eat, every day, several times a day. Food is set apart "from the rest of material culture"[29] not only because of its ubiquity, but also because "it is ingested, it is eaten, it goes inside."[30] Food is the site of a profound vulnerability—we cannot live without food and we cannot obtain the food we need without working in cooperation with nature and with other people. Food is such a powerful carrier of cultural constructions of identity and community because food is literally the vehicle for the interpenetrations of individuals that form a community, in the interpenetrations of animal, vegetable, mineral that form an ecosphere. Food is the site of a radical openness to the world. In the book of Ruth season and setting are too frequently viewed as backdrop; instead Ruth's context is a metaphor for human interdependence. Plot, character, and setting unite.

V

The book of Ruth is a story of crisis: Ruth and Naomi's inability to provide bread for themselves. Even though the famine has ended in Bethlehem the story does not end until Ruth marries Boaz and the two women's continual access to grain is secured. Throughout the narrative Ruth is legible through her relationship to food—she enacts both gender and class in her gleaning and her acceptance of grain from Boaz. Yet she also changes the way she is read and recognized through her changing relationship to food. First she adopts Israelite foodways and connects to networks of bread production; second she has sex with and marries Boaz. Her marriage to the wealthy patriarch changes her class status and thus her place in food production. She eventually becomes more and more intimately incorporated into the Israelite fold.

Although Ruth's relationship to Obed is the focus of chapter 8, Ruth's story of incorporation would not be complete without some discussion of how she becomes a mother. Food, sex, and reproduction are intertwined in the book of Ruth, and Obed is the final product of Ruth's incorporation into the community (4:13). The last scene in the story is Obed lying on Naomi's breast while the women of Bethlehem name him and proclaim him Naomi's son (4:14–17). There is, at least, the suggestion that Naomi becomes the boy's wet nurse, feeding him with her own body (4:16). Ruth has disappeared. Is Ruth erased from the narrative because she is a Moabite? Is there a bias against the Moabite which persists and erupts here in the book's final scene?[31] Perhaps, but there are other possible and more positive readings.

Gloria Anzaldúa weaves food in and out of her writing about life in the Borderlands. Through food practices Anzaldúa explores her own gender, class, ethnicity, nationality, sexuality. Anzaldúa forges her bonds to land, family, and community through food, but she also uses food to express her differences from and dissatisfaction with the way her community defines her identity and establishes her roles.[32] In Judith Butler's analysis:

> Anzaldúa asks us to consider that the source of our capacity for social transformation is to be found precisely in our capacity to mediate between worlds, to engage in cultural translation, and to undergo, through the experience of language and community, the diverse set of cultural connections that make us who we are. . . . She is asking us to stay at the edge of what we know, to put our own

epistemological certainties into question, and through that risk and openness to another way of knowing and of living in the world to expand our capacity to imagine the human. . . . What she is arguing then, is that it is only through existing in the mode of translation, constant translation, that we stand a chance of producing a multicultural understanding of women or, indeed, of society.[33]

As a border crosser, Ruth inhabits the margins. As she seeks incorporation into the larger Bethlehem community, she adopts the foodways and integrates into the food systems of the community. By doing so she performs her gender, her class, her status as foreigner. By doing so she moves through different roles. In the end she resists a final incorporation—giving her body over as food—and she leaves the narrative. She claims her legitimacy in the Israelite community but refuses a complete assimilation, leaving her transformation open, remaining a mediator between two worlds. Yes, the final scene can be read as erasure, but it can also be read as resistance, a seeking of recognition and legitimation but still on her own terms, a reimagining of kinship and community through the sharing and the withholding of food.

· 6 ·

RUTH AND BOAZ

R uth and Naomi arrive in Bethlehem at the beginning of the barley harvest.[1]
The fields and the threshing floor dominate the central two chapters of the
book of Ruth. The woman Ruth moves in and out of the fields and on and off of the
threshing room floor; the activities of the harvest structure the narrative time, the
actions of the protagonists, and their characterization. The two women are destitute. They have crossed the border between Moab and Judah, across the Dead Sea
(the lowest point in the world), and come to Bethlehem, on foot, with nothing.
They have no capital to use their land to produce their own food, and no trade to
earn money to buy their own food. Obtaining grain, in particular, was essential for
survival. Ruth and Naomi's only option is charity, and the laws of Israel do provide
for "the poor and the alien" through gleaning (Lev 19:9, 23:22, Deut 24:19).
Watching Varda's documentary on contemporary gleaners I am struck by their
poverty. Many read Ruth as a charming tale, a sweet story of friendship and perse-
verance. We have forgotten (or do we ignore?) the dirty desperation of poverty. The
social circumstance is embodied in the posture—gleaners must stoop to gather their
food. Varda assembles images first of rural then urban gleaners, stooping over,
bending down, looking through the leftovers of the farmers' markets before the
street cleaners sweep the trash away. Over her images a French rapper sings: "Yeah,
food, grub; it's bad, sad, man. To bend down is not to beg but when I see them sway
my heart hurts! Eating that scrap-crap; they have to live on shit-bits; they've got to
frisk for tidbits left on the street, leftovers, rough stuff with no owners; picking up
trash like the streetsweeper . . . ; it's always been the same game, will always be the
same pain."[2]

The arrival of Ruth and Naomi in Bethlehem at the beginning of the barley harvest and Ruth's gleaning during the barley harvest are details that further character-
ize the two women as poor, destitute.[3] Today's poor do not glean wheat or barley;
they no longer grind their own grain to make their own bread. In Paris the bakeries
throw out all the unsold bread from the day before between six and seven in the
morning. Alain Fonteneau[4] pulls a *batard* out of his bag, next a farmhouse loaf
rolled in oats, beautiful artisan breads turned trash. Today's poor glean in the dump-
sters outside of bakeries.

Ruth goes to the fields to glean for herself and her mother-in-law and it is here where she meets Boaz. Chapter 2 is fraught with difficulty. Whose idea was it to glean? How should the dialogue between Ruth and Naomi be read? What exactly is Ruth doing when Boaz arrives at the field? Why is the overseer's conversation so garbled? Why does Ruth misrepresent Boaz's directions when she returns to Naomi? This chapter also raises questions about the role of God. Is *chance* a code word for *God* or is chance just happenstance? These questions underscore the play of the narrative, its complexity and its ambiguity. Readers are especially inclined to elide the questions that arise about Ruth's character and consequently read her as embodying loyalty, *hesed,* kindness, bravery, self-sacrificial love. She has even been seen as representing God. Ruth's actions are, however, exaggerated and her speech is misleading. She is playfully mendacious, a trickster in the fields and on the threshing-room floor.

Ruth Meets Boaz

Just as Ruth and Naomi's first spoken words reveal essential facets of their character, Boaz's first dialogue does as well. When Boaz arrives in the fields, after greeting the overseer he asks: "To whom does this woman belong?" (2:5). Boaz's first question parallels one of his last statements: when he is before the men at the gate he speaks of acquiring Ruth, using the language of commerce (4:5). Those who wish to spin a romantic tale out of the terse biblical narrative often puzzle over the fact that Boaz speaks of Ruth as if she were property. If this is a love story, then how could he denigrate Ruth in this way? Translators sometimes alter his words in order to make his speech conform with contemporary notions of love and romance, notions that include mutual respect and female autonomy and equality.[5] Boaz's question is perhaps shocking to our modern ears, but it certainly is consistent with the basic patriarchal orientation of ancient cultures. Boaz is the patriarch—rich, male, an established and respected figure in his community; Ruth is poor, female, a stranger. Such a power differential does not preclude a love affair but it does challenge readers to be aware of what the two principals import into the narrative.

The supervisor first identifies the woman in a way that acquiesces to Boaz's belittling: "'The girl [*na'arah*] is a Moabite who came back with Naomi from the fields of Moab'" (Ruth 2:6). He calls her a *na'arah*—girl or servant girl. He then notes her foreignness, twice, and fails to mention her familial relationship to Naomi. She seems like a stray dog here, following along unbidden and unwanted. From the fields of Moab to the fields of Bethlehem, Ruth follows behind and picks up what others leave.

To this point the Hebrew is clear. The next part of the supervisor's answer, however, is incomprehensible. In his answer the supervisor repeats a dialogue he had with Ruth, a dialogue otherwise unattested in the text. He continues: "She said

'Please, let me glean and gather among the sheaves behind the reapers.' So she came, and she has been on her feet from early this morning until now, without resting even for a moment'" (NRSV; Ruth 2:6–7). Or he says: "She requested permission to glean, and to gather grain among the sheaves behind the reapers. She arrived and has been waiting from daybreak until now; thus she must have spent little time at home" (Sasson).[6] Or he says: "'She said 'May I glean stalks of grain and gather them in bundles behind the reapers?' She came and stood from then the morning and until now; this is her sitting the house a few" (Linafelt's literal rendering).[7] Or he says: "[ ]." (Campbell's use of brackets to indicate throwing up of his hands).[8]

The problems with the Hebrew are multiple and are at the level of both syntax and meaning. The first line of questioning is about what Ruth asked; the second line is about what she did. The supervisor says that Ruth asks to glean *ba'amarim*. The *bet* is a prepositional particle that has a wide variety of meanings. It is most frequently translated "in" or "on," which in this case means "among" or "between" the sheaves. However, gleaners do not glean "among the sheaves"—gleaning by definition takes place behind the sheaves. Is Ruth asking for special privileges?[9] Some commentators think so, but others think that it "stretches credulity to the breaking point to believe that Ruth would make a request so contrary to customary practice."[10] The particle *bet* does have a wide range of meanings, so it has also been suggested that it introduces an adverbial phrase, in which case Ruth's request is to glean and gather "into bundles," which is an acceptable activity.[11] However, if she is not asking for a special privilege, why ask anything at all? It is her right to glean and gather and bundle—permission is unnecessary. In either case Ruth's speech is strange.

The second issue arises in the supervisor's description of what she has been doing. Has she stood there all day in the hot sun waiting for Boaz? If she did ask the supervisor to gather "among the sheaves," he would not have had the power to grant such permission. Or has she been working so hard all day that she has hardly taken a break in the house? Is her industry, diligence, and dedication being emphasized? Or is she drawing unnecessary attention to herself? Another possible rendering of the verses says she "tarried a little in the house," which may have been off limits. In this case Ruth is behaving presumptuously.

The interpretive ink spilled all over these verses has focused on what they mean for Ruth's actions and Ruth's character. Commentators tend to give Ruth the benefit of the doubt—that is to say that the majority understand her words and actions to conform to a preexistent portrait of her as diligent and deferential. However, the words can equally be translated in ways that portray her as bold, even insolent. Another possibility explored recently by Jonathan Grossman is that the words attributed by the supervisor to Ruth are not accurate. Most interpreters assume that the supervisor is a reliable narrator—that Ruth really did ask him something when she arrived in the fields and that their dialogue is accurately relayed to Boaz.[12] Grossman points out that even if Ruth did speak to the supervisor, her words are conveyed by and therefore shaped by the supervisor. Ultimately his speech tells us nothing more than what he thinks about her.[13] The supervisor is misrepresenting Ruth and the reader literally sees his mendacity in the jumbled speech that comes out of his mouth. He stammers and stumbles over his words.

Grossman's understanding of the supervisor's lies entails a prejudice born of the character's hatred and mistrust of Moabites.[14] It is an ethnic prejudice, a xenophobia. The supervisor may be expressing bigotry toward Moabites, although I am cautious about understanding his references to Ruth's ethnic identity as automatically prejudicial. There is, however, another aspect of his dislike of the poor widow. More pervasive than ethnic prejudice is class prejudice. The supervisor may be snubbing Ruth because she is one more poor woman come to profit from his hard work. Just because the poor are permitted by law to glean does not mean that they are welcomed into the fields. In Varda's film the owners and the overseers resent the intrusion—truckers dump produce without notifying the community and it rots away untaken; the owner of the grape vineyards stops the gleaners and the remains of the harvest are trampled into ground; the grocery store manager pours bleach on the food thrown into the dumpster behind the store, intentionally rendering it inedible. "Anyway," Varda remarks, picking overripe figs left from the harvest, good to eat but not for their commercial purpose of making into candied fruits, "half the people are stingy. They won't allow gleaning because they don't feel like being nice." Even in the contemporary culture of the United States, it is more permissible to harbor negative stereotypes about the poor and to believe that they did something to deserve their own poverty than it is to express negative sentiments about other ethnic or racial groups of people. Poor women, in particular, are subject to a host of negative stereotypes and double standards (for example, poor mothers set a bad example by not working whereas middle- and upper-class women damage their children by working outside of the home). These negative attitudes are often exacerbated by racial and ethnic prejudice—as the supervisor's response to Ruth may be—but the primary revulsion is to the poverty.

The supervisor is certainly not very nice. Yet despite his negative and maybe even deceptive portrayal of Ruth, Boaz approaches Ruth and responds kindly, albeit bombastically: "Now, listen, my daughter, do not go to glean in another field and also do not leave this one, but keep close to my young women. Keep your eyes on the field that is being reaped, and follow behind them. I have ordered the young men not to bother you. If you get thirsty, go to the vessels and drink from what the young men have drawn" (2:8–9). Boaz repeats himself, perhaps betraying his eagerness to have Ruth stay in his field. Is he sexually attracted to her already? Fewell and Gunn suggest that his motives here are more predatory than laudatory.[15]

In response to Boaz's words Ruth falls to the ground, her face in the dirt (2:10). Commentators generally see this as an example of Ruth's humility and her gracious-ness. Trible even calls Ruth's actions "appropriately deferential."[16] Yet if it is defer-ence, it is excessive, even bordering on self-humiliation. If it is thankfulness, then the action is unnecessary since Boaz did not give her permission to do anything she already could not do.[17] Her verbal response to Boaz draws attention to her status as a foreigner, twice, and then she goes even further in her groveling by telling him that she is not even like one of his servants. Instead of using the word the narrator has used throughout for servants (*na'arim*), Ruth uses the word *shifhah* to describe herself, a word indicating the lowest rung of servitude, and thus she denigrates her-self even further. Even though Boaz takes Ruth seriously, even though commentators follow his lead and take her seriously as well, I cannot. Boaz is acting the rich patri-arch, opening his hand to those who are in need. But Ruth does not need his munifi-cence to glean—it is her right under the law. It is no virtue to allow the homeless to eat out of your trash; it is no virtue to let the poor pick up after your harvesters. The joke may be lost on Boaz, but she is mocking his show of "generosity."

Ruth gets up off the ground and gleans for the remainder of the day. Her work is well rewarded. She returns home to Naomi with an ephah of barley—about two-thirds of a bushel, enough grain for several weeks.[18] Perhaps it's just me, but every time I watch *The Gleaners and I* I am surprised that there is no mention of Ruth. A man in a black robe stands in a field holding a red book, a book he calls "his Bible." I think for a moment that he is going to read the biblical injunctions concerning gleaning, scattered through Leviticus and Deuteronomy. I think that he is going to talk about Ruth who stands among the "alien corn" while he himself stands amid the tall grasses. They sway back and forth in the breeze. But he doesn't—he is, instead, holding the French penal code and he begins to explain the French laws on gleaning. I hear the biblical laws echoing in the background of the French laws— Article R-26.10: "Gleaning is allowed from sunup until sundown. . . . Gleaning occurs after the harvest"; a law from November 2, 1554, "allows the poor, the wretched, the deprived, to enter the fields once harvesting is over." I hear the judges at the end of Ruth making their pronouncements about who owns what field, who owns what woman. Perhaps it *is* just me. Ruth is my subtext and I see her wink at me as she stands in the spaces between Varda's scenes.

Ruth first takes what she needs and then gives the rest to Naomi. When she tells Naomi in whose field she had gleaned, Naomi responds with enthusiasm. When Ruth tells her the name of the man who owns the field in which she gleaned, Naomi reveals to Ruth that Boaz, the very man who Ruth mocked with her deference, is her relative (2:20). Rather than being mortified by her gaff Ruth continues to poke fun. She relays to Naomi a conversation with Boaz that misrepresents Boaz's words in a way calculated to get a rise out of her mother-in-law. Boaz tells Ruth to stick close to his girls and even warns his boys to leave her alone (2:9)[19] yet Ruth tells Naomi that Boaz told her to stick close to his boys (2:21), much to Naomi's chagrin. Why does Ruth erroneously report Boaz's words?[20] Throughout this chapter, Ruth's speech—both direct and indirect—is exaggerated, misleading, mocking. She is laughing at Boaz, at Naomi, and ultimately at God.

God

Standard documentary filmmaking positions the camera as the omnipotent eye, uncovering truths otherwise hidden to the casual observer. The voice narrating the film is disembodied, the filmmaker remains out of the frame, hiding his or her hand. The documentary filmmaker presents the objective, omnipotent, God's-eye view. Robert Flaherty's *Nanook of the North* (1922) is generally acknowledged as the first documentary film. The questions that this film raises about the space between narrative art and reality, fiction and fact, the subject of the film and the filmmaker still shape documentary and documentary-film theory. According to the typology of Bill Nichols, the documentary can be classified according to four stylistic categories, and the history of documentary is largely the history of the movement from one style to the next.[21] Nichols calls the first stage "direct-address." Documentaries like *Nanook of the North* seek to hide the work and perspective of the director from the audience. The camera follows the subject as if it were an omniscient eye, and the disembodied narrator speaks from above in a technique called the "voice-of-God" narration.

Other documentary filmmakers, however, have challenged such objectivity. The second phase of documentary style and history is called *cinéma vérité*, a kind of "documentary purity" which causes the filmmaker to intrude as little as possible— no commentary, no interview of the subjects, no asking them to perform before the camera;[22] the third phase is a return of the direct-address but with the narrative told through interview rather than "voice-of-God." The fourth phase is self-reflexive, "moving toward more complex forms where epistemological and aesthetic assumptions become more visible. These new self-reflexive documentaries mix observational passages with interviews, the voice-over of the filmmaker with intertitles, making patently clear what has been implicit all along: documentaries always were forms of re-presentation, never clear windows onto 'reality'; the filmmaker was always a participant-witness and an active fabricator of meaning, a producer of cinematic discourse rather than a neutral or all-knowing reporter of the way things truly are."[23] As Nichols notes, the self-reflexive strategy in documentary filmmaking has always been an underemployed albeit present aspect of documentary film. Yet since the 1970s it has been used with increasing frequency. Varda was an early proponent of the self-reflexive documentary. She disrupts the omnipotent eye by turning the camera on herself and by highlighting the subjectivity of its gaze.

In *The Gleaners and I, Les Glaneurs et La Glaneuse,* Varda, as previously mentioned, is also the subject of her own documentary. She gets involved by calling a local food bank on the day the truckers dump the potatoes and then takes on the role of the gleaner as she herself gathers the food. Her own body intrudes into the frame[24] as she holds the camera with one hand and picks up heart-shaped potatoes with the other. As *la glaneuse,* "the gleaner" in the title, Varda's camera documents not only her actions but also her aging. She runs her fingers through her thinning hair with one hand and follows the gesture with her camera in the other. She zooms in on her own hand, lingering over its wrinkles and discolorations. She stands, camera in hand, in front of a full-length mirror. We see what she sees; we watch her passage of time.

The documentary certainly has its serious moments and its serious themes. At the same time "Varda's sense of fun and play"[25] permeates the narrative and prevents the self-reflective moments from becoming self-indulgent, prevents the serious from becoming morose. Varda is clearly filming that which interests her, even if it bears no obvious relationship to the subject of the film. Some of the images are quiet—a man sitting on a bridge watching the river roll by as the sun rises. Others are playful—a dog standing by the side of the road with a bright red boxing glove tied around its neck. No commentary or explanation accompanies such random images—the viewer is following her eye, picking up whatever happens to cross her path, drawing the connections and making the meaning.

As demonstrated in *The Gleaners and I,* the role of the filmmaker is not to orchestrate and manipulate. Like a gleaner, the filmmaker is to be open to chance and accident. Speaking of an artist whose medium is found objects, Varda remarks, "He draws with objects, he accommodates chance." Varda unintentionally leaves the camera on and the lens cap off as she walks through a field. The camera captures images of the brown grasses and the lens cap, dancing to the rhythm of Varda's stride. Such mistakes happen—we have all accidentally shot pictures of the inside of our bag or the road on which we were walking. But most of us throw our mistakes into the trash or leave such clips on the editing room floor. Like her urban gleaners, however, Varda goes through the trash, picking up what others leave behind. The sequence of the dancing lens cap is not cut and discarded—it is a part of the film, taking its place alongside the other images. Varda is not just a gleaner in her stooping to pick up heart-shaped potatoes; she is a gleaner of images, collecting them with her camera, assembling them into art in the editing room.

Where is God in the book of Ruth? Where is the omnipotent eye, directing the actors from above? God is notably absent. In his book *The Theology of the Book of Ruth,* R. M. Hals puts forth the definitive argument in modern biblical scholarship for a deep theological purpose in the book of Ruth. Despite the fact that the text itself attributes only two actions to God, and both of these are not as unambiguously positive as commentators assume (more on this below), many choose to see God precisely where God is not mentioned. Hals argues that God acts throughout the book of Ruth, is behind every circumstance, directing every action of every character. The reason the author is not explicit about God's involvement is because "the Book of Ruth is then a story about the hidden God."[26] Edward Campbell's understanding of the theology of Ruth follows Hals's reading and also represents a common interpretation of divine absence. He writes: "It is correct to observe that God's activity in the Ruth book is very much that of the one in the shadows, the one whose manifestation is not by intervention but by a lightly exercised providential control. It is equally correct to say as well that God is the primary actor in the drama."[27] Campbell sees God hidden in the role of chance, bringing Ruth to Boaz's field and bringing Ruth to Boaz's attention. Some commentators think that God is so obviously present that the point does not need to be argued but simply asserted. Robert Hubbard writes: "The reader is probably to react smilingly, 'Accident? Of course not!'"[28] The gaps in the narrative invite the reader to enter and make his or her own meaning. These commentators fill in the gap with God.

Other commentators, however, believe that chance is just that—chance.[29] The word used in the Hebrew to describe Ruth's finding of Boaz's field is *miqreh* (2:3), a word that literally means "chance, accident." Ruth gleans in Boaz's field "by chance." The word is used a handful of other times in the biblical text, most prominently in the book of Ecclesiastes. The book of Ecclesiastes is rich and complex, even contradictory; even so, it does not endorse a conventional view of God's providential incursion into human affairs. In Ecclesiastes chance is chance and it comes to human and beast alike, the righteous and the wicked without distinction (see Eccles. 2:14–15, 3:19, 9:2–3 for examples). In at least one biblical passage *miqreh* is directly contrasted with God's presence. When the Philistines seek to discover the cause of the plagues affecting their community, they ask whether they come from God or *miqreh*—chance (1 Sam. 6:9).[30] Why should the word carry a meaning that is the antithesis of its plain meaning only in the book of Ruth?

Readers find God in the story in order to domesticate its more radical and disturbing theological message. Even when God is explicitly discussed, most of the references to God come from the characters themselves either asking for God's blessings or attributing their hardships and their successes to God. In the two verses in which God is the subject of the verb God's providence is neither unambiguous nor unambivalent. The verses may be stock phrases, indicating nothing about God's actions; or God may be acting. Even with the later possibility, though, the reader should not feel sanguine about God's role in the world. In both cases God's actions are after extended periods of inaction, extended periods that lead to hardship in the lives of the characters. At best these actions of God point to God's fickleness not to God's steadfast love.

The first verse to address God is 1:6. Naomi decides to return to Judah because she had heard that "Yahweh had visited his people to give to them bread." The famine that precedes this bounty is not directly attributed to God, only the end of the period of want. Why had it taken at least ten years for God to visit God's people? Who else was God visiting? Had the time slipped away? This verse is linked with the one in 4:13 in which Ruth's conception of Obed is attributed to God, thus an inclusio is formed. These two verses are the only two in which God is the subject of a verb in active voice.

Naomi's speeches in chapter 1 are replete with invocations of the divine. When Naomi stops and tells her daughters-in-law to return to their mother's house, she blesses them, asking for Yahweh to do them *hesed* as they have done to the dead and to herself (1:8). Naomi continues, asking God to give the women rest in the house of a husband (1:9). Naomi links her daughters-in-law's *hesed* with God's *hesed,* but God is being asked to model human action; the situation is not the other way around. Again, those who take Hals's and Campbell's position see this correlation between divine and human action in a positive light. For example, Campbell says *hesed* "is more than ordinary human loyalty; it imitates the divine initiative which comes without being deserved."[31] However, it is God who is shown to be lacking. God is never shown in this book to be acting with loyalty. Otherwise what is the explanation for the famine that lasts at least a decade; for the deaths of Elimelech and his sons; for Ruth's and Orpah's apparent infertility? Later interpreters see the problem and posit punishment (see the Targum and the Midrash, for examples). Even Campbell's reading implies that God had the power to lift the famine because God caused the famine to punish the Bethlehemites: "For the Ruth story-teller, God's activity is intimately bound up with the mundane affairs and interrelationships of human beings. True, in 1:6 and in 4:13 the narration will refer to those 'acts' of God which we would call providential. After a period of famine (1:6), Yahweh has now 'visited' his people and given them food. This word 'visit,' Hebrew *pqd,* has profound theological overtones, for in the dynamics of the covenant relationship between God and his people it indicates the sovereign God's assessing the loyalty of his vassal people and bringing upon them either blessing for their obedience to him or cursing for their rebellion."[32] Yet a punishment is not even hinted at in the text itself.

Naomi's second speech intending to dissuade her bride-daughters from following her ends on a startling image: "for the hand of Yahweh has been sent out against me" or, according to Sasson's translation: "for the Lord's hand has struck me"[33] (1:13). With the addition of Naomi's assessment of God in her own life—that he has hit her, slapped her across the face—it becomes even more impossible to maintain that a positive theological view is presented in the book of Ruth. At the beginning of her first speech she asks God to act with *hesed* even though she acknowledges at the end of her second speech that God has failed to act this way so far, at least toward her. It is not that God is the model for Ruth. It is that Ruth is the model for God—at least, this is what Naomi is asking, for God to look at Orpah and Ruth and act according to their example. It is not as one commentator has said, "God is a Moabite widow."[34] The theological problem is that God has precisely not been acting like a Moabite widow, because if God had been acting with as much love and loyalty as Ruth and Orpah, Naomi would have never been in this painful situation.

After Orpah kisses Naomi goodbye Ruth now uses God-language in her vow to Naomi. She vows to make Naomi's god, her god (1:16). Considering how Naomi has just characterized the actions of this god, Ruth's adoption of Naomi's god may mean bringing down God's arbitrary wrath on her too. She seems to acknowledge as much in the next verse. Ruth evokes the Lord's name as the guarantor of her vow to Naomi, asking God to kill her if even death comes between her and Naomi (1:17). As far as Ruth can tell, God is good at meting out death, which is precisely what Naomi herself proclaims when she arrives to her hometown.

Naomi enters Bethlehem and remarks that she went away full but the Lord has brought her back empty (1:21). Naomi thus attributes the deaths of her husband and sons, and possibly even the infertility of her sons' marriages, to God's actions. She continues that the Lord "has testified against her." This phrase has garnered a lot of attention because it is the only instance in the biblical canon where God is the subject of this particular verb (*'anah*). Consequently the Greek translation of the Septuagint (LXX) and the Latin Vulgate both emend the pointing (the vowel markers) in order to change the simple active form of the verb (*qal* of *anah*) to the intensive active form (*piel* of *anah*), meaning "to oppress, humiliate." Many commentators and translators follow this meaning. The problem with this verb, though, is that it never occurs followed by the preposition *bet,* as it does in Ruth 1:21. Others, including Sasson and Campbell, follow the Masoretic text (MT), and agree with them in believing that the statement is "couched in and flavored by juridical terminology."[35] Without vowels the consonantal verbal root could mean both, and perhaps the reader is to understand "testified against" but that the testimony was tinged with oppression and humiliation. God has testified against, oppressed, and humiliated Naomi. The final phrase of this verse is "and Shaddai has caused evil to me." Shaddai is not a common name for God in the scripture. It is employed most in the ancestor stories of Genesis and in Job. The Job allusion here is particularly apt because Naomi is a Joblike figure here—she is beset by tragedy through no fault of her own. Yahweh is the subject of these three phrases: God empties, testifies against (humiliates and oppresses), and inflicts evil. If God is as present as Campbell and Hals assert, God's is a presence that is most unwelcomed.

81

The next reference to God is spoken by Boaz. When Boaz and his workers greet each other, they use what are probably standard salutations, invoking God's presence and blessing: "And behold, Boaz came from Bethlehem. He said to the reapers, 'Yahweh be with you.' And they said to him, 'Yahweh bless you'" (2:4). These are stock phrases; thus there is no more need to read an active and good god here than there is in understanding everyone who says "goodbye" today in English to be invoking God's presence and blessing.[36]

When Boaz greets Ruth (2:12) he blesses her and asks (like Naomi earlier) that "the God of Israel, under whose wings you have sought refuge" reward her deeds. Sasson notes parallels with the Arabic "May God give you" which is a formulaic phrase "automatically addressed to beggars and other seekers of help"[37] In other words Boaz may be responding without thinking, giving her the brush off, which is why Ruth speaks again. According to Sasson Ruth is trying to secure permission to glean in the sheaves—special privileges—and Boaz refuses her at first. It is also possible to understand Boaz's invocation of God's goodness and Ruth's good behavior as another instance when God is asked to model God's own actions according to what Ruth deserves. Like Naomi's first speech the stock pious phrases mask a deep irony and subtle criticism of God's *hesed.*

How does Ruth regard her own relationship to divine providence? Even though Ruth never directly addresses the question, she does respond to other characters' references to the divine. When Boaz blesses her, "May the Lord reward you for your deeds, and may you have a full reward from the Lord, the God of Israel, under whose wings you have sought refuge" (2:12), Ruth responds, "May I continue to find favor in your sight, my lord" (2:13). Ruth calls Boaz *'adoni,* "my lord," rather than using that title to refer to God.[38] As argued above Ruth is mocking Boaz's show of generosity in this scene. Is she also mocking the pious platitude that God has anything to do with her survival? Ruth recognizes the situation. She shifts the focus from God (who has done and can do nothing for her) to Boaz, who can, by calling Boaz "my lord." Boaz then provides her food, and finally permission to glean among the sheaves. Later in verse 3:9, it is Boaz whom she asks to spread his garment over her, using the same Hebrew word (*canaf*). She seeks refuge not under God's wings but under Boaz's robe.

When Naomi hears that Ruth had spent the day gleaning in Boaz's field, she expresses an ambiguous blessing: "Blessed be he to the Lord, who has not forsaken his *hesed* to the living or to the dead" (2:20). In the opening phrase she seems to be asking for God's blessing on Boaz. To whom, then, does the *who* (*asher*) refer? To the Lord or to Boaz? On whose *hesed* is Naomi remarking? Most translations ascribe the *hesed* to God and not Boaz—for example, the Jewish Publication Society translation capitalizes the masculine pronoun—"His kindness"—in order to make the referent clear. But the relative pronoun could be referencing Boaz instead.[39]

Understanding Boaz to be the possessor of the *hesed* according to Naomi makes this verse parallel to her earlier statement about Ruth and Orpah's *hesed*—in both cases people demonstrate *hesed* and God is asked to take note and perhaps even to start acting with *hesed* too.

Boaz remarks in 3:10, when he realizes that it is Ruth who is lying next to him in the dark, with a phrase identical to Naomi's, except in object: "Blessed be you to the Lord, my daughter" and then notes Ruth's *hesed*. This may be another indication that the *hesed* of which Naomi speaks in 2:20 is Boaz's and not God's. Boaz again references God in this scene when he makes his oath to Ruth to get the legal matters sorted out and to take care of her (3:13). In doing so he swears "as the Lord lives," which is a formulaic expression much like our "by God" or "I swear to God," both of which are used quite casually in everyday speech by people with a wide range of theological commitments or lack thereof.

After the matters of woman and land are settled, "all the people at the gate and the elders" bless Ruth. "May the Lord make the woman who is entering your house like Rachel and like Leah who together built up the house of Israel" (an allusion to sons since the word *to build* and the word for *sons* have the same root). The blessing continues: "from the seed which the Lord will give to you from this girl" (4:11–12). The blessing proves effective. Ruth conceives: "and the Lord gave her conception and she bore a son" (4:13). This is the inclusio of which I spoke earlier—God gives fertility to both the earth (1:6) and woman (4:13), but this is less comforting than it appears on the surface since it implies that God had been withholding fertility for no known reason. These are either formulaic phrases—attributing the fertility of both soil and womb to God—or they both indicate God's arbitrariness. No reason is given for sending the famine or the infertility in the first place. Readers who wish to justify God's actions can infer a system of reward and punishment or can affirm the platitude that God works in mysterious ways. But the plain meaning of the situation betrays a more frightening worldview and a more complex divine. God works in arbitrary ways. Or, as Linafelt remarks, God works in limited ways: "One must be careful, then, not to attempt to build a theological reading of the book based on preconceived notions of God's omnipotence and omnipresence. While such categories sit well in systematic theology, they are rather foreign to biblical narrative in general and to the book of Ruth in particular. . . . To the extent that the book of Ruth has a 'theology,' it is one that is less traditional but also less simplistic than has generally been recognized. It is a theology that refuses to see the human characters in the drama as puppets of God's providence and that, because of this refusal, may ultimately prove more relevant to the modern world than we might suppose."[40]

The gleaner knows that the world is a harsh place where poor people are left to fend for themselves. The life of a gleaner is a life of chance. The gleaner relies on finding castoffs, what is dropped, disregarded, or disavowed. What sequence of events, what infinite chain of cause and effect brings the gleaner and her object together at the same time, in the same place? Instead of calling out to God for help, Ruth laughs as does Agnès Varda—together they are imps, pixies, playing with chance and delighting in a world ordered not by God but by gleaners.

The Book of Ruth

Jane Hamilton's novel *The Book of Ruth* is not obviously connected to the biblical story.[41] There is no young widow, no foreigner, no love affair between women. The reader does not even discover that the female narrator's name is Ruth until toward the end of the novel (although it can be inferred and assumed much earlier). Why, then, a title that links the novel so decisively to the biblical book? Through her work Hamilton provides an astute commentary on the book of Ruth as well as an exploration of what it means to be human. I see three ways in which Hamilton's novel connects to the biblical story: 1) the setting of agricultural poverty; 2) the exploration of what it means to be compassionate; and 3) the absence of God.

Ruth lives in Honey Creek, Illinois, a small rural community near the border of Wisconsin. It is the kind of place where everyone knows one another, where one could "miss the town if you drive through listening to your favorite song or telling a story about your neighbor,"[42] where few of the inhabitants ever leave the precincts. Ruth herself leaves Honey Creek for the first time only after she is a married woman with a child, and even then she goes only to another town in Illinois. She never crosses the state border. She grows up in an aging farmhouse in abject poverty. The entire community is struggling, but her family is particularly troubled. Her mother is a bitter, hard, abusive woman; her father drives off in the middle of the night without a word; her brother is exceptionally intelligent and lives in a world of his own; her only happy family memory is of a hot night when her father accidentally dropped a scoop of ice cream on her head and they all laughed and laughed. "It wasn't until I was ten that I realized our family must be the ones with the wrung-out hearts, and that other people's faces shone with sadness for us."[43] The novel is full of images of tending chickens, watching cows, canning produce grown in the backyard. Hamilton's book paints an unflinching portrait of a poverty so brutal that it crushes the humanity out of almost everyone save the few who have the right combination of talent and luck to escape its confines. The story of Ruth is a story of women, the rural poor, the ones who barely have anything and then end up losing that too.

Ruth is considered stupid and slow, nearly retarded, by her immediate family and her teachers. The only people who sees possibilities in her are her Aunt Sid, who lives in a neighboring town, and an aging neighbor Ruth visits named Miss Finch. The reader, however, knows that despite her parochialism, her coarse speech, and her ignorance she is intelligent because she can recognize complexity; she understands nuance. Her curiosity and creativity make her seem stupid to those around her who have neither; their opprobrium reinforces her natural shyness; her silence confirms their assessment of her intellectual capabilities.

The opening sentence of the novel states the theme of human compassion that connects to the biblical story: "What it begins with, I know finally, is the kernel of meanness in people's hearts."[44] At first glance meanness may seem to be the opposite theme of the biblical book's *hesed*—compassion, loving-kindness, loyalty. But what the novel explores are the ways in which meanness and compassion are found intertwined in everyone and how the struggle to be human is the struggle of one's compassion against one's meanness. This is not simply a restatement of the classic Christian doctrine of original sin or a dualistic war between good and evil, darkness and light. It is far more complex. The meanness is in everyone, but some get singled out and made into scapegoats for the entire community so that others can deny the meanness in their own hearts. Ultimately Ruth has compassion for those with the meanness because it compels them and it obscures that which is good in them, because the community blames them for its own meanness. As a child she even feels sorry for Hitler and for the serpent in Genesis 3. As an adult she feels sorry for her husband—the man who brutally murders her mother by beating her to death and nearly kills Ruth too in the same way, all in front of their two-year-old son.

The interplay between meanness and goodness is not a metaphor for Christian theology because Ruth rejects Christian theology from the opening pages of the book. The novel is full of biblical allusion—Ruth does grow up attending church every Sunday and continues to do so until the Sunday her husband murders her mother—but it is also clear about Ruth's opinion on religion. "In the Bible it starts with the spirit of God moving upon the face of the water, but I don't buy those ideas."[45] Ruth has an almost instinctual suspicion of biblical myth and story, present from her earliest memories and encouraged by her Aunt Sid's explanations of metaphor and symbol. She dismisses the virgin birth, miracles, Jesus' resurrection, angels, heaven. But she does come to see and connect with the underlying message of compassion and doing good, caring for other people simply because they are human. Her rejection of Christian theology and any kind of literal understanding of the scriptures goes hand in hand with an embracing of the biblical ethic, albeit an ethic that is grounded in a this-worldly orientation.

The third way in which the novel connects deeply with the book of Ruth is in God's absence. God's absence is, in the final analysis, the ground on which Hamilton's Ruth's compassionate ethic is built. As a child she would escape her home and go out into the night. She would lie on the ground and look up at the stars: "For a split second I had the sensation all through my body that there wasn't a reason for our being on the planet. We were hurtling through space and there wasn't any logic to it. It was all for nothing. Such a thought made me feel so lonesome I had to turn over on my stomach and cry for all the world."[46] She cries for the lamb who lost its leg to a dog, for hungry people, for her blind neighbor, for the soft grass, for "the loveliness in the night," for her own adolescent pains, for feeling "just as fragile as the tender green shoots" of grass.[47]

Her husband Ruby beats her near to death and murders her mother on a Sunday, when they had just gotten home from church. The minister's sermon was on one of his favorite themes—eternal life.[48] The phrase "We shall not die but live" weaves its way in and out of her consciousness as she is going through the horror. But it is not a comfort; it is a darkly ironic counterpoint to the brutal reality of death—painful, meaningless death. Earlier in the novel Ruth heard her minister in church say a phrase that struck her as funny. It also floats back into her consciousness after she runs outside and stands on the porch: "I ran, my broken hands trailing behind me like caught fish. I knew my hair was plastered to my bloody skull. I ran out the front door and I stood panting, leaning against the house, tasting the blood in my mouth, thinking the words, 'You shall not die but live. The dung heap shall smile.' It occurred to me, I'm the dung heap, and someday I'm going to laugh my head off."[49]

Ruth survives. After Ruby kills her mother he returns to finish with her. He begins to beat her again but then stops. He hears his son scream "Daddy!" and at that moment remembers that Ruth is pregnant again. He drops the fireplace poker and goes inside where the police later find him watching a Laurel and Hardy movie on television and drinking from a carton of milk. Just as a series of small, mundane acts and irritants unleashes the whirlwind of violence that engulfs the family on that fateful day, one reminder of his paternity ends Ruby's slaughter. Who lives and who dies hinges not on monumental, premeditated decisions but on the vagaries of one man's emotions on any given Sunday.

While in the hospital Ruth suffers several visits from her minister, and it is in one of her conversations with him that the theology of *The Book of Ruth* is finally and most fully expressed.

> He said, "My dear, our kingdom on earth is not complete."
>
> It was the only sentence that hit me, out of the whole long jumbled prayer: "Our kingdom on earth is not complete." He squinched up his eyes while he was saying we get our reward in heaven, his favorite place. I couldn't stand his voice so I said, "Listen here, Rev, I don't know what the hell you're talking about, our kingdom not being complete. Don't you have one marble knocking around in your theological head? Do they have plaster casts up in heaven? I never heard them mentioned in your big black book there. My hands are going to be cured in no time and don't tell me Jesus could do it. For your information, Jesus is a crackpot."

The Rev stared. I loved every minute of his dumb gaze. I said, "You ever heard them little frogs screwing their heads off down in the marsh in the spring?"

He didn't say anything; he looked without blinking his eyes, a mannerism that was familiar. "Huh?" I said. "You ever heard the racket? Don't tell me anything about the resurrection. Go down to the stinky marsh in spring and listen, and you'll hear what's come to life, what's reborn. They aren't any bigger than a quarter. They was dead before, them frogs was, all winter, and there they are come to get some satisfaction. They call out the words *Urgent, Urgent.*"

"Well, yes," he said, like an idiot.

"Don't tell me our kingdom ain't complete. Don't be one of them big fat greedy assholes, Rev. If those chubby knees of yours can hold your weight, kneel down sometime in early spring and sniff a bloodroot. Just because you can't take it all in with your senses doesn't mean the earth is half-baked. It's ideal, if you don't count the humans."[50]

Ruth espouses a theology rooted in the earth, a hope found every spring.

The reader occasionally sees the meanness in the heart of Ruth herself. As a child she tormented her younger brother and mirrored the behavior of her abusive mother both verbally and physically. He hates her and flees Illinois to get away, in part, from her meanness. While in the hospital she gives full vent to her anger and disappointment. She hurls insults at everyone (save her aunt Sid), cussing out the nurses, calling the doctors ugly names. Yet a day or so after her speech to the Rev she experiences her own rebirth—she feels the fetus inside of her kick. "And what came to me were words from the Bible: 'As the hart panteth after the water brooks, so panteth my soul after thee, O God. My tears have been my meat day and night, while they continually say unto me, Where is thy God?'"[51] And then she feels a wordless song well up in her, a song that moves her beyond the mere feeling of love. Her use of the psalm is an affirmation of life with all of its longing, tears, and divine absence. A simultaneous longing for God yet an acknowledgment of God's inaccessibility.

Another reoccurring allusion is to the beatitudes, particularly to the verse found in Ps. 37:11 and Matt. 5:5 that "the meek shall inherit the Earth." Whereas she plays with the idea through most of the novel, finding in it some comfort and truth, ultimately she rejects this as a pious platitude as well. She summarizes her ethical perspective in the last pages of the novel: "I know, certainly, that there's nothing to the Rev's guarantee that the meek are going to inherit the earth. No one inherits one single thing. It's something I've thought a lot about. We're only passers-by, and all you can do is love what you have in your life. A person has to fight the meanness that sometimes comes with you when you're born, sometimes grows if you aren't in lucky surroundings. It's our challenge to fend it off, leave it behind us choking and gasping for breath in the mud. It's our task to seek out something with truth for us, no matter if there is a hundred-mile obstacle course in the way, or a ramshackle old farmhouse that binds and binds. The Bible is right on one score: it doesn't do one bit of good to render evil for evil."[52] This final statement of the ethic underlies the role of chance in any individual's life. Throughout the book she occasionally wonders if one small change here or there in her life, her actions, the circumstances of her birth would have moved her life in a completely different direction. "I wonder if I'd been born just five miles the other side of town, would I have met Daisy? Would I have known Ruby? Would my story have happened to me or a complete stranger? I'd like to know exactly how much I'm to blame. Was it my character that triggered the events, or chance, that I woke up and found myself in Honey Creek with a big old dog howling to 'Rock of Ages'?"[53] There is no Providence, no God watching from above directing human life. One steamy July night Ruth and her best friend go to the lake to escape the heat, and there Ruth meets the man who will kill her mother and nearly kill her years later. What if that night had been just a few degrees cooler?

Neither book of Ruth is about God as much as it is about how humans are determined to make meaning out of the tragedy of their lives. Both ultimately affirm perhaps the most uniquely human activity—telling stories as the method of making meaning. As such *The Book of Ruth* is like the understanding of good and evil at the heart of the Hebrew Bible where both are mixed and mingled, even within the activities of the divine.

Ruth's Romance

Ruth continues to glean in Boaz's fields throughout the barley and into the wheat harvest. Soon gleaning will no longer be an option for Ruth and once again she and Naomi will experience a crisis in bread production. This time Naomi has a plan. Chapter 3 is laden with as many questions as chapter 2. What does Naomi's plan indicate about her character and how she regards Ruth? Why does Ruth agree to the plan? What happens on the threshing floor between Ruth and Boaz? What does this indicate about Ruth's sexuality? What exactly does Ruth ask Boaz to do for her and why does he agree to do it? How much grain does he give her at the end? There are multiple ways of answering these questions and thus multiple ways of understanding Ruth's character. The text leaves all of these questions open and such ambiguity points toward an interpretation that highlights Ruth's own ambiguity and her duplicitous character.

If her first day of gleaning is any indication, Ruth was successful in her work, accumulating enough grain to provide for Naomi and her own immediate bread needs and even obtaining extra grain for the future. However, since the harvests had come to an end, it would be natural for the women's thoughts to turn to how they would continue to provide for themselves. Any stores of grain would be helpful but they would not guarantee freedom from want until the spring, the next season of harvest and gleaning. Naomi may be worried about Ruth's security and well-being; she may be worried about her own. Ruth agrees to Naomi's plan to confront Boaz on the threshing-room floor. She may be worried about Naomi's security and well-being; she may be worried about her own. They may both be weary of poverty and the mental stress of not knowing from where one's next meal will come. Gleaners are subject to the vagaries of chance in more ways than are women married to rich property owners. Both Naomi and Ruth's feelings about each other remain uncertain.

Ruth's feelings about Boaz are also uncertain and the scholarship on the issue is just as bifurcated as the scholarship on Ruth's feelings toward Naomi. Either the story is a great romance or a realistic depiction of what women must do to survive in a patriarchal world.[54] Both interpretations are equally viable because of a narrative lack—neither Ruth's motivations nor emotions are indicated. When Naomi councils Ruth to go to the threshing room in the dark of night, she sounds more like a pimp than a matchmaker, more concerned with security and material benefit than romance and feelings.[55] Yet the predominant popular interpretation and even many scholarly interpretations domesticate Naomi's strange and perhaps dangerous plan by portraying it as just the little nudge needed to get two shy but smitten people together.

The drama of the romance is usually heightened by assumptions about prejudices concerning Moabites, assumptions about Ruth's and Boaz's ages, and assumptions about how Ruth looks. The gaps in the story are filled by imagining a young and attractive Ruth whose beautiful face captures Boaz's attention but whose beautiful spirit captures his heart. One rabbinical interpreter, Rabbi Johanan, thinks that she is so beautiful that "everyone who saw her ejaculated semen."[56] Boaz himself tells the reader that he is older than Ruth but readers regard their relationship differently depending on how much older they perceive him to be.[57] How romantic that these two people find love across the barriers of ethnic prejudice; how romantic that their love transcends concerns about the difference in their ages! A romance culminating in marriage, especially between an unlikely pair, especially when the man gets to exercise the power conferred on him by gender and class, is one of the major narrative plotlines in our Western culture. It is quite easy to impose such a plotline on the book of Ruth.

When the story is read as a romance the scene on the threshing floor constitutes the climactic moment of the plot, and readers are drawn to the scene. The literary artistry of the author invites such attention. There is a sense of darkness and mystery. It is midnight, everyone but Ruth has fallen into a drunken slumber, quiet pervades the barn. The narrator switches from calling Ruth and Boaz by name to referring to them simply as "the man" and "the woman" (3:8, 14, 16, 18).[58] She approaches the sleeping Boaz, uncovers his "legs," and lies down. Eventually, sensing another presence, cold from the exposure, or just restless in his sleep, Boaz awakens with a start: "And behold! A woman was lying between his feet!" (3:8). Whether or not Boaz's feet or legs are really his genitals (*feet* is a common Hebrew euphemism for male genitalia), waking to find oneself half naked and entangled with a woman is suggestive, to say the least. His immediate response—"Who are you?"—is not only an indication of the darkness of the scene and his confusion at the situation, but it is also the second time he has had to ask about the identity of this strange woman Ruth. With each interaction, rather than knowing her better, new questions arise.

Many scholars also circle around the threshing-room floor, peering through the dark, trying to get a good picture about what actually happened between the two people lying there on the floor together. What exactly did Ruth do to Boaz and did he, in turn, do anything to her? The language is rich, full of double entendre. The verb *to know* occurs six times, scattered throughout the chapter, acting as an ironic counterpoint to the lack of knowledge this chapter underscores. In Linafelt's interpretation the leitmotif points to the fact that Ruth knows more than Boaz in this scene. "It also points up the fact that the reader often cannot know precisely what is happening, but must instead negotiate constantly the pervasive ambiguity."[59] Each word adds layers of meaning: *to know* is also a euphemism for intercourse in the biblical scripture, suggesting perhaps that Ruth and Boaz did indeed "know" each other in the biblical sense.

For Campbell the ambiguity is intentional, but it is meant to suggest to the reader only that sex was quite possible and yet did not happen. Thus the righteousness of Ruth and Boaz is heightened. Refraining from intercourse before marriage is "what righteous living calls for."[60] However, Campbell's idea of righteousness is more informed by his own sexual ethic—or at least traditional Jewish and Christian sexual ethics[61] —than the one in the biblical material. The words and images are all full of innuendo[62] and the main reason to think that there was no sexual contact that night depends on one's importing to ancient Israel in general and the story in particular a sexual code. There is no law among the biblical laws that forbids all sex outside of marriage, or what is now termed "the sin fornication."[63] The law does forbid the free sexual congress of virgin daughters living in their father's house and of married women. The former may not have sex with anyone; the latter may have sex only with their husbands. Women who are not under the authority of either father or husband are free to engage in intercourse with any man. This is not to say that there would not have been limits imposed by custom and propriety, but there were no limits imposed by law. Prostitution, for example, was not the most glamorous profession, but it was not illegal and much biblical scholarship on prostitution is tainted by our own contemporary mores. Ruth and Boaz could have had sex without breaking any laws. The fact that he bids her to slip away before the sun is fully up indicates that propriety dictates that such things be done discretely—not that such things not be done. Even today certain sexual encounters are carried out with discretion despite the lack of legal or societal censure. Sasson notes: "Moreover, in opposition to the stance taken by most commentators, we do not think that Boaz was overly concerned with the opinion of others regarding the quality of his own morals: Biblical man displayed no evident scruples in contracting marriages in the manner arrived at by our protagonists."[64] There is at least an ambiguity here. The language bursts with sex and desire but refrains from stating that Ruth and Boaz consummated their affair. Such lack of specificity in the text leaves the reader wanting more, not fully satisfied, and thus enacts the desire it describes.

Sex and desire are certainly a part of the scene but is love? Positing a great love for Ruth on the part of Boaz is common in popular interpretations, from nineteenth-century English poetry to twentieth-century Hollywood movies. For example, Thomas Hood (1799–1845) imagines Boaz watching Ruth glean in his fields: "Sure, I said, heaven did not mean, / Where I reap thou shouldst but glean; / Lay thy sheaf adown and come, / Share my harvest and my home."[65] The sword-and-sandal movie *The Story of Ruth* (Henry Koster, 1960) also constructs a great love affair between the two characters. In the movie Boaz is only a little older than Ruth and as handsome as she is beautiful. (They are played by Stuart Whitman and Elana Eden, respectively.) He has to vie with the other relative-redeemer (unnamed in the biblical story but, following a traditional Jewish suggestion, called Tov in the movie) for Ruth's affection, and, once he has won Ruth's love must persuade Tov to release her from her obligation to marry him. However popular the image in tradition and imagination, the details of the biblical text do militate against a Boaz consumed by love. Boaz certainly notices Ruth during their first meeting—but then apparently fails to court her throughout the rest of the barley and wheat harvest seasons. If he had been in love with the woman, would he not have pursued her, as he does in the movie?[66] If Boaz had been consumed by a great passion, would he not have asked her to marry him, as he does in Hood's poem? Why would Ruth have to make the first move and even propose marriage herself?

Naomi explicitly says "He will tell you what to do" and yet Ruth is the one who takes control of the situation. There is a gap between what Naomi instructs and what Ruth does. She tells Boaz to spread his "wing" over her, echoing his language in chapter 2 but substituting Boaz himself for God (3:9). She is not waiting for God to provide but taking the initiative, taking what she needs and calling on Boaz to provide. By asking him to spread his wing over her Ruth may be asking him to marry her or inviting him to have sex or both.[67] She proclaims him "redeemer," also translated "next-of-kin" (NRSV) or "kinsman-redeemer" (NIV). There has been much discussion about what law Ruth is using to stake her claim on Boaz—what does it mean that she calls him redeemer? Many understand the proposal in terms of the laws of levirate marriage. According to Deut. 25:5–6, if a man dies before he has a son, his widow is to marry his brother. Their first son will be the heir of the dead man. However, too much in the story of Ruth counters this understanding. If the laws of the levirate apply, then why would Ruth have to confront Boaz on the threshing-room floor, in the middle of the night, months after she arrives in Bethlehem? The law as written in Deuteronomy explicitly binds only brothers who live together not distant relatives in other towns. Another line of interpretation sees Ruth citing the law of the redeemer. According to Lev. 25:25–28, if a poor relative has sold a piece of land, the next-of-kin can buy it back in order for the land to remain in the family. Yet Ruth's request seems to mention only herself and not a piece of property; alternatively, perhaps she is implying that marriage to her is legally connected to the purchase of the land. Boaz seems to take both of these meanings and separates them when he goes to the city gate to work out the legalities (4:1–10). Established codes and customs are referenced in the book of Ruth, but they are not adhered to precisely. People, especially people on the margins, often use law and custom in creative and imprecise ways in order to live and flourish.

As earlier in the narrative, Boaz behaves kindly although bombastically on the threshing-room floor: "Blessed are you to the Lord, my daughter; the last example of your *hesed* is greater than your first for you have not gone after young men, whether poor or rich. And now my daughter, do not fear. All that you say, I will do for you, for all of my people know that you are a woman of valor" (3:10–11). He may not be in love, but he may indeed be flattered by Ruth's attentions and enjoy the role of being protector and provider.

Ruth is named by Boaz as an *'eshet hayil,* a "worthy woman," "virtuous wife," or, more literally, "valorous woman" or "woman warrior." Such a title mirrors Boaz's own status as an *'ish hayil* (2:1) and alludes to Proverbs 31, the poem of the virtuous wife. Such an allusion recalls the portraits of women throughout the book of Proverbs. Proverbs presents a bifurcated picture of women—Woman Wisdom is countered by Dame Folly; the strange woman is countered by the virtuous wife. Ruth may be identified with the virtuous wife by Boaz's words, but a more careful examination of women in Proverbs and Ruth's character indicate that the compliment is more complex. The strange woman who is contrasted with the *'eshet hayil* in Proverbs is a woman who uses her sexuality to drag men into Sheol. The adjective *strange* may also be an indication that the woman is not just an adulteress but also a foreigner.[68] Ruth may embody all of the virtues explicated in Proverbs 31 and attributed to the perfect wife. But she also is the foreign woman who seduces the righteous Israelite man. The foreign woman is the *'eshet hayil;* the seductress is the virtuous wife. Ruth parodies Proverbs.

Boaz acknowledges another redeemer, closer kin to Elimelech than he. He does promise Ruth that he will attend to the matter first thing in the morning—but also recommends she spend the night with him anyway (3:12–13). At dawn she gets up to leave and he fills her apron with six measures of grain, perhaps mirroring how he just filled her womb with seed, certainly foreshadowing how he will soon impregnate her. It is common for the Bible to be vague about measurements, as it is in this case. It is also common for commentators to attempt to make plain what is left cloudy in the Hebrew. The estimates of how much grain Boaz gave Ruth range from 1,740 to 30 pounds.[69] The exact weight raises an issue of interpretation since every possible number is larger than one would expect anyone to carry comfortably. As a worker in the fields, Ruth would have been strong of arm, capable of carrying thirty, forty, even fifty pounds. However, as Sasson points out, women farmworkers would usually have baskets and ropes to carry such large amounts, whereas Ruth has simply her apron.[70] Boaz could not have been that concerned with discretion if he loaded her down with all of that grain. On the one hand if Ruth is trying to sneak back home, then she would want to be unencumbered. On the other hand a load of grain might provide an alibi if Ruth is seen coming from the threshing room. In addition to the metaphorical import of Ruth's grain-filled apron, the picture of a heavily laden Ruth trying to sneak home at dawn adds a certain comic, even bawdy, element to the scene as well.

When Ruth arrives home she tells Naomi that Boaz gave her the grain and said, "do not go back empty to your mother-in-law" (3:17). Just as she did when she first met Boaz, Ruth misrepresents to Naomi what he said to her (2:21). In this case also the words seem to be calculated to evoke an emotional response. When Naomi entered into Bethlehem months earlier, she proclaimed to the women of the village that God had brought her back "empty" (1:21). Ruth may be trying to comfort her mother-in-law, telling her that now she really will be full again. Ruth may also be trying to recall to Naomi that day when she effectively called Ruth a "nothing." These words, misrepresenting her encounter with Boaz, are the final ones that Ruth speaks in the story. As Amy-Jill Levine notes, "Having left her home, risked attack in the fields, placed both herself and Boaz in a compromising position, and twice lied to Naomi, she has done all a woman could do."[71]

Ruth leaves Boaz "before one person could recognize another" (3:14). When she returns to Naomi, Naomi asks, "Who are you, my daughter?" (3:16). She knows that it is Ruth and yet she does not know. Ruth finally leaves the narrative with a lie on her lips. Ruth's character and identity are open questions, even to the people closest to her, even to her closest readers.

· 7 ·

AGRICULTURAL
INTERLUDE NO. 3

In the spring we planted; in the summer we tended. The first vegetables ripened by mid-summer and by August we reaped the full bounty of our toil. We would pull the red Radio Flyer wagon across the creek, past the apple orchard and grape arbors to the first vegetable garden. My mother in cutoff shorts and bathing suit top would start down the first row of corn. My job was to follow behind, arms outstretched, and she would pick the ripe ears and stack them in my arms. When I could carry no more, I would retreat back through the row, corn leaves sharp against my skin, and deposit my load in the little red wagon. My little sister, meanwhile, would take my place until she too could not bear her load. I arranged my corn in neat stacks; she dumped hers and ran off to search for earthworms; I tried quickly to straighten the corn before my mother's voice found me, needing me from between the rows.

Naomi and her family flee a famine in Bethlehem and arrive in Moab searching for grain. Ruth and Naomi arrive in Bethlehem at the beginning of the barley harvest and Ruth gleans in the fields, filling her baskets with grain. Boaz and his men spend the night in the threshing room, sleeping amid the grain. After a midnight encounter Boaz sends Ruth home at daybreak, filling her apron with grain. Boaz speaks to the men at the gate, trading women and land good for growing grain. In the end Ruth and Naomi's future is secure, marrying Boaz who gives them continuous access to seed, to grain.

I

Grain is another character in the book of Ruth, omnipresent yet overlooked, ubiquitous yet unseen. The roots wrap around every letter in the text, its shoots sprout between the verses. More than just the typical travel guide is needed to tour this countryside. The food we call grain is the seed of certain grasses. The grass family, *Poaceae* or *Gramineae,* comprises a remarkable number of genera and species.[1] It is among the largest of the plant families and it has the widest distribution. Grass can be found on every continent, in every environment, from the African savannas to the plains of Antarctica, from the forests of Asia to the mountains of the Americas. Grass, its simple spear sticking straight up out of the soil, is nearly everywhere on this earth.

As humble as grass may seem, its simplicity belies its centrality. With its almost infinite shades of green, its sometimes brown or red or white, it carpets the earth. For the environment it is essential in the prevention of soil erosion; for animals it provides food and shelter and shade. The ancient Israelites consumed grains in many forms for nearly every meal. Even in twenty-first-century America, in one way or another our primary source of sustenance is grass.[2] Grass yields grain—rice, wheat, barley, corn, oats, sorghum. We eat grass in the manner of the cereal grains either in a nearly natural form (rice, corn, oatmeal) or processed into another product (bread, pasta, cracker); we eat it by eating animals that graze on the leaves of grass or are fed corn, a seed of grass (cattle, poultry, pig). Most sugar and many oils are also derived from grass, so grass is present in foods that outwardly bear no resemblance to other more obvious grain products (soda, marshmallow, ice cream). Almost all alcohols are made of fermented grasses (beer, whiskey, gin). All flesh is indeed grass.

This human reliance on grass extends back hundreds of thousands of years. Early in human evolution our ancestors forged an alliance with the grasses of the African savanna. The grasses would draw the game animals that our ancestors hunted; our ancestors set fires to clear dry grass and encroaching trees. Fresh grasses grew and spread, drawing more game; both human and grass species flourished.[3] As our species continued to develop and spread out across the earth, our symbiosis with grass remained vital but changed as humans developed agriculture. Grass no longer helped to bait food—grass became food.

The history of grain domestication takes us back to the dawn of civilization, when human beings first learned to band together and manipulate the environment to promote human flourishing. The discovery that wild grains could be gathered and made into flatbreads was early, and various kinds of flatbreads were a staple even in the diet of people during the Stone Age. Early humans simply gathered the grains from wild wheat, barley, rye, and oats. But by sometime between 12,000 and 10,000 B.C.E. people had begun to cultivate the cereal grains. Grain domestication arose independently in Southwest Asia (also known as the Fertile Crescent), China, and Mesoamerica with the earliest evidence of agriculture found in the Fertile Crescent—Mesopotamia and the Jordan River Valley.[4] People, probably women, discovered that they could take some of their gathered seeds and plant large fields to produce more seeds for food. Exactly when, where, and, even more intriguingly, why some hunter-gather societies developed agriculture to provide for their physical needs is unknown, and the questions generate much debate in anthropology and archaeology.[5] Whatever the initial reasons for the transition, such farming work produced a larger and more consistent food source. For this story we have traveled further back in time than the Iron Age, but we still find ourselves standing in the fields of Moab and Judah. Ruth gleans her barley and her wheat in the very areas men and women first began to plant, tend, and harvest. Her agrarian roots go deep, grow long.

Ruth's ancestors forged a dynamic relationship with the wild grains around them. Over the course of thousands of years the plants revealed their potentialities. The cereals of Southwest Asia were perfect partners in the dance of domestication: they had certain "botanical advantages." Southwest Asia

> has the largest number of large-seeded annual wild cereal and pod-bearing legume species . . . of any region of Mediterranean climate, all genetically programmed to germinate and grow through the short day-lengths of the wet winter and to remain dormant in seed form in the ground during the hot dry summer. Annual cereals tend to have larger grains as food stores during dormancy. Fortunately for humans, those cereals and legumes chosen for ultimate domestication also happened to be self- rather than cross-pollinating. In other words, useful characters developed as a result of human management would not be easily swamped out of successive generations by back-crossing with wild plants, especially if such modified varieties were planted beyond the normal ranges of the wild forms.[6]

Two wheat species, emmer (today more commonly known as farro and still used in Italian cooking) and einkorn, along with rye and barley, were the first grains that humans cultivated. Good bread wheat evolved by about 8,000 B.C.E. when emmer, itself a cross between wild wheat and goat grass, was crossed with a wild goat grass once again.[7]

Our dependence on and our debt to grass goes well beyond our foodways. We have shaped and changed and tamed the wild grasses, but they have shaped and changed and tamed us in return: "Civilization of the human race is directly attributable to the development of agricultural practices, which from the beginning have been most dependent upon grasses."[8] Planting, tending, and harvesting the fields reshaped both the natural environment and human culture and society. Technologies were spurred on by agricultural necessities: plows, sickles, the instruments of threshing. Grains were ground by hand until 800 B.C.E. when the technique for continuous milling was discovered in the Mesopotamia region. Once the knowledge was acquired machines could be built that harnessed the power of animals, wind, or water. What had been a time-consuming human labor, performed primarily by women, was no longer.[9] Gender relationships changed as men took over the processing of flour. Slowly the seeds grew to affect even aspects of culture that seemingly bear no relationship to food production. Humans had to adjust their rhythms to the cycles of the growing seasons; they had to structure their social groups to the labor of the fields. Mircea Eliade writes:

> We are used to thinking that the discovery of agriculture made a radical change in the course of human history by ensuring adequate nourishment and thus allowing a tremendous increase in the population. But the discovery of agriculture had decisive results for a quite different reason. It was neither the increase of the population nor the over-abundance of food that determined the course of history, but rather it was the *theory* that man evolved with that discovery. What he himself *saw* in the grain, what he himself *learnt* from dealing with it, what he *understood* from seeing how the seed lost its identity in the earth, it was all this that made up his decisive lesson. Agriculture taught man the fundamental oneness of organic life; and from that revelation sprang the simpler analogies between women and field, between the sexual act and sowing, as well as the most advance intellectual syntheses: life as rhythmic, death as a return, and so on. These syntheses were essential to man's development, and were possible only after the discovery of agriculture.[10]

The intellectual and spiritual legacy of agriculture can be seen on nearly every page of scripture. Not only is our flesh grass but so also are our minds, spirits, souls.

II

Not found only in the book of Ruth, grain (*dagan*) grows throughout the Hebrew Bible, commonly characterizing the bounty of the land (Gen. 27:28), paired with wine and oil (Deut. 7:13), given in sacrifice (Lev. 2:1–16).[11] Wheat grows in a variety of species: einkorn (*Triticum monococcum*); emmer (*Triticum dicoccum*); bread wheat (*Triticum aestivum*); hard wheat (*Triticum durum*). Yet in the biblical catalogue of grasses they are not distinguished: all are named *wheat* (*hittim*). *Corn* was a word in English before Europeans found the New World and all of the new vegetation therein; therefore there is corn before corn (*Zea mays*), meaning grain in general. Because of the King James translation and John Keats's poetry, Ruth is sometimes said to stand among the "alien corn," although what we commonly call corn today was unknown in Iron Age Israel. Instead Ruth would stand amid sheaves of both barley (*s'orim*) and wheat (*hittim*).

Although *grass* is a general word that covers a nearly endless variety of species and a field of grass contains more diversity than the one word suggests, English speakers do speak of plants with precision. Grass, herbs, greens, legumes, clover can all be found in a meadow and easily identified by anyone who kneels down and takes the time to inspect. We would never use the word *grass* to refer to herbs or plants more generally; we would never confuse a leek with what constitutes a suburban lawn. Yet the Hebrew Bible contains at least four different words that can be translated "grass," "green plant," "herb," "vegetation," "leek," "plant."[12] Since the Hebrew seems to use them all interchangeably, English translations vary considerably. Sometimes the word is clearly referring to that which humans eat and therefore may refer to plant life more broadly; sometimes the word is clearly referring to that which cattle eat. For example, the first man shall "eat the plants of the field" (Gen. 3:18) as a consequence of his eating of the fruit of the forbidden tree. This same plant is called grass and eaten by cattle in Deut. 11:15 ('esev). Another word (yereq, yaraq, yaroq) is an adjective or a noun, meaning the color green or green things, used to describe but also to name grasses and herbs and other plants of the field (for example, Exod. 10:15, Gen. 1:30, Job 39:8). The words for "reed grass" and "papyrus" ('ahu and gome') are the only Hebrew words that are carefully distinguished from these other grasses of field and earth, probably because reeds inhabit such a distinctive ecological niche (wetlands) and are associated with a foreign country, Egypt (Gen. 41:2, 18; Job 8:11).

When the words are used metaphorically, there are two primary resonances. The first is that human flesh is weak, fragile, and transient—like a blade of grass. Isa. 40:6–8 exemplifies this meaning. Isaiah is commanded to call out that "all flesh is grass and its hesed is like the flower of the field. The grass withers and the flower fades for the breath of the Lord blows upon it; truly the people are grass. The grass withers, the flower fades, but the word of our God will stand forever." The second is that humans are numerous, too many to even count—like a field of grass. After Isaiah proclaims that people can be destroyed as a wind can kill grass, he offers hope to Israel using a similar metaphor. In chapter 44 God's spirit (breath or wind) is poured out, causing the people to be restored. Their descendents will "spring up like grass" beside a flowing stream (Isa. 44:3–4). In many ways these metaphors do capture the human experience of grass and yet they also miss the biological reality of these nearly ubiquitous plants. Grass can survive and thrive naturally in environments in which human beings cannot—Antarctica, for example. As a single blade grass may be fragile, but as a species it is remarkably hearty, able to adapt to and survive in a wide range of environments. Grasses are, by some estimates, "the most highly evolved plants on earth."[13] They are not as weak as we may think; they are even more populous than we may imagine.

Yet there is something even in this that is analogous to the human. We are the most highly evolved and successful mammal on earth—we have survived and thrived in ways that our basic biological equipment would seem to belie. We have a weak protective covering—no scales, no blubber, no fur, no feather. We do not have sharp teeth or nails. We cannot outrun most other species. Our sense of smell is pitiable, our sight and hearing passable. It is only our brains and our opposable thumbs that give us the advantage. We have used these assets to spread out over the earth and occupy nearly every space that a piece of grass can. Even Antarctica is not just for intrepid explorers and hearty scientists anymore—it has become a tourist attraction.

III

I have never traveled to Antarctica; I suspect I never will. Less than two months after my doctor delivered my son (just after midnight we finally succeeded, through push and pull, to bring my boy into the world), she sailed there just to see the cold. I dream of other grasses. Many years ago, sitting in the Missouri sun with a baby boy not my own, I talked about photosynthesis and Walt Whitman, spoke the words of Isaiah and sang the "Song of Myself." He happily pulled and plucked spears of summer grass, his fists full of green.

IV

Our relationship to grass is somewhat paradoxical. Even though we depend on the seeds that certain grasses produce, grass remains one of the only plants humans cannot eat—in fact most animals cannot eat grass because we lack the ability to digest the cellulose that constitutes the grass's cellular walls. Only those of us with two stomachs can do the hard work of grass digestion, and even they need the help of specialized bacteria. The rest of us can consume only the grass's seeds, and people can do so only after a certain amount of processing.

At the end of chapter 3, in another instance of the intertwining of agricultural and human fertility, Boaz fills Ruth's apron full of seed. A seed is the future hope of any plant. The plant uses leaves to gather sunlight and elements from the air, its roots to gather water as well as minerals from the soil. The nutrients and energy are packed into a tiny package, an embryo wrapped up tight. And there it lies latent, waiting for the right conditions to converge before it consents to be born. Here we intervene. A seed is "an invaluable resource for us and other creatures of the animal kingdom who are unable to live on soil and sunlight and air."[14] We take the seed, pound and grind and mix and boil and bake. We take the seed and commandeer its life for our own, consuming sunlight, air, and soil in the way most productive for our own bodies. Allan Nation, editor of a magazine on alternative agricultural practices called *Stockman Grass Farmer,* notes: "All agriculture is at its heart a business of capturing free solar energy in a food product that can be turned into high-value human energy."[15]

In its essence our reliance on grass is really a reliance on the sun for energy. As the grass farmer Joel Salatin remarks, "these blades are our photovoltaic panels."[16] All plants consume sunlight directly through the process of photosynthesis. Having no photosynthetic abilities, animals then eat the plants or eat other animals that eat plants. The energy from the sun is stored as calories, and calories are what power the human and all other bodies. Our atoms were forged in the core of stars and then scattered throughout the universe by the exploding of a dying star. Atoms made in stars then assemble into organic bodies that still need the stars to consume. Our bodies are constructed of star-made atoms whose life persists because they are star-fed.

Walt Whitman chose to title the collection of his poetry *Leaves of Grass* (1855–1892) as if each line of poem were a fragile blade. The title also draws the reader's attention to his poem "Song of Myself," which opens with an image of the poet lying in the grass:

> I celebrate myself, and sing myself,
> And what I assume you shall assume,
> For every atom belonging to me as good belongs to you.
> I loafe and invite my soul,
> I lean and loafe at my ease observing a spear of summer grass.[17]

The "you" the poet is addressing is the reader but also may be the spear of summer grass. The substance of all flesh is drawn into the substance of the green grass; the poet, the reader, and the grass converge.

Such convergences between nature and the self, the whole cosmos and humanity, are a hallmark of Whitman's philosophy and are reflected in his poetry. The first stanza of the poem continues to connect, intimately, the human body to the soil: "My tongue, every atom of my blood, form'd from this soil, this air."[18] And such organic interconnectivity extends throughout time and the generations: "Born here of parents born here from parents the same, and their parents the same."[19]

Grass is a reoccurring image in Whitman's poems, as they focus on the natural world, from the humble blade to the grander cosmos: "I believe a leaf of grass is no less than the journey-work of the stars."[20] Whitman was inspired by the science of his day and even seems to anticipate our modern knowledge of astronomy and the ways in which all of the elements that compose the world—animate and inanimate alike—were forged in the core of stars. What journey did the atom in any blade of grass take, from that ancient exploding star expelling its substance across the universe to this particular earth configuring and reconfiguring its elements into infinite varieties of matter? An atom in a spear of summer grass could one day be an atom in a human body, which will most certainly be part of a plant again as grass grows on the grave. In Ruth the plot, characters, and setting converge to demonstrate human interdependence. When the grains in Ruth are viewed not just as prop but as character, interdependence goes deeper and farther. The interdependence in Ruth is not just between human beings but between humans and plants, animals, soil, sun, stars as well—the entire universe coalesces in a seed of barley carried home in Ruth's apron to Naomi.

Rather than publishing multiple volumes of poetry, Whitman simply kept adding to his one *Leaves of Grass*. The book went through nine editions, growing and changing each time. He added new poems and rearranged the order of the old in all editions up through the eighth (1881). In the ninth and final edition, sometimes called the "Death Bed Edition," seemingly satisfied with what came before, he simply added his new poetry to the end. In the final "annex" in his final edition, the pen-ultimate poem, preceded only by a farewell missive musing on possible ways of living on ("Goodbye My Fancy!"), Whitman returns to the images of vegetation. The image of seeds in the soil becomes a metaphor for the unending regeneration of all life:

> Unseen buds, infinite, hidden well,
> Under the snow and ice, under the darkness, in every square or cubic inch,
> Germinal, exquisite, in delicate lace, microscopic, unborn,
> Like babes in wombs, latent, folded, compact, sleeping;
> Billions of billions, trillions of trillions of them waiting,
> (On earth and in the sea—the universe—the stars there in the heavens,)
> Urging slowly, surely forward, forming endless,
> And waiting ever more, forever more behind.[21]

Like the book of Ruth, Whitman's poem "Unseen Buds" connects the seed to the fetus, the reproduction of flora to human reproduction. Whitman continues by loosely connecting the latent seeds to the stars, the engines that power the generation of it all.

Photosynthesis is a type of remarkable alchemy by which inorganic elements are transformed into organic compounds. This chemical process, which takes place in the leaves of green plants, "opens a gateway from the inorganic to the organic world,"[22] a gateway through which the eons of animals and other plants have passed, one by one, from fruit fly to brontosaurus, from orchid to live oak, from sand flea to human being. Had photosynthesis not developed 3.8 billion years ago on our planet, no other life would exist. Look backward. Devolve and dediversify us all, moving faster and faster as climates change and species come and go, as seas rise and fall and continents drift. Look backward to a time without oxygen gas, without ozone, when cyanobacteria shuttered and sparked, took in the carbon dioxide from the air and the heat and light from the sun, and created a molecule of oxygen gas and organic carbon.[23] The door opens up to all life—not in a spear of summer grass but in a single cell.

Ruth stands amid the tall barley grasses, domesticated thousands of years before her gleaning. She looks up, stretches, and shields her eyes with her hand. The sun, our star, which formed five billion years ago when the gases and dust from a solar nebula coalesced into a spinning ball, shines hot and bright. Her feet, perhaps sandaled, are dusty with the soil of our earth, a planet that formed with the leftovers of that nebula 4.6 billion years ago. Tonight she will eat the sunlight and soil stored in the seeds, captured by these blades of grass.

(RUTH) AND OBED

Questions of kinship dominate the daytime talk shows.[1] So ubiquitous are shows that feature the problem of paternity that I would wager that there is no one currently reading this chapter who has not caught at least a few minutes of one and can picture the format perfectly—photograph of smiling baby is projected on the screen behind the protagonists in the paternity drama, audience murmurs appreciatively on cue. The mother vacillates between the emotions of love for her child and righteous indignation at the baby's father if she is sure but he accuses; or in other cases bravado and embarrassment if it is she who is uncertain. The host is handed a sealed envelope and then, like the emcee at an awards show, slowly opens, reads, pauses, looks up with portent, and announces the results to 99.985 percent accuracy. The man either sinks to his knees in despair and disappointment or jumps up and pumps his arms as if he has just won the lottery—both yes and no results elicit such responses depending upon the man's feelings toward the child. In a few cases none of the men lined up on stage is the father of the smiling baby, and the mother abashedly shakes her head trying to remember with what other man she might have had sex nine months before her bundle of joy arrived. In these shows the baby is the object of the inquiry of possession. I can imagine a follow-up genre that is a possible but yet unrealized potentiality—in a few more years we may see the baby, now an adult, reflecting back on his or her drama of paternity.

Questions of kinship compound when the child is the result of reproductive technologies. Now it is possible for the sperm, ovum, and womb to come from three different people—none of whom are the parents who will raise the child. The dramas of the parents are frequently media fodder, and we are only just now hearing the voices of the test-tube-baby-now-adult and sperm-bank-child-now-teenager, each with his or her own issues surrounding paternity, maternity, and how to relate to identity. As more of these people become adults, how will they tell their own stories of origin? How will they understand their culture, ancestry, kinship?

Because we are now awash with new technologies and a 24/7 media industry that feeds off of our voyeuristic impulses, it may be tempting to posit a time in the distant past when kinship was clear, a matter of blood and substance, and identity was certain, a matter of family and culture. However, as new appraisals of kinship emerge inspired by modern technologies and contemporary lifestyles, these new appraisals are revising prior assumptions and theories about how people relate to one another. The technologies may be new but the complexities and uncertainties are ancient.[2]

One such complicated ancient kinship question is found in the book of Ruth. At the end of the book the desired child is born but a curious displacement takes place, a displacement on top of a displacement. As soon as Ruth and Boaz marry, "the Lord gave her conception and she bore a son" (Ruth 4:13). Boaz certainly provides the sperm and thus half of the genetic material for the boy; yet he is not the boy's father legally—Ruth's first husband is. When Boaz "acquires" Ruth he publicly declares that the transaction is in order "to maintain the name of the dead, so that the name of the dead will not be cut off from his kindred and from the gate of his place" (4:10). Ruth certainly provides the egg and the womb, yet she is not the boy's mother in their community. After the boy is born Naomi takes Obed to her own breast, and it is she who is publicly acknowledged as his mother: "And the women of the neighborhood gave him a name, saying 'A son has been born to Naomi'" (4:17). Rather than Ruth and Boaz, the boy's parents are "really" Mahlon and Naomi. The reconfiguration and extension of kinship relations, which today rely on twenty-first-century reproductive technologies, are not really new. They have been present in society for millennia—the people who give the genetic plan to the child are not necessarily the child's parents in the legal and/or social spheres. Legal, social, and biological parenthoods are not always coterminous.

The history of the anthropological study of kinship has been shaped by a bias for heterosexual blood relations as the natural foundation of kinship patterns across time and place. Such bias was first challenged by David Schneider's pioneering work on American kinship in the late 1960s.[3] Schneider was the first to redefine kinship as a system of symbols instead of a network of blood relations. For Schneider kinship is not a being but a doing and the theory he developed generated a new anthropological understanding of kinship.[4] Kinship is still an object of inquiry, but, in the words of theorist Judith Butler, it "remains a contested analytic concept," one which "helps to constitute what it describes."[5] How kinship is defined affects more than what anthropologists talk about at conferences. Our understanding of kinship goes to the heart of our deepest held values of family, friendship, community. Our understanding of kinship also has social and legal ramifications. It is within this context that Butler explores the question of kinship. Drawing on the new anthropology, Butler defines kinship as a "set of practices that institutes relationships of various kinds which negotiate the reproduction of life and the demands of death." Kinship practices, then, "emerge to address fundamental forms of human dependency, which may include birth, child rearing, relations of emotional dependency and support, generational ties, illness, dying, and death (to name a few)."[6] Kinship is constituted not just by biology but also by "community and friendship," "the regulations of the state," as well as "property relations" both material and human.[7]

One can observe all of these facets of kinship operating in the story of Ruth. Naomi and Ruth's relationship already challenges our conventional notions of what constitutes family. They are related only through marriage, a marriage now over due to the death of the spouse. According to kinship studies of ancient Israel, "the extended or joint family, not the biological family, was most important."[8] The joint family was rooted in the biological relationships between men, with women coming in through marriage. Naomi, Ruth, and Orpah find themselves without the ties that bound them together, three nonbiologically related females, their legal obligations to each other at an end with the deaths of the biologically related men. Orpah, although clearly upset by the parting, does accept that the bonds have been dissolved; she returns to her mother's house. Ruth, in contrast, protests and, through a vow, binds herself to Naomi with a new contract of mutual dependency, one that is strictly voluntary. The story of Ruth is about, at one level, the fluidity of kinship and that family is more a matter of choice than blood or even legal obligation.

The Family Ruth Chooses

Whether from an anthropological or sociological perspective, the relationship between mothers- and daughters-in-law is not one that has received a lot of attention in contemporary Western culture. Even today a woman binding herself to her mother-in-law, especially after the death of the man who tied them together, would make an odd story. And when the relationship does garner attention, it is defined by the popular, and arguably sexist, wisdom that mothers- and daughters-in-law never get along. Their relationship is too fraught with jealousy as they compete for the affections of the same man. In an essay on the book of Ruth Marianne Hirsh discusses her own search for positive cultural representations of the mother- and daughter-in-law relationship, a search influenced by her own positive relationship with her husband's mother. "When one recent study finds that a high proportion of mothers-in-law and daughters-in-law report that they have 'no problems' with each other, the researchers repeatedly express their surprise. At a recent feminist psychology conference, I attended a workshop on mother-in-law/daughter-in-law relationships and was amazed at the terrible anxiety that pervaded the room."[9] Ruth and Naomi's relationship—whether romantic or platonic, whether irenic or tense—confounds our normative scripts of association.

Mona West in her commentary on Ruth specifically makes the connections between the families formed in Ruth and contemporary family patterns that do not conform to the heterosexual nuclear norm: "All of these actions indicate Naomi, Ruth and Boaz's decision to create their own family and define their own understanding of kinship and responsibility to one another within the context of the inheritance and kinship laws of ancient Israel. These actions are similar to the ways in which Queer people of today create families."[10] Although West does not refer directly to the new anthropology on kinship, her language calls it to mind, reflecting specifically the work of Kath Weston on gay and lesbian kinship in a 1991 work entitled *Families We Choose*.

Ruth and Naomi's bond also crosses ethnic, religious, and cultural divisions in ways that challenge conventional kinship relations. At the heart of acceptable kinship patterns is a balance between two competing taboos: incest and miscegenation. Again, quoting Butler's analysis of the material: "Marriage must take place outside the clan. There must be exogamy. But there must also be a limit to exogamy; that is, marriage must be outside the clan, but not outside a certain racial self-understanding or racial commonality. So the incest taboo mandates exogamy, but the taboo against miscegenation limits the exogamy that the incest taboo mandates."[11] The twin taboos of incest and miscegenation are the specters that haunt the story of Ruth.

Earlier I argued that we cannot discern the attitudes toward Moabites embedded in the text. Most analyses rely on reading Ruth in conjunction with select passages in Genesis, Numbers, and Deuteronomy. Reading Ruth alone fails to present the negative assessment of Moabites that reading Ruth in combination with these other texts produces. There are shades of incest and miscegenation present in Ruth alone, but these anxieties are amplified when Ruth is read together with the other biblical material about Moabites. According to the biblical story, the Moabites are the descendents of Moab, the son of Lot and his daughter. To compound further the taint of such an origin, Lot's daughter initiated the sexual contact after rendering her father helpless through drink (Gen. 19:30–38). The Moabites continue to be associated with licentiousness throughout the scriptures (Num. 25:1–5). As a Moabite Ruth shares in this originary incest and carries the taint of licentiousness, drunkenness, and deception. By forming kinship bonds with a Moabite, miscegenation and incest come together.

But incest appears at another juncture of the story as well, one that does not rely on reading Ruth with Genesis. If Naomi is the mother and her son the father, then Obed is, in effect, a product of incest too. Ruth is often read as a book that argues for the acceptance of Moabites in the Israelite community—a kind of social critique of the Israelite prejudice against them. Is the original incest of father-daughter "undone" by the symbolic incest of mother-son? Perhaps if there is a social critique, it is operating at this deeper level as well.

Of course Naomi's and Mahlon's incest is only symbolic since, to state the obvious, Mahlon is dead and did not actually have sex with his mother. Their relationship through Obed has biological, social, and legal aspects but it is not sexual.

Speaking of the greater implications of international adoption and donor insemination for heterosexual and same-sex couples, Butler notes the ways in which these
practices "constitute a 'breakdown' of traditional kinship that not only displaces the
central place of biological and sexual relations from its definition but gives sexuality a domain separate from that of kinship, which allows for the durable tie to be
thought outside of the conjugal frame, and thus opens kinship to a set of community ties that are irreducible to family."[12] Naomi and Mahlon's parentage can certainly be understood as a kind of international adoption and donor insemination
worked out without modern technologies. Even if Naomi and Ruth never had a sexual relationship, the way in which this book redefines kinship at the beginning as
the family you choose and at the end removes the link between sexuality and parenthood, opens it up to queer readings, ones that go deeper and further than the
question of whether or not the two women had sex. Naomi and Ruth transgress the
borders of Israel and Moab, transgress borders of conventional kinship, glean in
the fields, and, since their kinship "is seen to be self-consciously assembled from a
multiplicity of possible bits and pieces,"[13] glean their family ties as well.

The Story of a Sandal

Law and narrative are interwoven throughout this book, but law comes to the fore
only in the first half of chapter 4 of Ruth. Instead of resolving all of the issues,
the legal discourse among Boaz, the other redeemer, and the men at the gate raises
more questions than it answers. Who is the other redeemer and why didn't Ruth
approach him first? Why does the writer withhold the man's name? How does Boaz
know of the field and why does he take it upon himself to offer it for sale? What
does the legal ritual of the sandal entail?

We have before us only the world of the text. We have no direct access to the
laws and customs that structured the lives of Bethlehemites in the Iron Age. We can
infer only from biblical texts, ancient Near Eastern law codes from the same time,
and cross-cultural observation of other subsistence societies. Law in illiterate cultures is less mandate written in stone and more lived relationship. This situation
would have obtained in Israel through most of its history. Although it is reasonable
to assume that some law codes were committed to writing during the period of
the monarchies (tenth through seventh centuries), the bulk of the Mosaic law was
not written until the Babylonian exile (586–538 B.C.E.) and not codified until the
Persian period (538–333 B.C.E.).[14] In the biblical material the phrase *a torah of
Moses* ("a teaching of Moses") starts to appear in the Persian period texts (Ezra).
Even in times and places where written codes exist, not everyone had access to the
codes since the bulk of the population was still illiterate. Who, then, was invested
with the authority of interpreting, applying, and enforcing these codes? If we

approach the matter from our legal context—vast arrays of written codes, systems of dissemination, interpretation (judges), application (lawyers), and enforcement (police)—then we are naturally puzzled by the inconsistencies of the situation present in Ruth, especially compared to the legal codes in Leviticus and Deuteronomy. If we, instead, look at the legal material from the perspective of an oral culture, a different situation emerges, one in which different rules may exist in different villages (even today certain laws are subject to state or even municipal variation), where community standards may be more flexible than the laws presented in the first five books of the Bible.[15] Even the narrator of Ruth acknowledges that the legal practices described in Ruth's final chapter are no longer practiced. Ruth 4:7 reads: "Now this was the custom formerly in Israel concerning redeeming and exchanging: to confirm all words, a man took off his sandal and gave it to his neighbor, and this was the custom of testimony in Israel." Ruth's original readers are not familiar with the practice. How does Ruth's author know about it? Why should readers thousands of years later assume the author had access to some special knowledge about law and custom in Iron Age Bethlehem and that therefore his or her understanding and explanation is the correct one? Not only do we have no idea what law and custom structured relationship in Iron Age Bethlehem—neither does the author of Ruth.

Ruth's final chapter opens with Boaz at the city gate. The unnamed relative of Elimelech comes by and Boaz explains to him the situation of Naomi's land. Boaz refers to the man as *peloni 'almoni*—a sing-song phrase roughly equivalent to the English *so-and-so*.[16] Once Mr. So-and-so agrees to buy Naomi's land, Boaz announces that the day he buys the land, he is also buying Ruth in order to maintain the name of her dead husband Mahlon. Or Boaz announces that on the day Mr. So-and-so buys the land, Boaz is buying Ruth in order to maintain Mahlon's name. The alternative redeemer backs down from his pledge to buy the land and Boaz gets both the land and the woman (4:1–6). As explained in chapter 6 above, the interpretive issue is this: whether the men are negotiating about Ruth and the land in the context of levirate marriage (Deut. 25:5–10) or the law of the redeemer (Lev. 15:25–28)? And is Ruth attached somehow to the land or are the land and marriage to the young widow separate issues? The lack of clarity in terms of the legal issues results in a lack of clarity about the second unnamed relative and his motives. If he redeems the land then must he also marry Ruth? A common explanation for his refusing both the land and the woman is that he does not want to marry a Moabite. Or are land redemption and marriage separate issues? In this case he may be worried that any progeny Ruth would produce with Boaz would later claim the land he just bought. Neither law fits the situation or the story precisely; different attempts to elide the problems require the emendation of the text or the jettisoning of different parts of the story; different solutions result in different appraisals of character.

Sasson's understanding of the relationship between buying Ruth and buying the land offers the simplest explanation of what is going on at the city gate.[17] When the unnamed redeemer agrees to buy the land, Boaz declares his own intention of marrying Ruth not that the other man has to take Ruth and the land. It is not that Mr. So-and-so would be required to take Ruth along with the land; it is that Boaz's declaration of marriage and his intention of raising up an heir to Mahlon puts Mr. So-and-so's future claim to the land in jeopardy. He would expend time and capital in the development of the land only to have to turn it over to Mahlon's heir when he came of the age to claim it. There is no prejudice against Moabites; there is only a practically minded man calculating the return on his investment.

Understanding Ruth to be attached to the land is a long-standing interpretation. In the MT it is Boaz who declares his intention to marry Ruth. However, the Masoretes believed that the unnamed redeemer was obligated under the law of levirate marriage to marry Mahlon's widow. They altered the Hebrew text of Boaz's words in verse five so that he declares that Mr. So-and-so had to marry Ruth, not that he is going to marry the woman himself. The change the Masoretes made in the text does not shed light on the intention of Ruth's author; it indicates only that the rabbis, over a thousand years later, did not understand the precise legal matters either.

An additional reason for the confusion about whether Mr. So-and-so is obligated to marry Ruth is the ritual he performs to indicate that he has given up his right of redemption: Mr. So-and-so must remove his sandal (4:7–8). The ceremony with the sandal may allude to the ceremony of the release of the levirate, although the ritual is not exactly the same. In Deuteronomy 25 if a man refuses to marry his brother's widow, she goes to the elders who sit at the gates of the city to explain the situation. The recalcitrant brother is then summoned. If he fails to yield to their persuasion, then the widow must pull off his sandal and spit in his face (Deut. 25:7–10). There are certainly similarities between what Deuteronomy requires in a case in which a widow is spurned by her brother-in-law and what Mr. So-and-so does at the end of Ruth, but there are some differences as well. To state the obvious, Ruth does not expectorate in the would-be redeemer's face. Ruth is, in fact, not present at the gate at all.

Some commentators use Ruth as evidence for an actual legal practice otherwise unattested in the scripture. For example, LaCocoque writes: "It is hard to believe that such a complex legal maze was imagined by the author of Ruth for poetic needs only. It is likely that the narrator alludes to a situation of long ago in Israel when all those intricate substitutions and correspondences were possible."[18] He then goes on to claim that the laws surrounding levirate marriage underwent development through time and that the period of Ruth represents a time when the laws applied not only to brothers but also to any kin. Other commentators think it more likely that the detail serves a literary rather than a historical purpose. For example, Linafelt points out that the author "has a penchant for archaizing, for making use of words or syntax that appear to be ancient and thus give the story an ancient feel."[19] A detail about an ancient ceremony may be another such moment of, in Linafelt's words, "historical color." From a literary perspective "the shoe is rich in symbolism."[20] Its removal may even introduce another bawdy element into the narrative since taking off a sandal may be a sexual reference, the sandal a symbol of male genitalia.[21]

One shoe on and one shoe off, Mr. So-and-so limps out of the narrative. In a chapter that three times repeats the phrase "the name of the dead man" (4:5, 10 [twice]), repeats Mahlon's name twice (4:9, 10), contains a blessing from the elders that includes a prayer that Boaz and Ruth will have children and "bestow a name in Bethlehem" (4:11), and then ends with a double genealogy, replete with the names of men, the point is clear. Mr. So-and-so has lost his chance for the immortality that names and sons confer. If virility is also confirmed through the begetting of sons, the anonymous redeemer is unnamed and unmanned when he strips himself of his sandal.

Gaps between the Mosaic legal material and other narratives are common in the scriptures. For example, Abraham serves meat and dairy to his three angelic visitors (Gen. 18:7–8) and Jacob marries two sisters (Gen. 29:21–30). Gaps between the Mosaic legal material and extrabiblical legal documents also sometimes appear. For example, among the Jews of the Persian military outpost of Elephantine, widows could inherit directly from their husbands. Law in lived practice may have been quite different, at different times and in different places, than the written law code. In the case of the book of Ruth the ambiguity of the legal material is resonant with the other ambiguities throughout the text. The book of Ruth presents a creative play on the idea of law and custom rather than a rigidly followed set of prescribed mandates.

West's commentary on Ruth focuses on the interplay between law and narrative in the story and sees it as essential to the "artistry and message" of the entire book.[22] In fact references to various laws are rich in the book of Ruth: Naomi alludes to the levirate law in 1:12–13 and there may also be allusions to it in 4:7–10. The law of the redemption of land is referenced throughout the story as it is a major motivating factor in the plotline—see 2:20; 3:9, 12–13; 4:1, 3, 4, 6, 7. The laws of gleaning are also essential to the unfolding of both plot and character.[23] For West "the legal material should be viewed as a creative matrix for plot movement and character development."[24] The ambiguity of the law allows the characters to go beyond the letter of the law in their interactions with one another and even to manipulate the law in order to affirm their relationships with one another. From West's queer perspective, "the strategies we find in Ruth are essential to our very survival in a society and a culture that invoke and create laws with narrow definitions of family and procreative privilege in order to exclude us and perpetuate hatred and violence against our community."[25]

Haunted by Hidden Twins

- Ruth is blessed in the name of Tamar, the unconventional levirate bride, veiled and seductive after the sheep shearing, mother of twins (Gen. 38).
- Her youngest, Perez, supplants his older twin brother, and Zerah disappears from the genealogies, red ribbon tied around his wrist (Gen. 38:27–30).
- Boaz is the descendent of these twins, according to the genealogy at the end of Ruth's tale (Ruth 4:18–22).
- Sasson suggests, based upon the oddities of the Hebrew, that the story may have originally been about Ruth's own bearing of twins.[26]
- Jesus, descendent of all these twins according to Matthew, has a twin, according to the Gospel of Didymus Jude Thomas, which means "twin," Jude "twin."
- B. D. Wong fathers twins, but Boaz, the elder, dies.[27]

B. D. Wong is an actor most acclaimed for his title role in the Broadway production *M. Butterfly,* most familiar in his reoccurring role as the court psychologist in the television drama *Law and Order.* Wong and his partner Richie Jackson brought all the reproductive technology of late-twentieth-century America into their service when they decided to have children. Jackson's sister Sue Barez donated her ova, Wong provided the sperm, and Shauna Berringer, a third party found via an agency, gestated the fertilized union in her uterus through a process called gestational surrogacy. Together the four conceived twins—none of them had "ever been all together in the same room, city, or state."[28] Biologically the mother was Jackson's sister, the father Wong. Legally Wong and Jackson managed to get a California court order to allow them to put their names on the birth certificate as the parents, no others. If recent court cases are any indication, Berringer had the potential to sue for custody herself, claiming both biological and legal connections to the products of her womb.[29] The biological and legal disjunctions are multiple.

Berringer had first gone into preterm labor on May 19—two months before the boys were due. The doctors managed to stop this labor, and they gave her steroids to help develop the fetuses' lungs in case she went into labor again. She did nine days later, and this time the contractions could not be stopped. The night that Berringer delivered the twins, Wong happened to be with her in California but Jackson was at the couple's home in New York City. Wong had to call Jackson to tell him that Berringer had gone into labor again, that the first boy had died but the second lived. They talked about what to name their baby boys. They already had some names picked out (although Berringer knew, neither father knew the sex of the twins), and now, during a transcontinental phone call in the hours after midnight but before the dawn, the men had to chose what to call the living and the dead.

> We agreed from the beginning that the first name of one baby, boy or girl, would be Jackson, Richie's family name. We put my dad's original Chinese name, Foo, in the middle if he were a boy because we both liked the way it tripped off the tongue. Jackson Foo Wong. . . .
>
> The other name we had chosen, if the babies were boys, was Boaz Dov Wong. Richie and I were immediately both drawn to the name Boaz, a name from the Old Testament; "Dov" is the Hebrew word for "peace."[30] My father's "American initials" and my brothers' initials are all "BDW," and we wanted to continue that tradition.
>
> On that night, coast-to-coast long distance, the question became whose name was whose? Richie and I both wanted a child named Jackson (to keep both our surnames alive in the family). But living, or in memoriam? After some thought, the name Boaz Dov seemed like the only choice for the mighty sacrificer. A biblical name and the Hebrew word for peace. It was easy to "give up" my BDW monogram for a name that sounds like the name of a fleet-footed heavenly messenger. What's a monogram when someone has given their whole life?[31]

This passage resonates with the book of Ruth in multiple ways, on levels superficial and significant. In terms of the former, while Jackson was waiting for word about the fate of the twins, he was killing time by watching reruns of *Oprah*. Oprah is the namesake of Orpah, named after the biblical character with a transposition of two letters. They chose the name Boaz for one of their boys. Nurses enfolded Wong from the moment he entered the hospital until so many months later when he finally emerged with his one living son, much as the women of Bethlehem form an unnamed chorus that surrounds Naomi to council and support.

Deeper than these surface coincidences, Wong and Jackson's quest for a family outside of the conventional nuclear triad mirrors the atypical alliance of mother- and daughter-in-law that is at the heart of the book of Ruth. There are no generational differences between Wong and Jackson, but their union does cross ethnic, racial, and religious boundaries. Wong is Chinese American; Jackson is Jewish American. Wong's family are recent immigrants, settled on the West Coast; Jackson's are from the East.

The ideals of sacrifice and strength interweave themselves through both the book of Ruth and Wong's memoir. Boaz, whose name means "strength," dies as a consequence of Twin-to-Twin Transfusion Syndrome (TTTS). In this syndrome one twin gives all of his or her blood to the other twin. The condition can be fatal for both twins since the donor will almost always be anemic and the excess blood in the recipient's body can result in heart failure: "When Boaz was born, he was about two pounds, five or six ounces, pale and anemic. He had given his brother nearly all of his blood, and at that point they, as one doctor put it, 'demanded to be born,' because they must have sensed their own distress. . . . Jackson couldn't have tolerated much more of Boaz's blood than he'd already been given at the time of their birth. If they had stayed much longer in utero, they would surely both have perished. I figure they must have known all of this. So they made a break for it, and Boaz gave everything he had in the effort, including, of course, his life. . . . The little guy gave his blood and everything he had to his brother so his brother would have the best chance possible."[32]

Wong and Jackson imagine that Boaz initiated the preterm labor in order to prevent his brother from dying, thus sacrificing himself to improve his twin's chances for life. As sacrifice and strength are intertwined, so are the highs and lows of human life—fullness and emptiness, birth and death, bad luck and good. For Naomi, Moab is both life and death; it is a land of agricultural bounty but is also the land in which her husband and sons are buried. The fruitful land is also a grave. For Ruth, the death of one husband leads her to another one and ultimately a son of her own. No reasons are given for the deaths of the men. Chance may be as responsible here as it is for leading Ruth to Boaz's field. Wong feels simultaneously grief and elation as one of his sons lies dead and the other holds on miraculously to life, both in the neonatal intensive care unit: "It's not fair, it's not fair. Why is life so unfair? Where's the raft, the preserver, the plank of wood randomly floating by to grab on to? Then, with a turn of your body and a few paces, your head breaks the surface of the water, and the oxygen nourishes you brain, and suddenly, you're swimming circles around *unfair.* You passed *fair* way back in the first lap. With a stop, a step, and a start, you're quickly approaching grateful and gaining on *lucky.*"[33] Life's gifts are enmeshed in life's sorrows, both subject to change and chance.

Finally the two narratives, so different in terms of time and consequence, come together in the deeply human desire to memorialize both the living and the dead. Both capture how children are living memorials to their parents, bearers of their parents' names, their characteristics both biological and social, their histories. Both struggle with the best ways to carry on the names of the dead. Both textualize the living and the dead. Wong writes: "As the short paragraph of Boaz Dov Wong's life came to a close, there opened an entire bookful of material on the humble journey of Jackson Foo Wong."[34] In many respects Wong's memoir is an attempt to make Boaz immortal through the telling of his tale and to will Foo into life through the force of writing—the memoir is largely based on e-mails Wong wrote during the period Foo was still in the neo-natal intensive care unit, balanced between life and death. The written name survives the death of the person who bore it—Foo lives and Boaz lives on.

Feeding Obed

In addition to the questions of kinship the final scene in Ruth raises an even more basic question: as Naomi stands in for Ruth as the mother of Obed, as she takes the boy to her breast and becomes his nurse, does this mean that she actually nurses the infant (4:16)? Whereas some scholars such as Edward Campbell reassure the reader that this is not the case, others including Amy-Jill Levine assume that she does indeed nurse the boy.

Campbell simply states in his comment on the verse: "Obviously, this has nothing to do with wet-nursing."[35] Campbell's dismissal seems reliant on the fact that the word *breast* or *bosom* can refer to either male or female anatomy (2 Sam. 12:3), and the word for nurse is not used for wet nurses but only caretakers who can be either male or female (2 Kings 10:1, 5).[36] Campbell is correct—just as in English *bosom* can refer to a male chest. However, I do not think that the author of Ruth is trying to imply that Naomi had a flat, masculine chest rather than round, female breasts. Whereas Campbell is also correct that the word *nurse* means caretaker, he is not correct when he states that it never means a caretaker who also breast-feeds. In Num.11:12, when Moses is berating God for not properly providing food for the wandering Israelites, he points out that he did not conceive or give birth to these children (as God did) and asks why he should be asked to carry them in his bosom like a nurse carries a suckling child. The words in Num. 11:12 for *bosom* and *nurse* are the same words used in Ruth 4:16. In the context of Moses' conversation with God it is clear that the words mean that the children are deriving nourishment from the bosom of this nurse.

Perhaps Campbell's dismissal of even the possibility that Naomi may be nursing Obed is really a result of his understanding of Naomi's age and the biology of lactation. Although the book of Ruth is silent about the ages of its main characters, there is a dominant interpretation that understands Naomi to be well into her middle ages if not already a senior citizen, and Campbell does see both Naomi and Boaz as comparable grandparent figures.[37] She would have to be at least old enough to have had two sons, both of whom grew up and were married for ten years before they died. Naomi may be as young as forty or as old as sixty. In addition to age there is also the fact that Naomi did not give birth to Obed—she may be his mother in her community but she is not his biological mother. Can a nonbiological mother who is somewhere between forty and sixty years old even begin to lactate? An exploration of the biology of lactation is necessary to answer this question.

A woman's breasts begin to prepare for lactation soon after conception, growing during pregnancy due to the ovarian and placental hormones that are now present in the pregnant woman's blood. Even though some milk is produced during the pregnancy, it is not until after birth that full milk production ensues. The exact mechanism by which milk is inhibited before birth but initiated at delivery is unknown, but it involves the complex interactions of the hormones estrogen, prog-esterone, and prolactin. What is known by scientists, doctors, midwives, nurses, doulas, mothers, and anyone else who has had experience with child-bearing is that the action of an infant sucking on the breast is the stimulus that begins and main-tains lactation.

The stimulus of sucking triggers the release of prolactin and another hormone called oxytocin, both from the pituitary gland. The former hormone promotes milk production and the later hormone causes the muscles around the alveoli in the breast to contract and thus expel the milk. The suckling stimulus is so central to lactation that even a woman who has given birth can quickly lose her milk if she is not nursing frequently enough, and sucking can initiate lactation even in women who have not just given birth. Whereas this phenomenon is most common in pre-menopausal women, it has also been observed in older women. The oldest woman in a documented case of nonmaternal lactation began to nurse her grandchild after the death of his mother when she was sixty years old and had birthed her last child when she was forty-two. It took a few days for her milk to come in—but it often takes a few days with new biological mothers as well. Adoptive mothers can also nurse their children. There is a device called a supplemental nurser which consists of a tube that is taped to the breast next to the nipple. The infant sucks on the nip-ple and the tube transmits formula into the baby's mouth, thus simulating natural breast feeding. In some women the sucking of the infant will eventually stimulate lactation and the adoptive mother will be able to nurse her baby naturally.[38]

In light of the biology of lactation it would seem as if Campbell's quick dismissal of the possibility of Naomi actually being Obed's wet nurse is unwarranted. The book of Ruth is a fictional short story and in the world of fiction anything can hap-pen. However, different assumptions about kinship, the ages of the protagonists, and the biology of lactation shape different interpretations of the story. Different assumptions shape interpretation because there is an ambiguity here—just as read-ers wonder what Ruth does between Boaz's legs on the threshing-room floor (Ruth 3), readers also are left to wonder what Obed does between Naomi's breasts. Suggestively the text itself connects Boaz, Ruth, and Naomi in the process of fertil-ity and reproduction. At the end of both chapters 3 and 4 Boaz fills Ruth with seed: grain in 3:15 and semen in 4:13. Ruth then hands this seed over to Naomi, as food in 3:17 and as her son in 4:16.

If it is at least possible that Naomi becomes Obed's wet nurse, what, then, is the purpose of this strange relationship? For those who wax romantic over Ruth and Naomi's relationship, Ruth giving Naomi her child is the culmination of her love for Naomi. As Nielsen writes: "The close relationship between Ruth and Naomi is one of the most important ongoing themes that has held the book together from first to last. Everything that Ruth has done has been stamped with loyalty to Elimelech's family and with her love for Naomi. In one sense Ruth takes Naomi's place when she marries Boaz to perpetuate Elimelech's family. What the aging widow was unable to do for her deceased husband the young, still fertile, Ruth can achieve. The child is therefore not so much Ruth's as the family's represented here by Naomi."[39] For those who understand the romance to be lesbian, Naomi does not replace Ruth as Obed's mother but instead displaces Boaz as Obed's father. In such cases Obed has two mommies.[40]

Since the book of Ruth is a biblical story considered sacred by both Jews and Christians and since the woman Ruth is a key figure in the genealogy of the messiah, however that messiah is named and defined, theological interpretations of Ruth's displacement have also arisen. LaCocque argues that "a whole theological perspective opens up before us on the theme of substitution."[41] Ruth is for him a paragon of self-abnegation for the benefit of others. First Ruth takes Naomi's place in the levirate system as wife for Boaz; Naomi then takes Ruth's place as mother of Obed and Obed takes Boaz's place as a redeemer (which he is called in 4:17). Ruth's exemplary selflessness is seen when she does not even insert herself into the mothering of Obed but hands him completely over to her mother-in-law.

Less sanguine understandings of Ruth and Naomi's relationship label the exchange at the end of the book of Ruth as "sexploitation." Naomi may be using Ruth as a surrogate much as Sarah employed the womb of Hagar or Rachel and Leah used their slaves Zilhah and Bilhah in their reproductive competition. Even though Ruth is not legally enslaved as Hagar is to Sarah, Wil Gafney argues that she initially came into the family through capture and rape not contract and consent.[42] Naomi then continues to "pimp" Ruth's body for her own benefit when she arranges the seduction of Boaz. Even though Gafney refrains from passing judgment on Naomi's actions, allowing for the possibility that Naomi was genuinely concerned for Ruth's future, Gafney concludes that it is still "troubling that Naomi procured her own salvation through the sexual and reproductive services of another woman."[43]

Sasson in his folkloric study of Ruth takes an entirely different tack in his analysis of the final picture of Obed lying on Naomi's breast. He compares the image of Obed on Naomi's lap and then at her breast, surrounded by the neighborhood women, to other images in ancient Near Eastern literature of goddesses suckling human infants. "*Ancient Near Eastern literature assigns female deities the task of establishing the fate, hence the future, of a newborn male; and that such a newborn, if human, is invariably a future king.*"[44] These images range through Mesopotamian and Egyptian texts, Old Babylonian and Akkadian. One of the many examples Sasson summons to support his thesis will suffice. The goddess Ninsunna in a text dating from about 2090 B.C.E. declares: "Shulgi, you sacred seed to which I gave birth / You holy semen of the [divinized king] Lugalbanda / On my lap I raised you / at my holy breast I determined the destiny for you / You are the best that fell to my portion."[45] The last scene in the book of Ruth references this common ancient Near Eastern motif albeit in a vestigial form.[46] The purpose of employing such a motif was to confer political legitimacy on David by demonstrating that David's grand-father Obed "had already enjoyed divine protection."[47] The similarities between the image of Naomi holding Obed to her breast and goddesses performing the same ser-vice to future kings is striking. Rather than David conferring legitimacy on Ruth (and to Moabites and mixed marriages by extension) Ruth and Naomi confer legit-imacy on David.

The history of wet nursing is difficult to trace because breast feeding, in general, was rarely commented on in ancient sources. It was (and is) a common activity exclusively done by women in a world where most texts were written by men. In the ancient Near East Old Babylonian and Egyptian materials indicate that wealthy women frequently gave their infants to wet nurses for periods from two to three years.[48] However, if the biblical text is a reliable reflection of social reality on this point, the women of Israel did not usually do the same.[49] In the Bible there are only three other passages about wet nurses: Rebecca's wet nurse Deborah (Gen. 24:59; 35:8); Joash's wet nurse (2 Kings 11:2–3); and Moses' wet nurse, who is really his own mother (Exod. 2:7–10). In Genesis and Kings a hired servant feeds the baby; in Exodus Pharaoh's daughter seeks a wet nurse from among the Hebrew slaves to nurse her Hebrew foundling. The history of wet nursing is ultimately a history of class, even though the class meanings mapped onto a nursing woman's body differ from culture to culture, from time to time. Certainly Pharaoh's daughter thought a slave woman the obvious choice for her newly adopted son. Perhaps Ruth's new position as wife of a rich man has moved her into a higher class than Naomi—but because of the linking of Ruth with Naomi this seems a difficult interpretation to sustain. What the examples of Moses and Obed do have in common, however, is the foreignness of the one *not* breast feeding. Despite the possible social critique of prejudices about Moabites, can the author of Ruth not quite allow this ancestor of David to suckle at a foreign woman's breast? He grew in a foreign woman's womb, but he can ingest only the milk produced by an Israelite body? "In the final ironic moment, Ruth . . . is erased from the text. Her mother-in-law nurses the child, the local women name him, and they even proclaim, 'A son has been born to Naomi' (4:17). This erasure removes the child from any Moabite stigma."[50] As at the begin-ning of the narrative, food, sexuality, reproduction, class, and ethnicity come together to form knots of complicated meaning.

It is also common for readers, both academic and lay, to assume that Ruth has feelings about this erasure. The assumption is based on our own idealizations of the maternal instinct and the mother-child bond, particularly the one formed during breast feeding. A curious aspect of the story is that Ruth was married to Naomi's son for ten years before he died, leaving no children behind. And yet in a few short

verses Ruth marries Boaz and conceives a child. This is certainly the biblical formula, and I reiterate that the story is a fiction and in fiction anything can happen,
but such a situation also raises questions of fertility. Ten years without conception
is unusual in any day and age. The obvious explanation is that Naomi's sons were
infertile. In the biblical world infertility is most often blamed on the woman
because of cultural values as well as an incomplete understanding of the mechanisms of conception.[51] To assume Mahlon's infertility, though, one also has to
assume that the couple wanted children and were trying to conceive. Although it is
much easier today to avoid conception even if one is sexually active, such techniques (and therefore, we can surmise, such desires) were not unknown in earlier
times.[52] Maybe Mahlon and Ruth did not have children because they simply did not
want them.

No matter the explanations for Ruth's displacement, the situation remains
strange. No matter how much a woman may love her mother-in-law, no mother
hands her child over to her. What adds to the peculiarity of the situation is the fact
that Naomi is in no way related to this child by blood; she is no longer Ruth's
mother-in-law. She is often referred to as Obed's grandmother, but biologically she
is not. Ruth is related to Naomi only through a now-ended marriage; Boaz is
Elimelech's kinsman. Perhaps Ruth had only Obed to replace herself, so someone
else could be responsible for Naomi. And once he was conceived and borne, she was
perfectly willing, maybe even happy, to return to a life unencumbered by children.
Readers romanticize both Ruth and motherhood in assuming that the conception
and birth of Obed fulfills a desire on the part of Ruth, even though the narrative
never indicates that she has such a desire. For example, Robert Hubbard comments:
"For a brief instant, Yahweh stepped from the shadows to center stage. By granting
Ruth motherhood, he finally paid the 'full wages' which her devotion to Naomi,
both earlier and later (2:11, 3:10), had earned."[53] Considering the dangers of childbirth in the ancient world as well as the damage it did to bodies before adequate
medical intervention was available, why should Ruth want children? Considering
how labor-intensive caring for a newborn is (and I type this with my own newborn
on my lap, between my breasts), what woman does not daydream of having a sub-
stitute, someone else whose breasts can nourish, at the very least in the hours
between midnight and six in the morning? Who would want to risk the dangers,
suffer the assault on the body, give over all of one's time and attention? Having a
child is in many ways contrary to a woman's best interests. As argued earlier, the
moment when Ruth hands Obed over to Naomi to breast-feed may be Ruth's resisting of a final assimilation into the Israelite community. She refuses to embrace fully
the role of good Israelite wife and mother when she declines to raise the son whom
she has borne.

Moving Obed from the object to the subject position, how would he tell his own story of origins and ancestors? How would a two-year-old Obed respond to the question, who is your *imah*? How would he respond to the same question at twenty-two? And how would we—or how should we—answer the same question? What is a mother? The one who provided half of your genetic material? The one who carried you in her womb for nine months, literally building your body with her own? What about the woman who later feeds you out of her body? Or is the real mother the one who cares for you not just physically but emotionally as well throughout your lifetime? If the same woman performs all of these roles and functions, then the answer is simple. But when these functions are divided and dispersed across multiple women, as in the book of Ruth, the question becomes much more difficult to answer. Before we turn to the studio audience, camera panning across the room, scanning the upturned faces, to ask the real mother of Obed please to stand up, we must first answer the more fundamental questions—what makes a family, who are my kin, how does "blood" define us in terms of culture, religion, ethnicity, and what does it mean to be a real mother?—all questions that the book of Ruth leaves suggestively open.

· 9 ·

THE STORY BEGINS
WHERE IT ENDS

Harvesters know secrets. They know how the green of the bean blends with the green of the leaf; how sometimes it is necessary to peek beneath a leaf and find a colony of beans, hidden by shape and shade. They know how to bend down and enter into the world of the plant, row by row, leaf by leaf, turning over, looking under, peering in to find the fruit. Even those fruits that beacon their ripeness with color still hide behind and beneath the leaves of the plant. A game of hide and seek. The baskets fill. They know that they are not alone in the game. Our gardens were bordered by young woods to the west, home of deer. A large brush pile stood next to the first garden, haven for rabbits and groundhogs. Fields stretched out behind as far as the eye could see behind the copse of blueberries. Birds filled the skies above. Sometimes my mother would go to the gardens in the morning, lawn chair under her arm, twelve-gauge shot gun held against her shoulder. Those were the days I did not cross the creek. I watched her disappear behind the orchard trees to take up her post in the gardens. Any shots fired were largely symbolic—a rabbit here, a groundhog there, a Pyrrhic victory against nature's prolific and exuberant bounty.

Ruth ends with a double genealogy. First Naomi's "son" is named Obed and the text immediately notes that "he is the father of Jesse, father of David" (4:17). Next the genealogy of David is extended further back to Perez with a *toledoth* formula: "And these are the generations of Perez: Perez begot Hezron, and Hezron begat Ram, and Ram begat Ammindab, and Ammindab begat Nahshon, and Nahshon begat Salmon, and Salmon begat Boaz, and Boaz begat Obed, and Obed begat Jesse, and Jesse begat David" (4:18–22). It may seem to contemporary English readers of Ruth that the genealogy functions as a neat ending, closing the narrative; however, in Hebrew narrative a genealogy always begins rather than ends a story.[1] Based on Ruth's divergence from all other Hebrew narratives, many historical-critical scholars propose that the genealogy was not original to the story of Ruth but appended later.[2]

There are, however, persuasive arguments that read the genealogy in other ways. For example, Linafelt argues that it was a part of the original composition of the text. First he presents a literary reading of the genealogy. As the book began with a male line subject to famine, infertility, and then death, it ends with a male line full and fertile. There may even be a connection between the ten years spent in Moab and the ten generations that descend from Judah through Boaz to David.[3] Second, Linafelt continues his literary reading to note the many connections between Ruth and the books of both Judges and Samuel. He uses this evidence to argue that Ruth was written to introduce the book of Samuel and that the genealogy therefore is not at the end of the story but at the beginning, the beginning of David's story. The placement of Ruth in the LXX and the Christian canon (between Judges and 1 Samuel) is not just a chronological ordering due to the book's narrative setting but possibly even intended by the author of the book.[4] To support his thesis Linafelt notes that the book of Ruth serves to link the book of Judges with the books of Samuel: Ruth begins with the phrase "In the days of when the judges ruled" (or, literally, "in the days of the judging of the judges") and ends with the word *David*. As Linafelt notes, "the reader has moved, in the space of four chapters, from the period of the judges to the period of the monarchy, making the book of Ruth a natural connector between the book of Judges and the books of Samuel."[5]

The Greek-speaking Jews of the Diaspora who assembled the LXX placed Ruth between Judges and Samuel. This ordering was adopted by the Christians when they canonized the LXX as their Old Testament. The Hebrew-speaking Jews of Judah placed Ruth in the final section of the Tanak, the Ketuvim or Writings, between the Proverbs and the Song of Songs, linking wisdom and love. The final genealogy may be an afterthought, tacked on by an editor who wished to adopt Ruth as David's great-grandmother. The final genealogy may have been written intentionally to introduce David's story. The final genealogy, out of place when compared to the arrangement of other Hebrew narratives, may also be the book's way of resisting the "happily ever after" ending a reader generally imposes on this idyllic tale. The genealogy is indeed a beginning for it opens Ruth up and begins every one of Ruth's afterlives. The gleaner becomes the gleaned as artists, writers, theologians, directors, rabbis go to her story to pick and sort from all it has to offer, carrying home according to their need, creating according to their vision.

Jewish Liturgical Uses of Ruth

There is no harvest in May in northeastern Ohio, but the seasonal cycles celebrated by Jewish holidays are not the cycles of any Diaspora community. The holidays tie the Diaspora into the rhythms of the land of Israel; the first grain harvests in Israel are in April. Many Jewish holidays have an agricultural component with a historical overlay. Shavuot (literally "Weeks" and also known as "the Festival of Weeks"), celebrated fifty days after Passover, is a late-spring harvest festival imbued with additional meanings from Israel's salvation history: Shavuot also marks the day that the Ten Commandments were given to Moses on Mount Sinai. According to the Bible, in the time of the Temple Shavuot was a pilgrimage festival and involved gifts of grain as well as animal offerings in the Temple in Jerusalem. Num. 28:26–31 reads: "And on the day of the first fruits, when you offer a grain offering of new grain to the Lord at your festival of weeks, you shall have a holy convocation; you shall not work at your occupations. And you shall offer a burnt offering, a pleasing odor to the Lord: two young bulls, one ram, seven male lambs a year old. And their grain offering shall be of choice flour mixed with oil, three-tenths for each bull, two-tenths for one ram, one-tenth for each of the seven lambs; with one male goat, to make atonement for you. In addition to the regular burnt offering with its grain offering, you shall offer them and their drink offering. They shall be without blemish." After the destruction of the Temple, the focus shifted to synagogue readings.

Traditionally many holidays are celebrated for two days in the Diaspora. Today in the synagogue there are two readings from the Torah (the Torah reading and the Maftir, or "Additional," passage) and a reading from the Prophets called the Haftarah on each day of Shavuot. Such a reading structure corresponds with any Shabbat or holiday—the central liturgical moment in the synagogue is the Torah reading followed by the Haftarah. Shavuot also includes the reading of the entire book of Ruth. Thus it joins four other Jewish holidays that are marked by the reading of a book from the last section of the Jewish Bible called the Ketuvim, or "Writings." These five books are collectively called the Megillot, or the "Five Scrolls," and are Song of Songs (Passover), Ruth (Shavuot), Lamentations (Tisha B'Av), Ecclesiastes or Qohelet (Sukkot or the Festival of Booths), and Esther (Purim).

During Shavuot the Torah reading includes the giving of the Ten Commandments to Moses and the sacrificial rituals associated with the festival. On the first day of Shavuot the Exodus account is read (Exod. 19:1–20:23) followed by the passage in Numbers that recounts the Temple rituals on this day; on the second day of Shavuot the requirements for all three pilgrimage festivals (Passover, Shavuot, and Sukkot) are narrated along with some additional agricultural legislation (Deut. 15:19–16:17 or Deut. 14:22–16:17 if the second day of Shavuot falls on a Sabbath) followed again by the same passage in Numbers read on the first day of the festival. After the destruction of the second Temple in 70 C.E., reading about the Temple rituals substitutes for the doing of the rituals.

Ruth precedes the Torah. At one level Ruth is an appropriate reading because of its agricultural setting. The book begins with the barley harvest and ends after the final harvests of wheat, and the main action takes place in the fields and on the threshing floor. There is a harvest party in the story that plays a pivotal role in the plot. Agricultural law (joining the dual themes of law and harvest) are also key to the plot in Ruth since the laws of gleaning are what allow Ruth to be in Boaz's fields in the first place. But the differences between Ruth and the story of the giving of the

Torah run deep. The juxtaposition of the two narratives—a pericope so male-focused that it instructs the Israelites not to go near a woman for three days before the Decalogue can be revealed (Exod. 19:15) versus a book named for a woman that features the relationship between two women; a listing of laws versus a short story; the premier male prophet who experiences the divine directly versus a foreign widow who never receives a theophany—invites reflection and interpretation. In the words of Nehemia Polen Jewish interpretive practices entail "revealing meaning by hurling texts at each other and observing the resultant trajectories and the energies released."[6]

The Ten Commandments presume a male audience not just because of the instruction to avoid women but also by the wording of the legal formulations themselves. This is most evident in the command not to covet one's neighbor's wife (Exod. 20:17). Were women standing at the foot of Mount Sinai when the Torah was revealed? And, if not, are women members of the covenant community? Are women Jews? Such questions are asked not just by Jewish feminists;[7] the rabbis also asked these questions in their conversations about the foundational events at Sinai. Even though the rabbis responsible for the Talmud certainly constituted an androcentric association, the notion that women were not present at Sinai was preposterous. Women were, of course, equal members of the covenant community; women were, of course, Jews. How, then, did the rabbis place women at Sinai despite their exclusion by the plain meaning of the text? They decided that the command not to approach a woman was in order to allow the women to purify themselves so that they could stand at the foot of Mount Sinai. Rashi also had an ingenious way of inserting women into this scene. He decided that when Exod. 19:3 said "the house of Jacob" it was referring to the women and when it said "the children of Israel" it was referring to the men.[8] Reading the female-focused text of Ruth before the Ten Commandments are read reinforces the idea that women were there too, despite what the text of Exodus says.

The link between Moses and Ruth is complex and multifaceted. Bonnie Honig reads Ruth as a story of immigration. The welcome that Ruth receives, her own attraction to Israel, and her successful integration permit "citizens (who are perhaps jaded) to re-experience the fabulous wonder of founding, the moment in which the truth or power of their regime was revealed or enacted for all the world to see. Notably, Moab is (as President Clinton put it in a speech in the Middle East in the fall of 1994) 'the land where Moses died and Ruth was born.' Ruth is a vehicle through which the law comes alive again generations after the death of the lawgiver, Moses. She repeats the foreign-founder script first acted out for the Israelites by Moses. Ruth's immigration and conversion re-perform the social contract of Sinai and allow the Israelites to re-experience their own initial conversion, faith, or wonder before the Law."[9]

Even without accepting the theory that Moses was himself an Egyptian, the fact that he was raised by Egyptians and has an Egyptian name positions him as an outsider within his Hebrew community. Rather than being an oddity, myths of founding that involve a foreign hero, or at least one associated with foreignness, are common throughout the world. Israel itself has several. Abraham, the first patriarch of the Israelites, is also a foreign-founder. He is from Ur and his foreign status is preserved in the early credo that begins with the statement "My father was a wandering Aramean" (Deut. 26:5). Ephraim, the eponymous ancestor of the most important tribe in the North, has an Egyptian mother and he himself never steps foot in Israel; Judah, the eponymous ancestor of the most important tribe in the South, has a Canaanite wife and conceives twins with his daughter-in-law Tamar, most certainly a Canaanite herself. The insider can experience what is special about his or her own society anew through the eyes of the outsider who voluntarily joins.

Ruth, which uses law to its own purpose and presents a very complicated picture of law and custom—so complicated that readers and commentators are not really sure what laws are being invoked, which ones are being modified—is paired with a fairly clear, straightforward set of laws. Even though the Ten Commandments are not as simple as they first appear when they are more deeply probed, they are written in the form of unconditional apodictic law ("You shall not . . .") and are the basic foundations of the remainder of the legal codes. Pairing Ruth with the Ten Commandments pairs fast-and-loose with slow-and-stable. Which is supposed to tame which? Does Ruth's play with legal material and emphasis on *hesed* imbue the entire Mosaic corpus with the same? The rabbis themselves give this as the reason for the reading of Ruth on Shavuot: "That is why on Shavuot, the festival of first fruits, also the festival of the covenant, the giving of the Torah, we read the scroll of Ruth, the Torah of kindness, to prepare the way to receive the Decalogue itself as a Torah of kindness."[10] Or do the commandments tame and reign in the wayward Ruth? In this case Ruth has preceded them in the reading so that they can have the last word.

The final readings in synagogue on Shavuot are from the collection of texts called the Nevi'im, or Prophets, which includes Joshua, Judges, 1 and 2 Samuel, 1 and 2 Kings, Isaiah, Jeremiah, Ezekiel, and the Book of the Twelve (the twelve minor prophets). On the first day of Shavuot the custom is to read Ezek. 1:1–28 and 3:12. On the second day, if the synagogue follows the traditions that descend from the communities of central and eastern Europe (the Ashkanazi), Hab. 3:1–19 is read; if the synagogue follows the traditions of the Jews whose origins lay in the Iberian peninsula (the Sephardic), then Hab. 2:20–3:19 is read.

The juxtapositions again open up new interpretations of Ruth, the legal materials, and the prophetic passages. The chapter from Ezekiel consists of his call by God to become a prophet. It is the most mystical of all the prophetic calls as it entails a detailed description of the heavenly throne room; thus it is the basis for Judaism's first forays into mysticism (called Merkabah, or "the Chariot"). Short story, legislation, mystical vision—three distinct forms of religious experience and writing brought together here to illuminate one another. Particularly telling is that the Ezekiel reading begins with the mystical vision, skips the actual commission and instruction of Ezekiel, and ends with 3:12 when God's commands are complete and Ezekiel begins his transport back to Babylon. It is as if the rabbis who put these texts together had decided that the Torah readings contained enough of God's commanding voice and that such a voice needed to be balanced by a story of poor women on one side and visionary description on the other.

The giving of the law as depicted in Exodus also entails a mystical experience as God descends in smoke and fire. Rabbinic tradition connects the two passages by understanding God's descent at Sinai as the descent of the same divine chariot in which God rides in Ezekiel.[11] Both Moses and Ezekiel, then, experience the same vision. Habakkuk also speaks of God's chariot in his prayer (3:8), as God runs down the nations that have violated God's own people. The Habakkuk chapter is also the origin of the midrash that God offered the Torah to other nations before God approached the Israelites. The other peoples all refused but the Israelites accepted.[12] This midrash provides the rabbis with other resonances between Ruth and Sinai— rabbinic interpretation never is singular. Just as the people of Israel voluntarily accept the Torah on Shavuot, Ruth voluntarily accepts the Torah when she follows Naomi into Judah. Neither was under any obligation. "By that very act, in choosing an irrevocable commitment, she also becomes a personification of the people of Israel at Sinai."[13] Ruth, however, makes such a commitment without the spectacular theophanies experienced by Moses, Ezekiel, and Habakkuk.

Shavuot is not just about hearing Torah read in the synagogue. Yet there are fewer rituals and customs associated with Shavuot than with any other holiday. Compared to the elaborate and precise rituals of Passover and Sukkot (both of which last seven days in Israel and for Reform Jews; eight days for the rest of Diaspora Judaism), Shavuot is paltry. Judith A. Kates writes in her reflection on Ruth and Shavuot, "I knew nothing about Shavuot from childhood—at most a vague memory of flowers in the synagogue from the pious period of my adolescence. . . . The holiday had been muted in my youth even in the nominally Orthodox practice and teaching of my family's synagogue in the '40s and '50s."[14] Lasting only one or two days, requiring no special building project, cleaning project, or food, celebration of Shavuot is left relatively open. One would think that the holiday of the giving of the law would have accrued serious and intense ritual elaboration. But beyond decorating home and synagogue with flowers (a traditional component of most celebrations including every Shabbat) and eating dairy products, it did not. In Israel on secular kibbutzim, its harvest character is again paramount. Parades of tractors, hayrides, communal feasts all celebrate the first fruits of the harvest. Back in the land, Ruth is again a woman in the fields as the original meanings of the holiday come, once again, to the fore.

The day commemorating the giving of the Torah on Mount Sinai could have been a solemn holiday to match the serious nature of law. Yet Ruth interjects a sense of play and fun. The reason that there are so few set rituals for this day is a reflection of the flexible approach the book of Ruth takes toward law. Yes, law frames the entire narrative; but on closer inspection none of the laws fits exactly with the narrative. It is as if the rabbis are saying, yes, the law is the foundation, but "it is on earth and not in heaven." The people involved can and should interpret the Torah, always erring on the side of human flourishing and fertility. It is not just that the characters go beyond the requirements of the law; it is that what they do does not quite fit the law as we know it, as it is recorded in the Torah. The openness of the ritual opens up a space of creativity, which, in conjunction with law is precisely what the story of Ruth recommends.

Christian Liturgical Uses of Ruth

Shavuot plays a pivotal role in the Christian story although most Christians do not realize it. In Christianity Shavuot is transformed into Pentecost. According to the New Testament book the Acts of the Apostles, the disciples had gathered together in Jerusalem for Shavuot. Because Shavuot was one of the three pilgrimage festivals, the city was full of Jews from the surrounding countryside as well as from various Diaspora communities. It had been an eventful fifty days for the disciples. According to the Gospel of Luke, written by the same person who wrote Acts, their teacher Jesus had been arrested and executed on Passover, betrayed by one of his own (Luke 22–23). Two days later a group of women discovered that Jesus' tomb was empty and they told the disciples and other followers of Jesus. Later that day Jesus himself appeared to them, first to a group on the road to a village named Emmaus, next to others who were still gathered in Jerusalem (Luke 24).

Acts opens with Jesus' ascension into heaven while the disciples look on (Acts 1:1–11). Still debating the meanings of their experiences, the disciples, all observant first-century Jews, gather to celebrate Shavuot together: "And suddenly from heaven there came a sound like the rush of a violent wind, and it filed the entire house where they were sitting. Divided tongues, as of fire, appeared among them, and a tongue rested on each of them. All of them were filled with the Holy Spirit and began to speak in other languages, as the Spirit gave them ability" (NRSV; Acts 2:2–4). In other words they began to preach and all of the Jews of the Diaspora who had come to Jerusalem for Shavuot understood, each in his or her own language, what these illiterate Galileans were saying.

This story, told only in the Acts of the Apostles, marks the beginning of Christianity according to the Church traditions. Jesus ascends so that the Holy Spirit can descend and direct the spread of Christianity from the center in Jerusalem to the ends of the earth. The symbolism is clear. On the festival celebrating the day that Moses received the law from God on Mount Sinai establishing the covenant, God sends a new law through the Holy Spirit to replace the old covenant with a new one. Shavuot is appropriated and its meaning transformed. Christian supercessionism is imprinted in Christianity's understanding of its beginnings.

There is no mention of Ruth either in the Pentecost story or in any subsequent liturgy. It is likely that the reading of Ruth on Shavuot is a later Jewish practice and was not a part of the festival in the first century. The absence of Ruth continues on through Christian history. Not a single passage of Ruth is a part of any Christian lectionary, nor is it integrated into the liturgy of any holiday or Sunday service.[15] Although Ruth's vow to Naomi (1:16–17) is sometimes read in marriage ceremonies, it is included because of the wishes of the marrying couple not because it is officially part of the liturgical text. Ruth has only one point of entry into Christian ritual. She appears in the Gospel of Matthew in the genealogy as one of the ancestors of Jesus (Matt. 1:5).

The author of the Gospel of Matthew opens with a genealogy of Jesus that begins with Abraham and ends with Joseph, the man betrothed to Mary, Jesus' mother. There are several noteworthy features of this genealogy, features that demonstrate the plasticity of any genealogy in the biblical world. As discussed earlier, genealogies are genres that embed ideology in genetic connection. Matthew's genealogy gives the reader important information about Matthew's literary themes and theological orientation but little if any information about Jesus' history. For example, beginning the genealogy with Abraham signals a key theme of Matthew's account of the life of Jesus—Jesus is rooted in Jewish people, Jewish texts, Jewish history. The author of the Gospel traces Jesus' ancestry through the royal line of David— from Solomon through Jechoniah, Jesus' ancestors all sat on the throne in Jerusalem. Finally, another unique aspect of Matthew's genealogy is the inclusion of four women. It is unusual, in general, to include women in any biblical genealogy, but the particular women the author of the Gospel includes make the passage even stranger. The named women are Tamar, Rahab, Ruth, and the wife of Uriah (Bathsheba).

What unites these women is that they are all associated with non-Israelites, and they all have some kind of sexual "irregularity."[16] Tamar is a Canaanite. She dresses as a prostitute to trick her father-in-law Judah into having sex with her so that she can conceive her twins (Genesis 38). Rahab is a Canaanite prostitute (Joshua 2). Ruth is a Moabite who seduces Boaz on the threshing-room floor (Ruth 3). Calling

Bathsheba "the wife of Uriah" underscores the adultery of David when he took her and also her association with non-Israelites (2 Sam. 11). Uriah is a Hittite and Bathsheba may be as well. The women all point toward the fifth woman in Matthew's genealogy: Mary.

As part of Jesus' genealogy in Matthew, Ruth comes to the attention of various Christian theologians and biblical interpreters. When discussing Ruth early Christian commentators note her outsider status as member of a pariah nation (they too read Ruth in light of Deuteronomy and Genesis). Ambrose (fourth century), for example, writes: "For this woman who was an alien, a Moabitess, a nation with whom the Mosaic law forbade all intermarriage, and shut them totally out of the Church, how did she enter into the Church, unless that she were holy and unstained in her life above the law? Therefore she was exempt from this restriction of the law, and deserved to be numbered in the Lord's lineage, chosen from the kindred of her mind, not her body. To us she is a great example, for that in her was prefigured the entrance into the Lord's Church of all of us who are gathered out of the Gentiles."[17] Instead of understanding Ruth's integration into the Israelite community as a conversion to Judaism (as the rabbis do), early Christian commentators understand her entrance into God's community as an example of God's acceptance of Gentiles outside of the Torah.

Matthew's genealogy does not correspond exactly with either the genealogies of the Jewish Bible or the other genealogy of Jesus in the Gospel of Luke (Luke 3:23–38). But genealogies are about ideology not biology. Matthew includes Ruth in his genealogy of Jesus to foreshadow Jesus' mission—rooted in the people of Israel but ultimately open to all the nations (Matt. 28:19). Matthew is also commenting on the status of Mary—the way in which Ruth pursued Boaz to conceive Obed may be unconventional, as Mary's conception of Jesus is, but it is all part of the divine plan. For the Church Fathers Matthew's inclusion of Ruth is about their own inclusion as Gentiles. Many take their inclusion even further by reading Ruth as a supercessionist narrative. As Ruth left her parents behind in the idol-filled land of Moab, the new people of God must leave their parent Judaism behind. In this anti-Jewish twist Ruth's entering the land of Israel is really her leaving the people of Israel.[18]

Despite the understanding of Ruth as the Church promulgated by certain Church Fathers, Ruth's attendance in church has been confined to some wedding ceremonies (and who doesn't love a wedding) and to Sunday schools to tell stories to children (perhaps she missed Obed after all). Consequently Ruth has been free to wander in and out of more secular contexts. Peter Hawkins wonders if it is ignorance of Ruth because of her absence in Christian liturgy that has allowed for some of the creative interpretations of the figure in poetry and literature. For example, Hawkins notes that the strangest aspect of Keats's reference to Ruth near the end of his poem "Ode to a Nightingale" is not that the allusion intrudes unexpectedly but that it depicts a scene that is not in the biblical text:

> The voice I hear this passing night was heard
> In ancient days by emperor and clown:
> Perhaps the self-same song that found a path
> Through the sad heart of Ruth, when, sick for home,
> She stood in tears amid the alien corn.

Ruth cries only when Naomi threatens to leave her behind in Moab—in other words she only cries at the prospect of staying home, not at the reality of leaving home. Hawkins asks how Keats could have "gotten away with" such a mistake. His answer is that "Keats could have his way with Ruth, so to speak, because she was and is, a relative unknown 'amid the Gentiles.'"[19] A space of creative play opens up through the liturgical appropriation of the story in religious community—in the case of Christianity it is the naming of Ruth in a prominent place (the Gospel of Matthew is the first book in the New Testament) without the reading of Ruth in any official capacity. She becomes a name without a clearly known story and therefore she is left to play in other arenas, far from home.

Ruth and the Spirit of Exile

The Israeli director Amos Gitai has a series of films focused on the Jewish legend of the golem. The golem is a creature brought to life by magic, often to perform some task for its creator. There are many versions of the legend of the golem, whose body is usually formed out of the earth, animated by the name of God. Instructions for the creation of a golem can be found in the Talmud, the Jewish mystical text the Sefer Yezirah, and commentaries on the Sefer Yezirah. Some of the most popular stories of the golem arose in the sixteenth century around the Maharal of Prague (1513–1609). In order to protect the members of his community, who were subject to various forms of anti-Jewish violence, the Maharal created a golem. Gitai gleans from the Sefer Yezirah and the Ashkanazi folk tales to bring his own golem to life.

The movie *Golem: The Spirit of Exile* (1991) has a double introduction. In the first a man paces while recounting the story of David and Goliath, ending not with David's triumphant victory over the giant but with David's claim to be armed with faith. This first scene introduces one of the characteristic ways Gitai employs biblical text. In 1 Samuel 17 David does not claim to be armed with "faith" in opposition to Goliath's more conventional weapons. Rather David confronts Goliath "in the name of the Lord of hosts, the God of the armies of Israel, whom you have defied" (1 Sam. 17:45). Throughout *Golem: The Spirit of Exile*, Gitai subtly manipulates biblical texts in order to avoid explicit references to God. In the second introductory scene another man discourses on the Jewish mystical idea that the Torah precedes creation and the Hebrew letters are the building blocks of creation (from the Sefer Yetzira). He walks through a dark landscape, passing human figures lying silent and still on the ground. Toward the end of his discourse he kneels down next to one of these figures and gestures over it. When he stands and moves away, the figure rises up out of the mud, called to life. As she takes her first tentative steps the man proclaims: "You are the Spirit of Exile: the collective soul of all who wander the earth. I created you from the dust of the earth. Go. Protect the wanderers, the nomads, the exiles from all evil and hardship inflicted by their persecutors. Protect them and guide them."[20] The Golem has been brought to life.

Gitai does not employ a linear narrative structure; rather the story is told in vignettes, some of which are surreal, evocative, like a dream. After the Golem comes to life and receives her commission, the narrative of the movie begins, a story of a family living in Paris. A couple (later identified as Elimelech and Naomi) appear to be riding the elevator up through the Eiffel Tower. Outside the Golem floats; she is describing a terrible drought and famine, using the language of Jeremiah 14. Without pause she slides into the book of Ruth. While the Golem recites scripture in French, the woman echoes some of the words of Ruth in Hebrew.

The dialogue throughout the film is almost entirely quotation from biblical text. The book of Ruth is the narrative frame: the family is from Bethlehem, the two sons are married to French women. The father of the family dies in a construction accident; the sons are murdered, targeted because they are foreigners. Naomi advises her daughters-in-law to return to their mothers' homes. As in the biblical text one leaves but the other pledges her devotion and remains with her dead husband's mother. According to the movie French law dictates that burial in French soil is reserved only for the French. The widow must send her husband and sons back to Bethlehem; her property is confiscated (is she being evicted or is the property to offset the price of the transport of the corpses?), and she is offered a one-way ticket back to her home country. Paris is no welcoming Moab. Rather than returning to Israel, Naomi and Ruth, each with a single suitcase, instead board a barge and begin to wander the seas.

The rest of the Ruth narrative is played out with Gitai's own twists. Gitai's Naomi is young and beautiful, and the sexual charge between her and Ruth is evident. Naomi still instructs Ruth to seek out the stability of a relationship with Boaz, but, rather than a rich kinsman in Bethlehem, Gitai's Boaz is a French barge captain of African descent. A baby is born and Ruth hands him to Naomi. The movie ends with a conclusion that mirrors the double introduction to form an inclusio—the Golem speaks her own account of creation built upon the Hebrew alphabet and the final words return to the story of David and Goliath: "You come to me armed with a sword, a spear, and a javelin. I come to you armed only with my beliefs." As the book of Ruth ends with the word *David, Golem: The Spirit of Exile* ends with the words of David. The words are spoken while the camera pans through covered canals as if the viewer now too wanders the seas with the exiles.

Gitai explores the theme of exile, both voluntary and involuntary, on multiple levels. The story is about immigrants and it is told in three languages—French, Hebrew, and English (Elimelech seems to be a native English speaker, suggesting that his sojourn actually began in North America and moved through Bethlehem to Paris; he is an immigrant who dies in a land twice removed from the place of his birth). It is the rare viewer who would be able to watch the movie without subtitles, thus the linguistic alienation of the immigrant is at least in part reproduced in the viewing experience. In Gitai's story of the modern-day Ruth and Naomi no one finally returns home—except maybe the bodies of the dead men. There is no end to exile.

Perhaps even more profoundly, Gitai enacts his parable of exile in the biblical text itself. Biblical passages are unmoored from their contexts and left to wander in and out of other stories. Not only does the book of Ruth wander from Iron Age Israel to twentieth-century Paris to shape and be shaped by the modern world, but multiple other texts follow, inserting themselves here and there into the story of Ruth. The most prominent are the two other scrolls of the pilgrimage festivals—Song of Songs (read during Passover) and Ecclesiastes (read during Sukkot)—as if their attachment to pilgrimage has made them generally peripatetic. When Naomi prepares her husband's body for burial, she sings S. of S. 5:2–6—the passage about the beloved knocking on his love's door in the middle of the night. When she finally arises to answer him he is gone: "I sought him but did not find him; I called him but he did not answer," says Naomi along with the speaker in the Song, as she caresses the body of the dead man. When the sons are murdered in a pique of xenophobic violence, the fabric of Ruth is rent by grief and Qohelet steps in to speak his words of despair and pessimism (select passages from Eccles. 1–4, 6, 8). When Naomi tells her daughters-in-law to return to their mother's house, the Song of Songs returns to add another note of love and longing (S. of S. 8:8–10a).[21] Ruth and Naomi speak the words of the Song to each other, as do Ruth and Boaz, thus suggesting that both relationships are about love and sexual desire. As the men are killed, as the women are stripped of their belongings and expelled from the country, the Hebrew prophets act as a Greek chorus, accompanying the destitute widows, decrying the unjust treatment of the poor.

Throughout it all every reference to God has been removed from or altered in the biblical passages. Even in Gitai's version of Ruth's famous vow to Naomi, Ruth does not pledge to take Naomi's god. The line is simply omitted from Ruth's passionate words. Gitai's David may face Goliath armed with faith and beliefs, but the content of those beliefs is left open. The Hebrew alphabet is the only creative, metaphysical force; the Golem is the only supernatural presence. Even though she appears and disappears, taking various forms, not subject to the laws of nature, she fails to prevent the deaths of Elimelech, Mahlon, and Chilion. The Golem follows the exiles but seems unable to protect them. There is no God in Gitai's world of widows and sailors.

Forced out of Paris, Ruth and Naomi do create a new life for themselves, but there is no homecoming for Gitai's widows. There is no place for Ruth and Naomi in France (Moab), but neither does there seem to be a home for them in Israel. At the end of the movie, as if to underscore the endless exile, Naomi speaks the words that God first speaks to Abraham. She is sitting in the bathtub, facing a mirror, cutting her hair. The viewer peers into this private moment, looking over her shoulder. While she cuts, she recites in Hebrew, twice, "Go back to your country and your kindred, to your father's house, and you shall be a great nation." In Gen. 12:1–2 Abraham is commanded by God to leave his home in order to become a great nation, but Gitai's Naomi reverses the journey. After Naomi recites, the Golem reads Gen. 12:1–2 correctly, albeit in French rather than Hebrew. In the Bible Abraham goes into exile in order to settle the land of Israel. Later the people of Israel will be forcibly exiled from the land of Israel, exiled back to Abraham's homeland. In the contemporary world the exile ends with the creation of the state of Israel. On the one hand Abraham's command is reversed—go back in order to become a great nation, the nation of the modern state of Israel. Naomi does have a home to which she can return. On the other hand every return is still predicated on exile—to return to Israel one has to leave somewhere else. Who is in exile? Where is home? In the book of Ruth Naomi's exile takes her to Ruth's home; Naomi's homecoming is Ruth's exile. In *Golem: The Spirit of Exile,* the dialectic between exile and return is never resolved. Naomi cuts her hair in mourning.

Perhaps this is another way of understanding the haftarah reading of Ezekiel and Habakkuk on the days of Shavuot. Both prophets are positioned after the Babylonian destruction of Judah and the subsequent exile of some of the Judean people. Ruth, a story of return and coexistence with the foreigner, is a counterpoint to the prophets, voices of exile at the hands of the foreigner. Not only Jewish history but all human history is a play between expulsion and return, leaving and longing for home, however that home is defined. As Gitai's movie demonstrates the immigrant continues to wander in and out of different lands. Not only Jewish history but all human history is a tale of learning to live with people who are different. As Gitai's movie shows people both love and hate across difference—Mahlon and Chilion marry and are murdered by the French. Not only Jewish history but all human history is a struggle between powerful forces of exploitation and prophets who stand up to demand justice. As Gitai's movie suggests those who are in exile are still vulnerable to mob violence and state sanction. There may be a golem to follow the exiles, but there is no god to lead the way home.

The story begins where it ends. With the genealogy that opens Ruth up to all of her afterlives, the stories of Elimelech, Naomi, Ruth, Orpah, Mahlon, Chilion, Boaz, Obed are told over and over, forever reenacted anew. Famines reoccur in different lands, exiles never end, men and women continue to wander seeking security. Grasses grow and die and grow again. Women fall in love, vows are made that defy death, men and women find each other in the dark. Children are born and die and others are born. Names are restored, the dead are remembered, neighbors rejoice. In such a simple genre as the genealogy every name is the story of a life, every birth is the story of a hope. Ruth's genealogy takes the reader backward and points the reader forward in the unending drama of birth and death, the unending drama of life.

I have begun to harvest again. I bought four tomato plants, small and fragile but full of promise. Two plants were destroyed in a frenzy of canine exuberance. Two survived and slowly, slowly blossoms formed and bloomed into little green tomatoes, took in the sun and water, and bloomed into red fruit. They were mellow and sweet and mine. Ruth's gleaning reaped bounty; my harvest is meager. I need no apron but hold them all in my hand.

• NOTES •

Preface

1. Carol Meyers, "Returning Home: Ruth 1.8 and the Gendering of the Book of Ruth," in Athalya Brenner, ed., *A Feminist Companion to Ruth*, 98–99; see also Meyers, "Everyday Life: Women in the Period of the Hebrew Bible," in Carol A. Newsom and Sharon H. Ringe, eds., *The Women's Bible Commentary*, 244–51.

Chapter 1: Gleaning

1. Goethe uses the word *idyllisch* to describe the book of Ruth in *Noten und Abhandlungen zu besserem Verständnis des West-östlischen Divans: Hebräer.* Hermann Gunkel picks up Goethe's description and suggests that the genre of Ruth is a novella. Gunkel, *Reden und Aufsätze*, 65. The romantic designations continue through today. For example, the book of Ruth is called a "charming narrative of gracious family behavior" in Tikva Frymer-Kensky, *Reading the Women of the Bible*, 253.

2. Tod Linafelt and Timothy K. Beal, *Ruth and Esther*, xiii.

3. Linafelt's commentary presents "an unsettling interpretation." Linafelt, *Ruth*, xiii.

4. All translations are my own unless otherwise noted.

5. Linafelt, *Ruth*, xiii.

6. Naomi also doubles herself when she gives herself another name in 1:20.

7. Jack M. Sasson, *Ruth: A New Translation with a Philological Commentary and a Formalist-Folklorist Interpretation*, 159.

8. Jacob M. Myers arranges Ruth 1:17–18 into six bicola. Myers, *The Linguistic and Literary Form of the Book of Ruth* as discussed in Edward Campbell, *Ruth*, 11–12.

9. Campbell, *Ruth*, 13.

10. Campbell, *Ruth*, 13.

11. Campbell's translation. For the complete list, see Campbell, *Ruth*, 13.

12. Campbell, *Ruth*, 14.

13. Campbell, *Ruth*, 14. I explore other possible readings of such an oddity in chapter 3.

14. Campbell, *Ruth*, 24.

15. Judith A. Kates and Gail Twersky Reimer, eds., *Reading Ruth: Contemporary Women Reclaim a Sacred Story*, xviii. The number of essays in the volume that address issues of family and friendship also demonstrates the centrality of relationship in the book of Ruth.

16. Elizabeth Cady Stanton et al., *The Woman's Bible*. Stanton was not the first woman to engage the Bible. In every age women have read, discussed, and interpreted the scriptures. In

the nineteenth century Stanton was preceded by Maria Stewart, Sarah Grimké, and Anna Julia Cooper. See Gerda Lerner, *The Creation of Feminist Consciousness,* 138–66; Elisabeth Schüssler Fiorenza, ed., *Searching the Scriptures,* 1; and Christiana de Groot and Marion Ann Taylor, eds., *Recovering Nineteenth-Century Women Interpreters of the Bible.*

17. Stanton, *The Woman's Bible,* 2:39–40.

18. Stanton, *The Woman's Bible,* 2:41.

19. Stanton, *The Woman's Bible,* 2:43.

20. Stanton's wish was to assemble a committee of female translators and scholars to work on *The Woman's Bible,* but she was unable to get women from the academy to join her project because they feared such work would blemish their reputations. See Stanton, *The Woman's Bible,* 1: 9. She was, however, able to form a committee of other interested women, although she still did most of the interpreting and writing herself. The other members of the committee were Rev. Phebe A. Hanaford, Clara Bewick Colby, Rev. Augusta Chapin, Ursula N. Gesterfeld, Mary Seymour Howell, Josephine K. Henry, Mrs. Robert G. Ingersoll, Sarah A. Underwood, Ellen Battelle Dietrick, Lillie Devereux Blake, Matilda Joslyn Gage, Rev. Olympia Brown, Frances Ellen Burr, Clara B. Neyman, Helen H. Gardener, Charlotte Beebe Wilbour, Lucinda B. Chandler, Catharine F. Stebbins, Lousia Southworth, Baroness Alexandra Gripenberg, Ursula M. Bright, Irma von Troll-Borostvani, Priscilla Bright McLaren, and Isabelle Bogelot.

21. Louise Pettibone Smith, *The Book of Ruth,* 832. Considering that Smith begins her work on Ruth with a warning about the dangers of eisegesis and imaginative interpretations, I suspect that she would not approve of many of the current feminist studies that foreground imagination as a tool for interpretation.

22. See also Kathryn Pfisterer Darr, *Far More Precious than Jewels: Perspectives on Biblical Women,* 72–76, for her analysis of feminism's different treatments of Ruth.

23. Phyllis Trible, *God and the Rhetoric of Sexuality,* 170.

24. Many commentators choose not to translate this word. I too will use the Hebrew transliteration instead of attempting a translation. See Gordon A. Clark, *The Word* Hesed *in the Hebrew Bible.*

25. Trible, *God and the Rhetoric of Sexuality,* 173.

26. Esther Fuchs, "Status and Role of Female Heroines in the Biblical Narrative," in Alice Bach, ed. *Women in the Hebrew Bible: A Reader,* 78.

27. Fuchs, "Status and Role of Female Heroines in the Biblical Narrative," 78.

28. Cynthia Ozick, "Ruth," in Kates and Reimer, eds., *Reading Ruth,* 212.

29. Ozick, "Ruth," in Kates and Reimer, eds., *Reading Ruth,* 214.

30. George Aichele and Richard Walsh, eds., *Screening the Scripture: Intertextual Connections between Scripture and Film,* ix.

31. Aichele and Walsh, *Screening the Scripture,* xi.

32. Aichele and Walsh, *Screening the Scripture,* xi.

33. Aichele and Walsh, *Screening the Scripture,* xi.

34. Richard Walsh, *Finding St. Paul in Film,* 9. Using the word *precursor* takes the reader back to the introduction of *Screening the Scripture* where Jorge Luis Borges's short story "Kafka and His Precursors" is discussed. In this short story the researcher ends up seeing a wide range

of material echoing through Kafka's work, whether or not Kafka had the material. A precursor then is not identical to a source. Aichele and Walsh, *Screening the Scripture,* ix–x.

35. Jake Wilson, "Trash and Treasure: *The Gleaners and I,*" *Senses of Cinema.* Helen Carter, "Agnès Varda," *Senses of Cinema.*

36. Rémi Fournier Lanzoni, *French Cinema: From Its Beginnings to the Present,* 206–8.

37. Lanzoni, *French Cinema,* 209.

38. Lanzoni, *French Cinema,* 211.

39. Lanzoni, *French Cinema,* 237.

40. Athalya Brenner, *I Am . . . Biblical Women Tell Their Own Stories,* 4–5.

41. The suggestion that the book of Ruth was written by a woman was first made by S. D. Goitein in 1957. See Athalya Brenner, ed., *A Feminist Companion to Ruth,* 9–10. Brenner devotes a whole section of *A Feminist Companion to Ruth* to the question of female authorship (115–44). André LaCocque also argues for female authorship in *Ruth,* xvii.

42. Kirsten Nielsen, *Ruth,* 29.

43. William Rudolph as cited in LaCocque, *The Feminine Unconventional: Four Subversive Figures in Israel's Tradition,* 89.

44. For example, Campbell gives several reasons for David's taking his parents to Moab, one of which is his Moabite ancestry. See Campbell, *Ruth,* 59

45. Philip Davies, *In Search of "Ancient Israel."* Israel Finkelstein and Neil Asher Silberman, *David and Solomon: In Search of the Bible's Sacred Kings and the Roots of the Western Tradition.*

46. LaCocque, *The Feminine Unconventional,* 89.

47. See also LaCocque, *Ruth,* 13.

48. LaCocque, *Ruth,* 2.

49. Frymer-Kensky, *Reading the Women of the Bible,* 255. Others who support a postexilic dating include Frederic W. Bush, *Ruth, Esther,* and Linafelt, *Ruth,* who relies on Bush's linguistic argument (xx).

50. Frymer-Kensky, *Reading the Women of the Bible,* 256.

51. Roland Boer, *Novel Histories: The Fiction of Biblical Criticism,* 136–68.

52. Linafelt, *Ruth,* xviii.

53. Linafelt, *Ruth,* xx.

54. LaCocque, *The Feminine Unconventional,* 1.

55. Vanessa L. Ochs, "Reading Ruth: Where Are the Women?," in Kates and Reimer, eds., *Reading Ruth,* 291.

56. Ochs, "Reading Ruth: Where Are the Women?," in Kates and Reimer, eds., *Reading Ruth,* 292.

57. Campbell, *Ruth,* 28–32.

58. Woody Allen, "Hassidic Tales, with a Guide to Their Interpretation," in *The Insanity Defense: The Complete Prose,* 42.

59. Allen, "Hassidic Tales, with a Guide to Their Interpretation," 43. Once Varda's documentary was released, people from all over the world wrote to her about their own experience with gleaning. Many people also sent her objects that they had gleaned or that they had seen her glean. Varda documents this phenomenon in a second film entitled *The Gleaners and I: Two*

Years Later. When people hear that I am working on Ruth, they send me things too. Denise Greenwood, who teaches English at Albright College, sent me Allen's story through campus mail.

60. Nehama Aschkenasy, "The Book of Ruth as Comedy: Classical and Modern Perspectives," in Peter S. Hawkins and Lesleigh Cushing Stahlberg, eds., *Scrolls of Love: Ruth and the Song of Songs,* 31–44. LaCocque also understands that Ruth has comic although not farcical elements. *The Feminine Unconventional,* 119.

61. Aschkenasy, "The Book of Ruth as Comedy," 32–36; see also Raymond Chapman, "Comedy," in Tom McArthur, ed., *The Oxford Companion to the English Language,* 234–35.

62. Aschkenasy, "The Book of Ruth as Comedy," 36. Aschkenasy overreads certain elements of Ruth in order to make her point about how comedy is tragedy in reverse. For example, she admits that the narrator does not condemn the actions of Elimelech and his sons for moving to Moab and then marrying Moabite women, but she argues that the reader is supposed to understand this as a great and shameful offense against God. It seems to me that the deaths of the men are tragic enough without importing a supernatural reason for their demise.

63. Aschkenasy, "The Book of Ruth as Comedy," 35.

64. Frye calls comedy "the mythos of spring," as cited in Aschkenasy, "The Book of Ruth as Comedy," 32.

65. Aschkenasy, "The Book of Ruth as Comedy," 41–42.

66. Aschkenasy, "The Book of Ruth as Comedy," 34. Aschkenasy further explores this element of Ruth in "Reading Ruth through a Bakhtinian Lens: The Carnivalesque in a Biblical Tale," *Journal of Biblical Literature,* 437–53.

67. Aschkenasy, "The Book of Ruth as Comedy," 43.

Chapter 2: Agricultural Interlude No. 1

1. L. P. Hartley, *The Go-Between,* 17.

2. Campbell, *Ruth,* 49; Sasson, *Ruth,* 15.

3. Joshua, Judges, 1 Samuel, 2 Samuel, Ezekiel, Jonah, and Esther. Ruth and Esther open in identical ways: "And it was in the days of," which may be one indication that they were written during the same time period.

4. Sasson, *Ruth,* 15.

5. Translation into languages other than English is also challenging. For this verse the Syriac omits the infinitive construct; some Greek manuscripts omit "in the days of." Other Greek and Latin texts awkwardly render the Hebrew, preserving faithfulness to the Hebrew at the expense of clarity.

6. Linafelt, *Ruth,* 4.

7. M. F. K. Fisher, *The Gastronomical Me,* as cited in Carole Counihan and Penny van Esterik, eds., *Food and Culture: A Reader,* foreword.

8. According to the World Health Organization, iron deficiency is one of the top ten greatest global health risks. It affects two-thirds of all children and women of child-bearing age. J. R. Hunt, "Iron," in Benjamin Caballero, Lindsay Allen, and Andrew Prentice, eds., *Encyclopedia of Human Nutrition,* 82, 86.

9. MacDonald, *What Did the Ancient Israelites Eat? Diet in Biblical Times,* 80.

10. Philip J. King and Lawrence E. Stager, *Life in Biblical Israel*, 8.

11. MacDonald, *What Did the Ancient Israelites Eat?*, 13–14.

12. Daniel Hillel, *The Natural History of the Bible: An Environmental Exploration of the Hebrew Scriptures*, 11.

13. Translated by William F. Albright. James B. Pritchard, ed., *The Ancient Near East: An Anthology of Texts and Pictures*, 209. See also Oded Borowski, *Agriculture in Iron Age Israel*, 32–38.

14. Words used in Hebrew to refer to other countries include *'erets* ("land") and *gebul* ("territory"). When *sadeh* ("field") is used to refer to a country, the word is usually singular. In the book of Ruth the word for field is plural in four of its seven appearances, and instead of its normal feminine plural construct form, it appears in a masculine plural construct form. See Campbell, *Ruth*, 50, and Sasson, *Ruth*, 16.

15. Sasson, *Ruth*, 15.

16. J. Maxwell Miller, "Moab," in David Noel Freedman, ed., *The Anchor Bible Dictionary*, 4: 882–3.

17. Christopher J. Eyre, "The Agricultural Cycle, Farming, and Water Management in the Ancient Near East," in Jack M. Sasson, ed., *Civilizations of the Ancient Near East*, 177–78.

18. Hillel, *The Natural History of the Bible*, 142.

19. Hillel, *The Natural History of the Bible*, 146.

20. Hillel, *The Natural History of the Bible*, 157.

21. Hillel, *The Natural History of the Bible*, 26.

22. Hillel, *The Natural History of the Bible*, 17.

23. Borowski, *Agriculture in Iron Age Israel*, 87.

24. W. Robertson Smith, *Lectures on the Religion of the Semites*.

25. Mary Douglas, "Deciphering a Meal," in Counihan and van Esterik, eds., *Food and Culture*, 36–54; *Purity and Danger: An Analysis of Concepts of Pollution and Taboo*.

26. Marvin Harris, "The Abominable Pig," in Counihan and van Esterik, eds., *Food and Culture*, 67–79.

27. See also Nathan MacDonald, *Not Bread Alone: The Uses of Food in the Old Testament*, 17–46, for a review and analysis of Robinson, Douglas, Harris, and other scholars who have contributed to anthropological approaches to food in biblical times.

28. Sidney W. Mintz, "Time, Sugar, and Sweetness," in Counihan and van Esterik, eds., *Food and Culture*, 357.

29. Roland Barthes, "Toward a Psychosociology of Contemporary Food Consumption," in Counihan and van Esterik, eds., *Food and Culture*, 21.

30. Counihan and van Esterik, eds., *Food and Culture*, 2.

31. MacDonald, *Not Bread Alone*, 2.

32. In addition to the studies already referenced: Athalya Brenner and Jan Willem van Henten, eds., *Food and Drink in the Biblical Worlds*; Eleonore Schmitt, *Das Essen in der Bibel: Literaturethnologische Aspekte des Alltäglichen*.

33. Borowski, *Agriculture in Iron Age Israel*, 93–139; MacDonald, *What Did the Ancient Israelites Eat?*, 19–31; Jane M. Renfrew, "Vegetables in the Ancient Near Eastern Diet," in Sasson, ed., *Civilizations of the Ancient Near East*, 191–202.

34. MacDonald, *What Did the Ancient Israelites Eat?*, 9. MacDonald especially stresses the importance of class status in determining diet.

35. MacDonald, *Not Bread Alone,* 196. See also Stephen Mennell, Anne Murcott, and Anneke H. van Otterloo, *The Sociology of Food: Eating, Diet, and Culture,* 75–80.

36. Michael Pollan, *The Omnivore's Dilemma: A Natural History of Four Meals,* 3–4. Pollan relies on Paul Rozin, "The Selection of Foods by Rats, Humans, and Other Animals," in J. Rosenblatt, R. A. Hide, C. Beer, and E. Shaw, eds., *Advances in the Study of Behavior* (New York: Academic Press, 1976), 6: 21–76, for his discussion of the "omnivore's dilemma."

37. Claude Fischler, "Food, Self and Identity," in *Social Science Information* 27, 2 (1988): 278, as quoted in Mennell et al., *The Sociology of Food,* 13.

38. See, for example, the recent laws concerning "puppy mills" in Pennsylvania.

39. MacDonald, *What Did the Ancient Israelites Eat?*, 37–38.

40. Gloria Anzaldúa, *Borderlands / La Frontera: The New Mestiza,* preface.

41. Anzaldúa, *Borderlands,* 194.

Chapter 3: Ruth and Orpah

1. A version of this chapter was read at the Mid-Atlantic Regional Meeting of the Society of Biblical Literature, March 2010.

2. Laura Donaldson, "The Sign of Orpah: Reading Ruth through Native Eyes," in R. S. Sugirtharajah, ed., *Vernacular Hermeneutics,* 33.

3. Phyllis Trible, "Orpah," in Carol Meyers, ed., *Women in Scripture: A Dictionary of Named and Unnamed Women in the Hebrew Bible, the Apocryphal / Deuterocanonical Books, and the New Testament,* 134. See also Trible, *God and the Rhetoric of Sexuality,* 172: "Orpah is a paradigm of the sane and reasonable; she acts according to the structures and customs of society. Her decision is sound, sensible, and secure."

4. For example, Donaldson, "The Sign of Orpah."

5. Other important famine-compelled migrations in biblical narrative include Abraham's migration to Egypt in Gen. 12:10–20; Isaac's journey to Gerar in Gen. 26:1–16; the foundational event of exodus is predicated on a famine that propels the sons of Israel into Egypt to seek relief in Genesis 42–50; in 2 Kings 8:1–6 Elisha warns a woman about an impending famine and she settles in Philistia to avoid it.

6. Randall C. Bailey, "They're Nothing but Incestuous Bastards: The Polemical Use of Sex and Sexuality in the Hebrew Canon Narratives," in Fernando F. Segovia and Mary Ann Tolbert, eds., *Reading from This Place: Social Location and Biblical Interpretation in the United States,* volume 1, 121–38.

7. Frymer-Kensky, *Reading the Women of the Bible,* 259.

8. Frymer-Kensky, *Reading the Women of the Bible,* 259.

9. The geography is a little confused in these narratives. See Campbell, *Ruth,* 59.

10. This is assuming that the Targum precedes the Talmud. The dating of the Targum of Ruth is not certain. Opinions range from sometime before the destruction of the second Temple, a product of the Sadducees or another non-Pharisaic sect, through a post-Talmudic date based on the parallels with the Talmud and the Midrash thereby making the Targum dependent on these other works. With the judgment that "there are good reasons to think that

some elements in Tg. Ruth must be early, and it is difficult to find any that must be late," D. R. G. Beattie inclines toward an earlier dating. D. R. G. Beattie, *The Targum of Ruth*, 11–12.

11. Beattie, *The Targum of Ruth*, 19. The italics are in Beattie's translation and indicate where the Targumist added to the biblical text.

12. Ellen F. Davis, *Who Are You, My Daughter? Reading Ruth through Image and Text*, 9.

13. Jacob Neusner, *The Mother of the Messiah in Judaism*, 107, as cited in Davis, *Who Are You, My Daughter?*, 9.

14. Nielsen, *Ruth*, 44.

15. Frymer-Kensky, *Reading the Women of the Bible*, 260.

16. Davis, *Who Are You, My Daughter?*, xii–xiii. See also Ellen F. Davis, "Beginning with Ruth: An Essay on Translating," in Hawkins and Stahlberg, eds., *Scrolls of Love*, 11.

17. Davis, "Beginning with Ruth," in Hawkins and Stahlberg, eds., *Scrolls of Love*, 11.

18. Linafelt, *Ruth*, 14–15. For Linafelt, Orpah is contrasted to Ruth but only to heighten the extravagance of her response (15). See also Campbell, whose interpretation is similar. Campbell notes that Orpah is not negatively drawn in the text but she is Ruth's foil. As good as Orpah is, Ruth is more so (Campbell, *Ruth*, 82).

19. For example, farewell kisses are witnessed in Gen. 31:8, 2 Sam. 19:40, and 1 Kings 19:20. In Gen. 2:24 a man is said to leave his family to cling to his wife. Campbell, *Ruth*, 72.

20. Hebrew uses the same word for God and gods (*'elohim*). The only way to distinguish the plural from the singular noun is through the verb. However, certain phrases, like this one, have no verb and therefore the exact meaning remains ambiguous. Naomi is certainly acknowledging that Moabites have different deities than Israelites do. Such conflation between people-land-god was quite common in the ancient Near East. However, it is not clear whether or not Naomi is also making a distinction between monotheism and polytheism.

21. The Targum, the Septuagint (LXX), and the Peshitta add the detail that she did, indeed, turn and leave. Targum: "and went on her way"; LXX: "and she returned to her people"; Peshitta: "and she turned and went away."

22. See Sasson, *Ruth*, 17–19, for a fuller analysis of the meanings of the names.

23. Sasson, *Ruth*, 20.

24. See Nielsen, *Ruth*, 48; Linafelt, *Ruth*, 14–15.

25. Brenner, *I Am . . . Biblical Women Tell Their Own Stories*, 109.

26. Brenner, *I Am . . . Biblical Women Tell Their Own Stories*, 113.

27. Brenner, *I Am . . . Biblical Women Tell Their Own Stories*, 111.

28. Musa W. Dube, "The Unpublished Letters of Orpah to Ruth" in Brenner, ed., *Ruth and Esther: A Feminist Companion to the Bible*, 145–50.

29. Dube, "The Unpublished Letters of Orpah to Ruth" in Brenner, ed., *Ruth and Esther*, 145.

30. Dube, "The Unpublished Letters of Orpah to Ruth" in Brenner, ed., *Ruth and Esther*.

31. Dube, "The Unpublished Letters of Orpah to Ruth" in Brenner, ed., *Ruth and Esther*, 150.

32. R. S. Sugirtharajah, *Postcolonial Criticism and Biblical Interpretation*, 1.

33. Sugirtharajah, *Postcolonial Criticism and Biblical Interpretation*, 1.

34. Fernando F. Segovia, "Biblical Criticism and Postcolonial Studies: Toward a Postcolonial Optic," in R. S. Sugirtharajah, ed., *The Postcolonial Bible*, 56–61.

35. The phrase comes from the seminal work *Voices from the Margin: Interpreting the Bible in the Third World*, R. S. Sugirtharajah, ed.

36. Gale A. Yee, "'She Stood in Tears amid the Alien Corn': Ruth the Perpetual Foreigner and Model Minority," in Randall C. Bailey, Tat-siong Benny Liew, and Fernando F. Segovia, eds., *They Were All Together in One Place?: Toward Minority Biblical Criticism,*119.

37. Yee, "'She Stood in Tears Amid the Alien Corn,'" 119–20.

38. Musa W. Dube, "Divining Ruth for International Relations," in A. K. M. Adam, ed., *Postmodern Interpretations of the Bible: A Reader,* 67–79.

39. Dube, "Divining Ruth for International Relations," 73.

40. Dube, "Divining Ruth for International Relations," 74–75.

41. Dube, "Divining Ruth for International Relations," 77–78.

42. Dube, "Divining Ruth for International Relations," 77.

43. Dube, "Divining Ruth for International Relations," 78, n. 11.

44. Judith E. McKinlay, "A Son is Born to Naomi: A Harvest for Israel," in Brenner, ed., *Ruth and Esther,* 156.

45. Athalya Brenner, "Ruth as a Foreign Worker and the Politics of Exogamy," in Brenner, ed., *Ruth and Esther,* 160–61.

46. Archaeology has a difficult time distinguishing among the various Semitic peoples who populated the Levant because of the lack of differences in material culture. Perhaps this is another reason for the repetition of Ruth's ethnic identity in the biblical book—nobody would know she was a Moabite just by looking at her.

47. Haggard's novel is still popular. It has been made into a movie three times (1937, 1950, and 1985).

48. Haggard, *King Solomon's Mines,* 12–13.

49. Haggard, *King Solomon's Mines,* 91, 112–3.

50. Haggard, *King Solomon's Mines,* 6.

51. Haggard, *King Solomon's Mines,* 6.

52. Haggard, *King Solomon's Mines,* 5.

53. James Danly's endnotes in the Modern Library edition of Haggard's *King Solomon's Mines,* 238–39.

54. Haggard, *King Solomon's Mines,* 132–39.

55. Haggard, *King Solomon's Mines,* 184.

56. Haggard, *King Solomon's Mines,* 192.

57. Haggard, *King Solomon's Mines,* 208.

58. Haggard, *King Solomon's Mines,* 208.

59. Haggard, *King Solomon's Mines,* 190–91.

60. Haggard, *King Solomon's Mines,* 222.

61. See Alexandra Fuller's analysis in her introduction in the Modern Library edition to *King Solomon's Mines,* xv–xxv.

62. Donaldson, "The Sign of Orpah," 20–36.

63. Donaldson, "The Sign of Orpah," 21.

64. Donaldson, "The Sign of Orpah," 22.

65. Donaldson, "The Sign of Orpah," 24.

66. Thomas Jefferson, *Notes on the State of Virginia* (New York: W.W. Norton, 1982), 201, as cited in Donaldson.

67. Although Donaldson does not cite this example, Zane Grey's final novel, *The Vanishing American*, advocates this position. What is astonishing about his novel is that despite his sharp criticisms of missionaries on the Indian reservations and his obvious admiration for Indian culture and sympathy for their colonized plight, he holds up precisely this strategy—conversion, intermarriage, and thus absorption into the white race as the solution to the "Indian problem."

68. Donaldson, "The Sign of Orpah," 32–33.

69. R. S. Sugirtharajah, *The Bible and the Third World: Precolonial, Colonial and Postcolonial Encounters,* 109. Sugirtharajah is not speaking here specifically of Ruth but of a reading strategy of resistance using the Bible as a whole.

70. Audre Lorde, "The Master's Tools Will Never Dismantle the Master's House," 110–3.

71. McKinlay, "A Son Is Born to Naomi," in Brenner, ed., *Ruth and Esther,* 156.

72. Trinh T. Minh-ha, "Not You / Like You: Post-Colonial Women and the Interlocking Questions of Identity and Difference," in Gloria Anzaldúa, ed., *Making Face, Making Soul / Haciendo Caras,* 372.

73. Minh-ha, "Not You / Like You," 372.

74. Anzaldúa, *Borderlands,* 73.

75. Anzaldúa, *Borderlands,* 77.

76. Anzaldúa, *Borderlands,* 77.

77. Anzaldúa, *Borderlands,* 79.

78. Robert D. Maldonado, "Reading Malinche Reading Ruth: Toward a Hermeneutics of Betrayal," *Semeia,* 91–109.

79. Maldonado, "Reading Malinche Reading Ruth," 99.

80. Maldonado, "Reading Malinche Reading Ruth," 101.

81. Maldonado, "Reading Malinche Reading Ruth," 108.

82. Chris Weedon, "Postcolonial Feminist Criticism," in Gill Plain and Susan Sellers, eds., *A History of Feminist Literary Criticism,* 289.

83. Weedon, "Postcolonial Feminist Criticism," 298. Emphasis added.

Chapter 4: Ruth and Naomi

1. Robert Alter, *The Art of Biblical Narrative,* 74.

2. My count of the verses of dialogue.

3. Feminist interpreters still, largely, view Ruth and Naomi's relationship as an example of sisterhood, as do more popular and faith-based readings. See, for example, the essays in Brenner's edited volumes *A Feminist Companion to Ruth* and *Ruth and Esther* and in *Reading Ruth,* edited by Kates and Reimer; see also Marjory Zoet Bankson, *Seasons of Friendship: Naomi and Ruth as a Pattern,* and Renita J. Weems, *Just a Sister Away: A Womanist Vision of Women's Relationships in the Bible.*

4. Trible, *God and the Rhetoric of Sexuality,* 166.

5. Trible, *God and the Rhetoric of Sexuality,* 169.

6. Trible, *God and the Rhetoric of Sexuality,* 173.

7. Trible, *God and the Rhetoric of Sexuality,* 182.

8. Trible, *God and the Rhetoric of Sexuality,* 195.

9. Trible, *God and the Rhetoric of Sexuality,* 196.

10. Beattie, *The Targum of Ruth,* 20–21.

11. Jeannette H. Foster, *Sex Variant Women in Literature.* For the importance of this piece of literary scholarship see Caroline Gonda, "Lesbian Feminist Criticism," in Plain and Sellers, eds., *A History of Feminist Literary Criticism,* 170.

12. Foster, *Sex Variant Women in Literature,* 22.

13. Rebecca Alpert, "Finding Our Past: A Lesbian Interpretation of the Book of Ruth," in Kates and Reimer, eds., *Reading Ruth,* 92.

14. Alpert, "Finding Our Past," in Kates and Reimer, eds., *Reading Ruth,* 92.

15. When Foulata speaks the words to Captain Good in Haggard's *King Solomon's Mines,* the reader understands that she is very much in love with him.

16. Alpert, "Finding Our Past," in Kates and Reimer, eds., *Reading Ruth,* 94.

17. Alpert, "Finding Our Past," in Kates and Reimer, eds., *Reading Ruth,* 95.

18. Alpert, "Finding Our Past," in Kates and Reimer, eds., *Reading Ruth,* 96.

19. See Ken Stone, "Queer Commentary and Biblical Interpretation: An Introduction," in Ken Stone, ed., *Queer Commentary and the Hebrew Bible,* 11–34, for an analysis of queer biblical interpretation.

20. Mona West, "Ruth," in Deryn Guest et al., eds., *The Queer Bible Commentary,* 190.

21. West, "Ruth," 191.

22. Celena M. Duncan, "The Book of Ruth: On Boundaries, Love, and Truth," in Robert E. Goss and Mona West, eds., *Take Back the Word: A Queer Reading of the Bible,* 92–102.

23. Duncan, "The Book of Ruth," 95.

24. Duncan, "The Book of Ruth," 100–101.

25. The novel was made into a movie in 1991 called *Fried Green Tomatoes,* directed by Jon Avnet.

26. Fannie Flagg, *Fried Green Tomatoes at the Whistle Stop Cafe,* 47–48.

27. Flagg, *Fried Green Tomatoes at the Whistle Stop Cafe,* 48–49.

28. Flagg, *Fried Green Tomatoes at the Whistle Stop Cafe,* 80.

29. Flagg, *Fried Green Tomatoes at the Whistle Stop Cafe,* 81–82.

30. Flagg, *Fried Green Tomatoes at the Whistle Stop Cafe,* 88.

31. Flagg, *Fried Green Tomatoes at the Whistle Stop Cafe,* 191.

32. Flagg, *Fried Green Tomatoes at the Whistle Stop Cafe,* 198–99.

33. Anecdotally I have had several conversations with people who did not realize that the movie version depicted a lesbian relationship between Ruth and Idgie. Having read the book and seen the movie, I think that the book is clearer about their relationship than the movie is.

34. J. Cheryl Exum, *Plotted, Shot, and Painted: Cultural Representations of Biblical Women,* 129–32.

35. Exum, *Plotted, Shot, and Painted,* 169.

36. Exum, *Plotted, Shot, and Painted,* 170–71.

37. Campbell, *Ruth,* 24, 65.

38. Campbell, *Ruth,* 65.

39. Danna Nolan Fewell and David Miller Gunn, *Compromising Redemption: Relating Characters in the Book of Ruth,* 74.

40. See also Fewell and Gunn, "'A Son is Born to Naomi!': Literary Allusions and Interpretation in the Book of Ruth," in Alice Bach, ed., *Women in the Hebrew Bible: A Reader,* 233–34, in which they enumerate five silences between Ruth and Naomi that indicate that Naomi has hostile feelings toward Ruth.

41. Brenner, *I Am . . . Biblical Women Tell Their Own Stories,* 105.

42. Brenner, *I Am . . . Biblical Women Tell Their Own Stories,* 115.

43. Brenner, *I Am . . . Biblical Women Tell Their Own Stories,* 117.

44. Alter, *The Art of Biblical Narrative,* 74.

45. Linafelt, *Ruth,* 16.

46. Linafelt, *Ruth,* 16.

Chapter 5: Agricultural Interlude No. 2

1. A version of this chapter was read at the Mid-Atlantic Regional Meeting of the Society of Biblical Literature, March 2009.

2. MacDonald, *What Did the Ancient Israelites Eat?,* 19.

3. Many studies have focused on meat consumption in biblical times. The conventional wisdom—that meat was a rare treat—was established by the end of the nineteenth century and was based on the work of William Robertson Smith. Recently some scholars have challenged Smith's analysis using archaeological data and computer modeling. However, as MacDonald argues, such studies cannot indicate how much meat any individual Israelite consumed. Supplementing archeological with anthropological studies and being attuned to class and gender differences in food distribution, MacDonald presents a more nuanced conclusion about meat eating. As a poor widow in Iron Age Israel Ruth would rarely if ever have eaten meat. MacDonald, *What Did the Ancient Israelites Eat?,* 61–79.

4. King and Stager, *Life in Biblical Israel,* 93.

5. Carol Meyers, "Where the Girls Are: Archaeology and Women's Lives in Ancient Israel," in Milton C. Moreland, ed., *Between Text and Artifact: Integrating Archaeology in Biblical Studies Teaching,* 39.

6. Harold McGee, *On Food and Cooking: The Science and Lore of the Kitchen,* 516. I would like to thank Dr. Jennifer Rohrer-Walsh for bringing this book to my attention as we talked about food and shared Chinese takeout with our husbands.

7. In the English language there are even traces of the importance of class and gender status in defining one's role in bread production. The words *lord* and *lady* derive from the wealthy man and woman's roles in bread production and distribution. The word *lord* comes from the Anglo-Saxon *hlaford* meaning loaf ward, the master who supplies food; the word *lady* comes from *hlaefdige* meaning loaf kneader, the woman whose servants produce what her husband distributes. McGee, *On Food and Cooking,* 516–17.

8. Carole Counihan, "Bread as World: Food Habits and Social Relations in Modernizing Sardinia," in Counihan and van Esterik, eds., *Food and Culture,* 289. Carol Meyers, "Having Their Space and Eating There Too: Bread Production and Female Power in Ancient Israelite Households," *Nashim,* 14–44.

9. Iron sickles were not available to the Israelite farmer until sometime during the monarchy. Borowski, *Agriculture in Iron Age Israel*, 61–62.

10. See Carol Meyers, *In Search of Eve: Ancient Israelite Women in Context*, which argues that both men and women, adults and children had to contribute their labor to agricultural production in Iron Age Israel. Otherwise the survival of all would have been in jeopardy.

11. King and Stager, *Life in Biblical Israel*, 89. See also Borowski, *Agriculture in Iron Age Israel*, 62–69, for a more detailed account of the various methods of threshing and winnowing.

12. Borowski, *Agriculture in Iron Age Israel*, 66–67.

13. King and Stager, *Life in Biblical Israel*, 91.

14. King and Stager, *Life in Biblical Israel*, 40.

15. It is common for multiple grinders to be found in domestic structures. Meyers, "Where the Girls Are," 40–41.

16. Meyers, "Where the Girls Are," 40.

17. Meyers, "Where the Girls Are," 40–41.

18. King and Stager, *Life in Biblical Israel*, 17.

19. King and Stager, *Life in Biblical Israel*, 65.

20. There are French bakers who claim their starters are hundreds of years old.

21. Contrary to the assertion of King and Stager that salt was to season bread. King and Stager, *Life in Biblical Israel*, 65.

22. McGee, *On Food and Cooking*, 535.

23. King and Stager, *Life in Biblical Israel*, 4.

24. King and Stager, *Life in Biblical Israel*, 94.

25. Hildegard Lewy, "On Some Old Assyrian Cereal Names," *Journal of the American Oriental Society*, 203. Barley is almost never used for bread in modern times—perhaps another indication that barley was the bread grain of necessity. Now that wheat is cheap and plentiful, barley breads have all but disappeared. Compare barley production in 2002 with wheat and rice. In 2002, 21 million metric tons of barley compared to 579 metric tons of rice and 568 metric tons of wheat were produced worldwide (McGee, *On Food and Cooking*, 465). About half of the barley production is now fed to animals, and about a third is used to make a malt used primarily for alcohol production, secondarily in baked goods (McGee, *On Food and Cooking*, 469–70).

26. Carol Meyers, "'Women of the Neighborhood' (Ruth 4:17): Informal Female Networks in Ancient Israel," in Brenner, ed., *Ruth and Esther*, 122.

27. The English words *companion* and *company* mean in Latin "one who shares bread." McGee, *On Food and Cooking*, 517.

28. Counihan and van Esterik, eds., *Food and Culture*, 1.

29. Anna Meigs, "Food as a Cultural Construction," in Counihan and van Esterik, eds., *Food and Culture*, 105.

30. Meigs, "Food as a Cultural Construction," in Counihan and van Esterik, eds., *Food and Culture*, 104.

31. Amy-Jill Levine, "Ruth," in Newsom and Ringe, eds. *The Women's Bible Commentary*, 84.

32. See for example her poem "Cultures" in *Borderlands*, 120.

33. Judith Butler, *Undoing Gender,* 228.

Chapter 6: Ruth and Boaz

1. A version of this chapter was read at the Annual Meeting of the Society of Biblical Literature, November 2008.

2. Quotations from Varda's *The Gleaners and I* are from the English subtitles. I have added some of the punctuation for readability.

3. The activities of the poor in Israel continue to be marginalized. There is no entry on gleaning in King and Stager's otherwise comprehensive work *Life in Biblical Israel.* Both the *Anchor Bible Dictionary* and the *HarperCollins Dictionary* direct the curious from "Gleaning" to the entry on "Harvest, Harvesting." However, the harvest entries do not have a single word on gleaning.

4. Alain Fonteneau is not named in *The Gleaners and I.* Varda does, however, name him in her follow-up documentary *The Gleaners and I: Two Years Later* (2002). Fonteneau was unemployed but volunteered to teach French to immigrants. His story captured the public imagination, and he was featured in magazine and newspaper articles, interviewed on television talk shows, and revisited in Varda's second documentary.

5. Campbell, for example, puts the word *buy* in Ruth 4:5 in quotation marks. In his philological note he argues that the plain meaning of the verb does not obtain in this verse; rather the Hebrew word *qanah* should be paraphrased "marry as part of a legally valid commercial transaction" (*Ruth,* 147). See Sasson, *Ruth,* 123–25, for an extensive discussion of the use of *qanah* in 4:5. Sasson concludes that Boaz did buy Ruth by giving money to Naomi to compensate her "for the loss of a valuable helper" (124–25).

6. Sasson, *Ruth,* 38.

7. Linafelt, *Ruth,* 32.

8. Campbell, *Ruth,* 85. He later remarks: "It is likely that the precise meaning here will permanently elude us" (94).

9. Campbell, *Ruth,* 96; Sasson, *Ruth,* 47, 56.

10. Bush, *Ruth, Esther,* 114, as quoted in Jonathan Grossman, "'Gleaning among the Ears' — 'Gathering among the Sheaves': Characterizing the Image of the Supervising Boy (Ruth 2)," *Journal of Biblical Literature,* 704.

11. Bush, *Ruth, Esther,* 117; Linafelt, *Ruth,* 32. See Grossman "'Gleaning among the Ears,'" 703–5 for the various suggestions.

12. Grossman, "'Gleaning among the Ears,'" 705, 707.

13. Grossman, "'Gleaning among the Ears,'" 708.

14. Grossman, "'Gleaning among the Ears,'" 711.

15. Fewell and Gunn, *Compromising Redemption,* 40–44.

16. Trible, *God and the Rhetoric of Sexuality,* 176. See also Campbell, *Ruth,* 111.

17. Linafelt, *Ruth,* 38.

18. Sasson, *Ruth,* 55.

19. Harvesters appear to have been a rowdy bunch and women in the fields subject to their sexual harassment. See David Shepherd, "Violence in the Fields? Translating, Reading, and Revising in Ruth 2," *Catholic Biblical Quarterly,* 444–61.

20. In every case in the book of Ruth when a character reports a dialogue to another character, the dialogue is misrepresented; reported speech cannot be assumed to be accurate.

21. Bill Nichols, "The Voice of Documentary," in Alan Rosenthal, ed., *New Challenges for Documentary,* 48–49.

22. See also Brian Winston, "Documentary: I Think We Are in Trouble," in Rosenthal, ed., *New Challenges for Documentary,* 23.

23. Nichols, "The Voice of Documentary," in Rosenthal, ed., *New Challenges for Documentary,* 49.

24. Varda is aided by technology. She is using a digital camera, small and light, held in her hand. It can move with her and almost becomes an extension of her body.

25. Carter, "Agnès Varda." *Senses of Cinema.*

26. R. M. Hals, *The Theology of the Book of Ruth,* 16.

27. Campbell, *Ruth,* 28–29. For a survey of the commentators who agree with Hals and Campbell, see Linafelt, *Ruth,* 27–28.

28. Robert L. Hubbard, Jr., *The Book of Ruth,* 114, as cited in Linafelt, *Ruth,* 27.

29. Linafelt, *Ruth,* 28.

30. See also Deut. 23:11, in which *miqrah-laylah,* literally "accident-night," refers to men's nocturnal emissions, clearly not acts of a hidden God.

31. Campbell, *Ruth,* 81.

32. Campbell, *Ruth,* 80.

33. Sasson, *Ruth,* 22, 26.

34. John Holbert, *Reading and Preaching the Hebrew Bible: A Narrative Approach,* as quoted in Fewell and Gunn, *Compromising Redemption,* 94.

35. Sasson, *Ruth,* 35. See also Campbell, *Ruth,* 77.

36. The English *goodbye* is a contraction of the phrase *God be with you.* See also Linafelt, *Ruth,* 29–30.

37. Sasson, *Ruth,* 52.

38. Linafelt, *Ruth,* 37. Linafelt demonstrates an intentional blurring of Boaz and Yahweh ("the Lord") throughout the narrative.

39. Sasson, *Ruth,* 60.

40. Linafelt, *Ruth,* xvii.

41. A gleaner is open to chance. In the summer of 2008 I went to a used-book sale at the Leesport Farmer's Market, Leesport, Pennsylvania. It was the last day of the sale; the books had already been picked over for several days. On the last day the price was five dollars for a brown paper bag, which was handed to customers when they walked through the door. Anything that could be stuffed into that brown paper bag could be had. I started at the first row of books and slowly scanned with eye and hand, picking up, putting down, picking up again. I knew of Jane Hamilton, though I had never read any of her work. I had not even heard of this novel. I picked it up and put it in my bag.

42. Hamilton, *The Book of Ruth,* 2.

43. Hamilton, *The Book of Ruth,* 7.

44. Hamilton, *The Book of Ruth,* 1.

45. Hamilton, *The Book of Ruth,* 2.

46. Hamilton, *The Book of Ruth*, 60.

47. Hamilton, *The Book of Ruth*, 60.

48. Hamilton, *The Book of Ruth*, 288.

49. Hamilton, *The Book of Ruth*, 295. The earlier mention of the phrase *the dung heap shall smile* is on page 65. It may be a paraphrase of 1 Sam. 2:8 or Ps. 113:7, where God is praised for lifting up the poor from the "ash heap" or the "dung heap," respectively.

50. Hamilton, *The Book of Ruth*, 308–9.

51. Hamilton, *The Book of Ruth*, 311. The verse is the opening line of Psalm 42.

52. Hamilton, *The Book of Ruth*, 326.

53. Hamilton, *The Book of Ruth*, 4.

54. See Francis Landy, "Ruth and the Romance of Realism, or Deconstructing History," *Journal of the American Academy of Religion*, 285–317, for a close reading of the threshing-room floor scene. Landy's reading highlights the disjunctions that make the various understandings of Ruth and Boaz's relationship possible. His conclusion about Ruth's character is similar to my own: "But it [the narrative] also tells of the self, at least Ruth's self, that knows itself only through being never known" (312).

55. Fewell and Gunn argue that Naomi's plan is akin to "entrapment" (*Compromising Redemption*, 78).

56. As quoted in Beattie, *Jewish Exegesis of the Book of Ruth*, 190–91.

57. See Exum, *Plotted, Shot, and Painted*, 146–50, for an analysis of the difference age makes in the romantic plot.

58. Campbell, *Ruth*, 130.

59. Linafelt, *Ruth*, 46.

60. Campbell, *Ruth*, 132.

61. Both the Targum and Ruth Rabbah make it very clear that Boaz refrained from sexual intercourse with Ruth until after they married. Other Jewish rabbinical commentators also work to remove any hint of impropriety. See Beattie, *Jewish Exegesis of the Book of Ruth*, 158.

62. Linafelt, *Ruth*, 48–49.

63. See Daniel Boyarin, *Carnal Israel: Reading Sex in Talmudic Culture*; David Biale, *Eros and the Jews: From Biblical Israel to Contemporary America*; and Judith Romney Wegner, *Chattel or Person? The Status of Women in the Mishnah* for analysis of the biblical perspectives on sex and sexuality and how these perspectives were interpreted in Jewish tradition. See Kathy L. Gaca, *The Making of Fornication: Eros, Ethics, and Political Reform in Greek Philosophy and Early Christianity*, for an account of how Paul transformed the sexual ethic of the Jewish Bible (in his case the LXX) into the sexual ethic of Christianity.

64. Sasson, *Ruth*, 94.

65. Thomas Hood, "Ruth," in Robert Atwan and Laurance Wieder, eds., *Chapters into Verse*, 191.

66. There are similarities here with readings of David's affair with Bathsheba. It is often read as a great romance, one in which the protagonists break the laws of Israel because they are so in love. However, David has sex with Bathsheba once and then does not contact her again. Three months later she sends word to him that she is pregnant. If David had loved her, would he have failed to pursue her after their initial encounter?

67. Linafelt, *Ruth,* 54–55. The word for *wing* also means *extremity* and could imply *penis.*
68. Gale Yee, *Poor Banished Children of Eve: Woman as Evil in the Hebrew Bible,* 135–58.
69. Sasson, *Ruth,* 96.
70. Sasson, *Ruth,* 96
71. Levine, "Ruth," 83.

Chapter 7: Agricultural Interlude No. 3

1. Rick Darke, *The Color Encyclopedia of Ornamental Grasses: Sedges, Rushes, Restios, Cattails, and Selected Bamboos,* 30. Grass has more than six hundred genera and more than nine thousand species. Among the flowering plants it is surpassed by only the orchid family (*Orchidaceae*) and the sunflower family (*Asteraceae*).

2. Worldwide, more than half of all calories consumed come from grain products, not including the meats derived from animals that also consume grain. Total cereal grain production is two thousand million metric tons. Mark Nesbitt, "Grains," in Sir Ghillean Prance and Mark Nesbitt, eds., *The Cultural History of Plants,* 45.

3. Evan Eisenberg, *The Ecology of Eden,* 4–5.

4. Alison M. Smith et al., *Plant Biology,* 574–75. Agriculture also developed independently in the Andes and Amazonia and in eastern North America, but the first crops to be domesticated in these areas were not cereal grains.

5. Peter Bellwood, *First Farmers: The Origins of Agricultural Societies,* 19–25. See also Gary A. Wright, "Origins of Food Production in Southwestern Asia: A Survey of Ideas," in *Current Anthropology, Supp: Inquiry and Debate in the Human Sciences,* 109–39, for a survey of different anthropological models and their supporting evidence, especially the archaeological data.

6. Bellwood, *First Farmers,* 46–47.

7. Bellwood, *First Farmers,* 47; Smith et al., *Plant Biology,* 580.

8. Darke, *The Color Encyclopedia of Ornamental Grasses,* 30. See also Smith et al., *Plant Biology,* 574.

9. McGee, *On Food and Cooking,* 517.

10. Mircea Eliade, *Patterns in Comparative Religion,* 360–61.

11. The word *grain* appears 242 times in the Hebrew Bible.

12. The words are *yereq, 'eseb, hatsir, deshe'.* In Ps. 58:7 [Heb 58:8] the word *hitsav* may refer to grass but has also been translated *arrow.*

13. Darke, *The Color Encyclopedia of Ornamental Grasses,* 35.

14. McGee, *On Food and Cooking,* 452.

15. As quoted in Michael Pollan, *The Omnivore's Dilemma: A Natural History of Four Meals,* 188.

16. As quoted in Pollan, *The Omnivore's Dilemma,* 189.

17. Walt Whitman, "Song of Myself," in *Leaves of Grass,* 49.

18. Whitman, "Song of Myself," 49.

19. Whitman, "Song of Myself," 49.

20. Whitman, "Song of Myself," 72.

21. Whitman, "Unseen Buds," in *Leaves of Grass,* 416.

22. Smith et al., *Plant Biology*, 1. For the evolution of photosynthesis, see 4–7. For an explanation of the entire photosynthetic process, see 174–97.

23. Photosynthesis may even be older than this. There is evidence to suggest that nonoxygen producing photosynthesis had evolved by 3.8 billion years ago. Smith et al., *Plant Biology*, 5.

Chapter 8: (Ruth) and Obed

1. A version of this chapter was read at the Mid-Atlantic Regional Meeting of the Society of Biblical Literature, March 2008.

2. If recent scientific studies on animals that form pair-bonds for life are correct, the uncertainties are not even human, though the anxieties might be. From 10 to 70 percent of the progeny of these animals are not biologically related to the male in the bond. Natalie Angier, "In Most Species, Faithfulness Is a Fantasy," *New York Times*, March 18, 2008, sec. F.

3. David M. Schneider, *American Kinship: A Cultural Account*.

4. See Butler, *Undoing Gender*, 123, for her discussion of Schneider's work.

5. Butler, *Undoing Gender*, 123.

6. Butler, *Undoing Gender*, 102–3.

7. Butler, *Undoing Gender*, 103.

8. King and Stager, *Life in Biblical Israel*, 36.

9. Marianne Hirsh, "Reading Ruth with Naomi," in Kates and Reimer, eds., *Reading Ruth*, 310.

10. West, "Ruth," 193. See also West, "The Book of Ruth: An Example of Procreative Strategies for Queers," in Robert E. Goss, and Amy A. S. Strongheart, eds., *Our Families, Our Values: Snapshots of Queer Kinship*, 51–60.

11. Butler, *Undoing Gender*, 122.

12. Butler, *Undoing Gender*, 127.

13. Sarah Franklin and Susan McKinnon, "New Directions in Kinship Study: A Core Concept Revisited," *Current Anthropology*, as quoted in Butler, *Undoing Gender*, 126.

14. The standard dating of the biblical law codes understands the Book of the Covenant (Exod. 20:22–23:33) to be the oldest law code, perhaps arising before the monarchy; the Deuteronomic Code (Deut. 12–26) belongs to the seventh century B.C.E.; the Priestly Code (Lev. 1–16) and the Holiness Code (Lev. 17–26) to the sixth century B.C.E. The scholarly convention has, however, been challenged. See, for example, Philip R. Davies, *Scribes and Schools: The Canonization of the Hebrew Scriptures*, for an alternative understanding of when the Mosaic Torah came together. Davies sees the Torah as primarily a Persian Period document.

15. See Susan Niditch, *Oral World and Written Word: Ancient Israelite Literature*, for an appraisal of the ways in which orality interacted with textuality in the composition of the Hebrew Bible.

16. Sasson, *Ruth*, 105–7.

17. Sasson's discussion about all the legal wrangling at the gate is exhaustive. See Sasson, *Ruth*, 108–51.

18. LaCocque, *The Feminine Unconventional*, 101.

19. Linafelt, *Ruth*, 71.

20. LaCocque, *The Feminine Unconventional*, 103.

21. LaCocque, *The Feminine Unconventional*, 103–4.

22. West, "Ruth," 190.

23. West lists these references to law. West, "Ruth," 190.

24. West, "Ruth," 190.

25. West, "Ruth," 190.

26. Sasson, *Ruth*, 163–78.

27. I happened to hear B. D. Wong interviewed by Terry Gross on *Fresh Air* about his arduous journey into parenthood on June 11, 2003.

28. Wong, *Following Foo: The Electronic Adventures of the Chestnut Man*, 252.

29. Such situations had initially scared Wong and Jackson away from surrogacy. *Following Foo*, 235.

30. *Dov* is actually the Hebrew word for *bear,* which would emphasize the point Wong makes about Boaz's strength and courage. The word *dov* is derived from the verb *dbb* which means "to move gently, glide, glide over," which may capture the peaceful meaning Wong and Jackson were seeking.

31. Wong, *Following Foo*, 47–48.

32. Wong, *Following Foo*, 28–29.

33. Wong, *Following Foo*, 51.

34. Wong, *Following Foo*, 54.

35. Campbell, *Ruth,* 164.

36. Campbell, Ruth, 165.

37. Campbell, *Ruth,* 110.

38. Any number of books can be consulted for information about the biology of lactation. For a particularly comprehensive guide to lactation see La Leche League International, *The Womanly Art of Breastfeeding.*

39. Nielsen, *Ruth*, 93.

40. West, "Ruth."

41. LaCocque, *The Feminine Unconventional*, 99. See also Brian Britt, "Sacrifice and the Displacement of Mothers in the Book of Ruth and Coetzee's *Disgrace*," in Cheryl A. Kirk-Duggan and Tina Pippin, eds., *Mother Goose, Mother Jones, Mommie Dearest: Biblical Mothers and Their Children*, 37–49.

42. Wil Gafney, "Mother Knows Best: Messianic Surrogacy and Sexploitation in Ruth," in Kirk-Duggan and Pippin, eds., *Mother Goose, Mother Jones, Mommie Dearest*, 29.

43. Gafney, "Mother Knows Best," in Kirk-Duggan and Pippin, eds., *Mother Goose, Mother Jones, Mommie Dearest*, 35.

44. Sasson, *Ruth*, 235.

45. As quoted in Sasson, *Ruth,* 236.

46. Sasson, *Ruth,* 237.

47. Sasson, *Ruth,* 240.

48. Mayer I. Gruber, "Breast-Feeding Practices in Biblical Israel and in Old Babylonian Mesopotamia," *Journal of the Ancient Near Eastern Society*, 71.

49. Gruber, "Breast-Feeding Practices in Biblical Israel and in Old Babylonian Mesopotamia," 71.

50. Levine, "Ruth," 84.

51. There is one story in the Bible that implies that the husband may be responsible for the couple's infertility. In 2 Kings 4 Elisha wishes to reward a Shunammite woman for her hospitality. His servant Gehazi tells the prophet that the woman has no children "and her husband is old" (2 Kings 4:14).

52. See Robert Paul Seesengood, "Rules for an Ancient Philadelphian Religious Organization and Early Christian Ethical Teaching," *Stone Campbell Journal,* 217–33, for information about contraception and abortion in the ancient world.

53. Robert Hubbard, *The Book of Ruth,* 267, as quoted in Linafelt, *Ruth,* 77. Linafelt also notes that Ruth had never expressed any desire to become a mother.

Chapter 9: The Story Begins Where It Ends

1. Examples abound: 1 Sam. 1:1, which introduces the story of Samuel's birth; Esther 2: 5, which introduces the heroes of the book, Mordecai and Esther; 1 Chron. 1–9, which introduces Chronicles' history of the monarchy.

2. See Campbell, *Ruth,* 172, who notes that there is "all but universal agreement" to the appendix hypothesis, and Sasson, *Ruth,* 179–87, who examines some of the arguments concerning the appendix hypothesis but ultimately rejects it himself.

3. Linafelt, *Ruth,* 79–80.

4. Linafelt, *Ruth,* xviii, 80.

5. Linafelt, *Ruth,* 80.

6. Nehemia Polen, "Dark Ladies and Redemptive Compassion: Ruth and the Messianic Lineage in Judaism" in Hawkins and Stahlberg, eds., *Scrolls of Love,* 60.

7. See, for example, Judith Plaskow, *Standing at Sinai: Judaism from a Feminist Perspective.*

8. As discussed in Plaskow, *Standing at Sinai,* 27.

9. Bonnie Honig, "Ruth, the Model Emigree: Mourning and the Symbolic Politics of Immigration" in Brenner, ed., *Ruth and Esther,* 54–55.

10. Polen, "Dark Ladies and Redemptive Compassion," in Hawkins and Stahlberg, eds., *Scrolls of Love,* 74.

11. Michael Fishbane, Haftarah Commentary, in David L Lieber, ed., *Etz Hayim: Torah and Commentary,* 1321.

12. Fishbane, Haftarah Commentary, in Lieber, ed., *Etz Hayim,* 1325. The midrash is based on Habakkuk 3:6.

13. Judith A. Kates, "Women at the Center: *Ruth and Shavuot*" in Kates and Reimer, eds., *Reading Ruth,* 189.

14. Kates, "Women at the Center," in Kates and Reimer, eds., *Reading Ruth,* 187.

15. Although not a part of liturgy, the book of Ruth is a popular character in children's Bible story books and in children's Sunday school lessons. See Valerie A. Stein, "Know*Be*Do: Using the Bible to Teach Ethics to Children," *SBL Forum.*

16. Katherine Doob Sakenfeld, "Tamar, Rahab, Ruth, and the Wife of Uriah: The Company Mary Keeps in Matthew's Gospel," in Beverly Roberts Gaventa and Cynthia L. Rigby, eds., *Blessed One: Protestant Perspectives on Mary,* 21.

17. As quoted in Peter S. Hawkins, "Ruth amid the Gentiles," in Hawkins and Stahlberg, eds., *Scrolls of Love,* 79.

18. Hawkins, "Ruth amid the Gentiles," in Hawkins and Stahlberg, eds., *Scrolls of Love,* 78–81. Hawkins notes that there is "an alarming amount of animus against the Jews" in many of these Christian interpretations (80).

19. Hawkins, "Ruth amid the Gentiles," in Hawkins and Stahlberg, eds., *Scrolls of Love,* 76.

20. Quotations from Gitai's *Golem: The Spirit of Exile* are from the English subtitles.

21. The Song of Songs is one of only three texts to use the term *mother's house:* Ruth 1:8; Gen. 24:28; and S. of S. 3:4; 8:2.

• BIBLIOGRAPHY •

Aichele, George, and Richard Walsh, eds. *Screening the Scripture: Intertextual Connections between Scripture and Film.* Harrisburg: Trinity Press International, 2002.

Allen, Woody. "Hassidic Tales, with a Guide to Their Interpretation." In *The Insanity Defense: The Complete Prose,* 42–47. New York: Random House, 2007.

Alter, Robert. *The Art of Biblical Narrative.* New York: Basic Books, 1981.

Angier, Natalie. "In Most Species, Faithfulness Is a Fantasy." *New York Times.* March 18, 2008.

Anzaldúa, Gloria. *Borderlands / La Frontera: The New Mestiza.* San Francisco: Aunt Lute Books, 1987.

Aschkenasy, Nehama. "The Book of Ruth as Comedy: Classical and Modern Perspectives." In *Scrolls of Love: Ruth and the Song of Songs,* edited by Peter S. Hawkins and Lesleigh Cushing Stahlberg, 31–44. New York: Fordham University Press, 2006.

———. "Reading Ruth through a Bakhtinian Lens: The Carnivalesque in a Biblical Tale." *Journal of Biblical Literature* 126, 3 (2007): 437–53.

Atwan, Robert, and Laurance Wieder, eds. *Chapters into Verse.* Vol. 1, *Genesis to Malachi.* New York: Oxford University Press, 1993.

Bailey, Randall. "They're Nothing but Incestuous Bastards: The Polemical Use of Sex and Sexuality in Hebrew Canon Narratives." In *Reading from This Place: Social Location and Biblical Interpretation in the United States,* vol. 1, edited by Fernando F. Segovia and Mary Ann Tolbert, 121–38. Philadelphia: Fortress, 1995.

Bankson, Marjory Zoet. *Seasons of Friendship: Naomi and Ruth as a Pattern.* San Diego: Luria-Media, 1987.

Beattie, D. R. G. *Jewish Exegesis of the Book of Ruth.* Sheffield: Sheffield Academic Press, 1977.

———. *The Targum of Ruth.* Collegeville, Minn.: Liturgical Press, 1994.

Bellwood, Peter. *First Farmers: The Origins of Agricultural Societies.* Malden, Mass.: Blackwell, 2005.

Biale, David. *Eros and the Jews: From Biblical Israel to Contemporary America.* Berkeley: University of California Press, 1997.

Boer, Roland. *Novel Histories: The Fiction of Biblical Criticism.* Sheffield: Sheffield Academic Press, 1997.

Borowski, Oded. *Agriculture in Iron Age Israel.* Winona Lake, Ind.: Eisenbrauns, 1987.

Boyarin, Daniel. *Carnal Israel: Reading Sex in Talmudic Culture.* Berkeley: University of California Press, 1993.

Brenner, Athalya. *I Am . . . Biblical Women Tell Their Own Stories.* Minneapolis: Fortress, 2005.

———, ed. *A Feminist Companion to Ruth.* Sheffield: Sheffield Academic Press, 1993.

————, ed. *Ruth and Esther: A Feminist Companion to the Bible,* 2d ser. Sheffield: Sheffield Academic Press, 1999.

Brenner, Athalya, and Jan Willem van Henten, eds. *Food and Drink in the Biblical Worlds.* Semeia 86. Atlanta: Society of Biblical Literature, 1999.

Britt, Brian. "Sacrifice and the Displacement of Mothers in the Book of Ruth and Coetzee's *Disgrace.*" In *Mother Goose, Mother Jones, Mommie Dearest: Biblical Mothers and Their Children,* edited by Cheryl A. Kirk-Duggan and Tina Pippin, 37–49. Atlanta: Society of Biblical Literature, 2009.

Bush, Frederic W. *Ruth, Esther.* Word Bible Commentary. Dallas: Word Books, 1996.

Butler, Judith. *Undoing Gender.* New York: Routledge, 2004.

Campbell, Edward F. *Ruth.* The Anchor Bible 7. Garden City, N.Y.: Doubleday, 1975.

Carter, Helen. "Agnès Varda." In "Great Directors: A Critical Database," *Senses of Cinema* (2002). sensesofcinema.com.

Chapman, Raymond. "Comedy." In *The Oxford Companion to the English Language,* edited by Tom McArthur, 234–35. Oxford: Oxford University Press, 1992.

Clark, Gordon A. *The Word* Hesed *in the Hebrew Bible.* Sheffield: Sheffield Academic Press, 1993.

Counihan, Carole, and Penny van Esterik, eds. *Food and Culture: A Reader.* New York: Routledge, 1997.

Darke, Rick. *The Color Encyclopedia of Ornamental Grasses: Sedges, Rushes, Restios, Cat-tails, and Selected Bamboos.* Portland, Ore.: Timber Press. 1999.

Darr, Kathryn Pfisterer. *Far More Precious Than Jewels: Perspectives on Biblical Women.* Louisville: Westminster John Knox, 1991.

Davies, Philip. *In Search of "Ancient Israel."* Sheffield: Sheffield Academic Press, 1992.

————. *Scribes and Schools: The Canonization of the Hebrew Scriptures.* Louisville: Westminster John Knox, 1998.

Davis, Ellen F. *Who Are You, My Daughter? Reading Ruth through Image and Text.* Louisville: Westminster John Knox, 2003.

de Groot, Christiana, and Marion Ann Taylor. *Recovering Nineteenth-Century Women Interpreters of the Bible.* Atlanta: Society of Biblical Literature, 2007.

Donaldson, Laura. "The Sign of Orpah: Reading Ruth through Native Eyes." In *Vernacular Hermeneutics,* edited by R. S. Sugirtharajah, 20–36. Sheffield: Sheffield Academic Press, 1999.

Douglas, Mary. *Purity and Danger: An Analysis of Concepts of Pollution and Taboo.* New York: Routledge, 1966.

Dube, Musa W. "Divining Ruth for International Relations." In *Postmodern Interpretations of the Bible: A Reader,* edited by A. K. M. Adam, 67–80. St. Louis: Chalice Press, 2001.

Duncan, Celena M. "The Book of Ruth: On Boundaries, Love, and Truth." In *Take Back the Word: A Queer Reading of the Bible,* edited by Robert E. Goss and Mona West, 92–102. Cleveland: Pilgrim Press, 2000.

Eisenberg, Evan. *The Ecology of Eden.* New York: Knopf, 1998.

Eliade, Mircea. *Patterns in Comparative Religion.* Cleveland: Meridian, 1958.

Exum, J. Cheryl. *Plotted, Shot, and Painted: Cultural Representations of Biblical Women.* Sheffield: Sheffield Academic Press, 1996.

Eyre, Christopher J. "The Agricultural Cycle, Farming, and Water Management in the Ancient Near East." In *Civilizations of the Ancient Near East*, edited by Jack M. Sasson, 175–89. Peabody, Mass: Hendrickson, 2000.

Fewell, Danna Nolan, and David Miller Gunn. *Compromising Redemption: Relating Characters in the Book of Ruth*. Louisville: Westminster John Knox, 1990.

————. "'A Son Is Born to Naomi!': Literary Allusions and Interpretation in the Book of Ruth." In *Women in the Hebrew Bible: A Reader*, edited by Alice Bach, 233–39. New York: Routledge, 1999.

Finkelstein, Israel, and Neil Asher Silberman. *David and Solomon: In Search of the Bible's Sacred Kings and the Roots of the Western Tradition*. New York: Free Press, 2006.

Fiorenza, Elisabeth Schüssler, ed. *Searching the Scriptures*, vol 1. New York: Crossroads, 1993.

Flagg, Fannie. *Fried Green Tomatoes at the Whistle Stop Cafe*. New York: Random House, 1987.

Foster, Jeannette H. *Sex Variant Women in Literature*. Tallahassee: Naiad Press, 1985. Originally published, New York: Vantage Press, 1956.

Franklin, Sarah, and Susan McKinnon, "New Directions in Kinship Study: A Core Concept Revisited," *Current Anthropology* 41, 2 (April 2000): 275–79.

Frymer-Kensky, Tikva. *Reading the Women of the Bible: A New Interpretation of Their Stories*. New York: Schocken Books, 2002.

Fuchs, Esther. "Status and Role of Female Heroines in the Biblical Narrative." In *Women in the Hebrew Bible: A Reader*, edited by Alice Bach, 77–84. New York: Routledge, 1999. Originally published in *Mankind Quarterly* 23 (1982): 149–60.

Gaca, Kathy L. *The Making of Fornication: Eros, Ethics, and Political Reform in Greek Philosophy and Early Christianity*. Berkeley: University of California Press, 2003.

Gonda, Caroline. "Lesbian Feminist Criticism." In *A History of Feminist Literary Criticism*. Edited by Gill Plain and Susan Sellers, 169–86. Cambridge: Cambridge University Press, 2007.

Grant, Barry Keith, and Jeannette Sloniowski, eds. *Documenting the Documentary: Close Readings of Documentary Film and Video*. Detroit: Wayne State University Press, 1998.

Grossman, Jonathan. "'Gleaning among the Ears'—'Gathering among the Sheaves': Characterizing the Image of the Supervising Boy (Ruth 2)." *Journal of Biblical Literature* 126, 4 (2007): 703–16.

Gruber, Mayer I. "Breast-Feeding Practices in Biblical Israel and in Old Babylonian Mesopotamia." *Journal of the Ancient Near Eastern Society* 19 (1989): 61–83.

Gunkel, Hermann. "Ruth." In *Reden und Aufsätze*, 65–92. Göttingen: Vandenhoeck and Ruprecht, 1913.

Haggard, H. Rider. *King Solomon's Mines*. New York: Modern Library, 2002.

Hals, R. M. *The Theology of the Book of Ruth*. Philadelphia: Fortress, 1969.

Hamilton, Jane. *The Book of Ruth*. New York: Doubleday, 1988.

Hartley, L. P. *The Go-Between*. New York: New York Review of Books, 1954.

Hawkins, Peter S., and Lesleigh Cushing Stahlberg, eds. *Scrolls of Love: Ruth and the Song of Songs*. New York: Fordham University Press, 2006.

Hillel, Daniel. *The Natural History of the Bible: An Environmental Exploration of the Hebrew Scriptures*. New York: Columbia University Press, 2006.

Hunt, J. R. "Iron." In *Encyclopedia of Human Nutrition,* vol. 3, edited by Benjamin Caballero, Lindsay Allen, and Andrew Prentice, 82–89. Oxford: Elsevier Academic Press, 2005.

Kates, Judith A., and Gail Twersky Reimer, eds. *Reading Ruth: Contemporary Women Reclaim a Sacred Story.* New York: Ballantine Books, 1994.

King, Philip J., and Lawrence E. Stager. *Life in Biblical Israel.* Louisville: Westminster John Knox, 2001.

LaCocque, André. *The Feminine Unconventional: Four Subversive Figures in Israel's Tradition.* Minneapolis: Fortress, 1990.

———. *Ruth.* Continental Commentaries. Minneapolis: Fortress, 2004.

La Leche League International. *The Womanly Art of Breastfeeding.* New York: Plume, 2004.

Landy, Francis. "Ruth and the Romance of Realism, or Deconstructing History." *Journal of the American Academy of Religion* 62 (1994): 285–317.

Lanzoni, Rémi Fournier, *French Cinema: From Its Beginnings to the Present.* New York: Continuum, 2002.

Lerner, Gerda. *The Creation of Feminist Consciousness.* New York: Oxford University Press, 1993.

Levine, Amy-Jill. "Ruth." In *The Women's Bible Commentary,* edited by Carol A. Newsom and Sharon H. Ringe, 78–84. Louisville: Westminster John Knox, 1992.

Lewy, Hildegard. "On Some Old Assyrian Cereal Names." *Journal of the American Oriental Society* 76 (1956): 201–4.

Lieber, David L. ed. *Etz Hayim: Torah and Commentary.* New York: Jewish Publication Society, 2001.

Linafelt, Tod, and Timothy K. Beal. *Ruth and Esther.* Berit Olam. Collegeville, Minn.: The Liturgical Press, 1999.

Lorde, Audre. "The Master's Tools Will Never Dismantle the Master's House." In *Sister/Outsider.* Freedom, Calif.: Crossing Press, 1984.

MacDonald, Nathan. *Not Bread Alone: The Uses of Food in the Old Testament.* Oxford: Oxford University Press, 2008.

———. *What Did the Ancient Israelites Eat? Diet in Biblical Times.* Grand Rapids: Eerdmans, 2008.

Maldonado, Robert. "Reading Malinche Reading Ruth: Toward a Hermeneutics of Betrayal." *Semeia* 72 (1995): 91–109.

McGee, Harold. *On Food and Cooking: The Science and Lore of the Kitchen,* 2d ed. New York: Scribner, 2004.

Mennell, Stephen, Anne Murcott, and Anneke H. van Otterloo. *The Sociology of Food: Eating, Diet, and Culture.* London: Sage Publications, 1992.

Meyers, Carol. *In Search of Eve: Ancient Israelite Women in Context.* New York: Oxford University Press, 1988.

———. "Everyday Life: Women in the Period of the Hebrew Bible." In *The Women's Bible Commentary,* edited by Carol A. Newsom and Sharon H. Ringe, 244–51. Louisville: Westminster John Knox, 1992.

———. "Returning Home: Ruth 1.8 and the Gendering of the Book of Ruth." In *A Feminist Companion to Ruth,* edited by Athalya Brenner, 85–114. Sheffield: Sheffield Academic Press, 1993.

————. "Having Their Space and Eating There Too: Bread Production and Female Power in Ancient Israelite Households." *Nashim* 5 (2002): 14–44.

————. "Where the Girls Are: Archaeology and Women's Lives in Ancient Israel." In *Between Text and Artifact: Integrating Archaeology in Biblical Studies Teaching,* edited by Milton C. Moreland, 31–51. Boston: Brill, 2003.

Miller, J. Maxwell. "Moab." In *The Anchor Bible Dictionary,* vol. 4, edited by David Noel Freedman, 882–93. New York: Doubleday, 1992.

Miller, Toby, and Robert Stam, eds. *A Companion to Film Theory.* London: Blackwell, 2004.

Minh-ha, Trinh T. "Not You / Like You: Post-Colonial Women and the Interlocking Questions of Identity and Difference." In *Making Face, Making Soul / Haciendo Caras,* edited by Gloria Anzaldúa, 371–75. San Francisco: Aunt Lute, 1990.

Myers, Jacob M. *The Linguistic and Literary Form of the Book of Ruth.* Leiden: Brill, 1955.

Nesbitt, Mark. "Grains." In *The Cultural History of Plants,* edited by Sir Ghillean Prance and Mark Nesbitt, 45–60. New York: Routledge, 2005.

Newsome, Carol A., and Sharon H. Ringe, eds. *The Women's Bible Commentary.* Louisville: Westminster / John Knox, 1992.

Niditch, Susan. *Oral World and Written Word: Ancient Israelite Literature.* Louisville: Westminster John Knox, 1996.

Nielsen, Kirsten. *Ruth.* The Old Testament Library. Louisville: Westminster John Knox, 1997.

Plaskow, Judith. *Standing at Sinai: Judaism from a Feminist Perspective.* San Francisco: HarperCollins, 1991.

Pollan, Michael. *The Omnivore's Dilemma: A Natural History of Four Meals.* New York: Penguin Books, 2006.

Pritchard, James B., ed. *The Ancient Near East: An Anthology of Texts and Pictures,* vol. 1. Princeton: Princeton University Press, 1958.

Renfrew, Jane M. "Vegetables in the Ancient Near Eastern Diet." In *Civilizations of the Ancient Near East,* edited by Jack M. Sasson, 191–202. Peabody, Mass.: Hendrickson, 2000.

Rosenthal, Alan, ed. *New Challenges for Documentary.* Berkeley: University of California Press, 1988.

Sakenfeld, Katherine Doob. "Tamar, Rahab, Ruth, and the Wife of Uriah: The Company Mary Keeps in Matthew's Gospel." In *Blessed One: Protestant Perspectives on Mary,* edited by Beverly Roberts Gaventa and Cynthia L. Rigby, 21–31. Louisville: Westminster John Knox, 2002.

Sasson, Jack M. *Ruth: A New Translation with a Philological Commentary and a Formalist-Forklorist Interpretation.* Baltimore: Johns Hopkins University Press, 1979.

Schmitt, Eleonore. *Das Essen in der Bibel: Literaturethnologische Aspekte des Alltäglichen.* Studien zur Kulturanthropologie, 2. Münster: LitVerlag, 1994.

Schneider, David M. *American Kinship: A Cultural Account.* Chicago: University of Chicago Press, 1968.

Seesengood, Robert Paul. "Rules for an Ancient Philadelphian Religious Organization and Early Christian Ethical Teaching." *Stone Campbell Journal* 5, 2 (Fall 2002): 217–33.

Segovia, Fernando F. "Biblical Criticism and Postcolonial Studies: Toward a Postcolonial Optic." In *The Postcolonial Bible,* edited by R. S. Sugirtharajah, 49–65. Sheffield: Sheffield Academic Press, 1998.

Shepherd, David. "Violence in the Fields? Translating, Reading, and Revising in Ruth 2." *Catholic Biblical Quarterly* 63 (2001): 444–61.

Smith, Alison M., et al. *Plant Biology.* New York: Taylor and Francis, 2010.

Smith, Louise Pettibone. *The Book of Ruth.* Interpreter's Bible. Volume Two. New York: Abingdon Press, 1955. 829–52.

Smith, W. Robertson. *Lectures on the Religion of the Semites.* New York: 1889.

Stanton, Elizabeth Cady, et al. *The Woman's Bible.* 2 vols. Seattle: Coalition Task Force on Women and Religion, 1990. Originally published, New York: European Publishing Company, 1898.

Stein, Valerie A. "Know*Be*Do: Using the Bible to Teach Ethics to Children," *SBL Forum* 7, 2 (February 27, 2009). sbl-site.org

Stone, Ken. "Queer Commentary and Biblical Interpretation: An Introduction." In *Queer Commentary and the Hebrew Bible,* edited by Ken Stone, 11–34. Cleveland: Pilgrim Press, 2001.

Sugirtharajah, R. S., *The Bible and the Third World: Precolonial, Colonial and Postcolonial Encounters.* Cambridge: Cambridge University Press, 2001.

———. *Postcolonial Criticism and Biblical Interpretation.* New York: Oxford University Press, 2002.

———, ed. *Voices from the Margin: Interpreting the Bible in the Third World.* Maryknoll, N.Y.: Orbis, 1991.

Trible, Phyllis. *God and the Rhetoric of Sexuality.* Philadelphia: Fortress, 1978.

———. "Ruth." In *Women in Scripture,* edited by Carol Meyers, 146–47. Grand Rapids: Eerdmans, 2000.

———. "Orpah." In *Women in Scripture: A Dictionary of Named and Unnamed Women in the Hebrew Bible, The Apocryphal / Deuterocanonical Books, and the New Testament,* edited by Carol Meyers, 133–34. Grand Rapids: Eerdmans, 2000.

Walsh, Richard. *Findieng St. Paul in Film.* New York: T & T Clark, 2005.

Weedon, Chris. "Postcolonial Feminist Criticism." In *A History of Feminist Literary Criticism,* edited by Gill Plain and Susan Sellers, 282–300. Cambridge: Cambridge University Press, 2007.

Weems, Renita J. *Just a Sister Away: A Womanist Vision of Women's Relationships in the Bible.* San Diego: Luria Media, 1988.

Wegner, Judith Romney. *Chattel or Person? The Status of Women in the Mishnah.* New York: Oxford University Press, 1988.

West, Mona. "The Book of Ruth: An Example of Procreative Strategies for Queers." In *Our Families, Our Values: Snapshots of Queer Kinship,* edited by Robert E. Goss and Amy A. S. Strongheart, 51–60. New York: Harrington Park Press, 1997.

———. "Ruth." In *The Queer Bible Commentary,* edited by Deryn Guest et al., 190–94. London: SCM Press, 2006.

Weston, Kath. *The Families We Choose: Lesbians, Gays, Kinship.* New York: Columbia University Press, 1991.

Whitman, Walt. *Leaves of Grass.* New York: New American Library, 1980.

Wilson, Jake. "Trash and Treasure: *The Gleaners and I.*" *Senses of Cinema* 23 (2002).

Wong, B. D. *Following Foo: The Electronic Adventures of the Chestnut Man.* New York: Harper-Collins, 2003.

Wright, Gary A. "Origins of Food Production in Southwestern Asia: A Survey of Ideas." *Current Anthropology, Supp: Inquiry and Debate in the Human Sciences.* 33 (February 1992): 109–39.

Yee, Gale A. *Poor Banished Children of Eve: Woman as Evil in the Hebrew Bible.* Minneapolis: Fortress, 2003.

———. "'She Stood in Tears amid the Alien Corn': Ruth the Perpetual Foreigner and Model Minority." In *They Were All Together in One Place?: Toward Minority Biblical Criticism.* Semeia Studies 57. Edited by Randall C. Bailey, Tat-siong Benny Liew, and Fernando F. Segovia. Atlanta: Society of Biblical Literature, 2009. 119–40.

· SCRIPTURAL INDEX ·

· SUBJECT INDEX ·

• ABOUT THE AUTHOR •

JENNIFER L. KOOSED is an associate professor of religious studies at Albright College in Reading, Pennsylvania, and the author of *(Per)mutations of Qohelet: Reading the Body in the Book.*

Studies on Personalities of the Old Testament
James L. Crenshaw, Series Editor

GLEANING RUTH